THE BREAD BOOK

THE
BREAD
BOOK

Martha Rose Shulman

MACMILLAN
LONDON

First published 1990 by
MACMILLAN LONDON LIMITED
4 Little Essex Street London WC2R 3LF
and Basingstoke

Associated companies in Auckland, Delhi, Dublin, Gaborone,
Hamburg, Harare, Hong Kong, Johannesburg, Kuala Lumpur,
Lagos, Manzini, Melbourne, Mexico City, Nairobi, New York,
Singapore and Tokyo

ISBN 0–333–49424–5

A CIP catalogue record for this book is available from the
British Library.

Typeset by Rowland Phototypesetting Limited
Bury St Edmunds, Suffolk
Printed by Billings Bookplan Limited
Worcester

For Bill, again, with love

Contents

Note

The following recipes, in slightly different form, appeared in *Chez Martha Rose* by Martha Rose Shulman (Macmillan London, London, 1988, and Atheneum, New York, 1988): Mixed-grain Bread; Cornmeal and Millet Bread; Wholemeal Pain de Campagne; Cumin and Cornmeal Bread; Pesto Bread; Texas Cornbread.

The following recipes, in slightly different form, appeared in *Mediterranean Light* by Martha Rose Shulman (Bantam Books, New York, 1989): Italian Country Loaf; Breadsticks; Rosemary and Thyme Bread; Sicilian Bread; Fougasse; Sesame Bread Rings; Wholemeal Focaccia with Herbs; Wholemeal Pitta Bread; Socca; Carta Musica; Gazpacho Andaluz; Pappa al Pomodori; Italian Bread Salad; Fattoush; Chick-pea Fattet; Fattet with Chicken; Bruschette; Bruschette with Tomato Topping; Crostini.

Introduction

This is a book about one of my greatest passions: bread. It is not a definitive bread book, in that it doesn't have an exhaustive number of recipes for breads from around the world. Instead, it is a very personal 'how-to' book, with recipes for my favourite breads, the ones I have developed in my kitchen, and the breads I have been introduced to by other passionate bakers. Most important, it is a book designed to give the home breadmaker confidence about making successful bread. I want you to understand how dough feels (sticky!) and to learn how to work with it. A decent recipe will get you nowhere if you don't understand the principles of working with different kinds of dough.

Of all cooking activities, breadmaking is what I like to do best. I love the physicality of it. I adore working the dough, and watching flour and water turn into our most basic food. I also love bakeries. When I travel I always seek them out. While other tourists visit museums in Italy, I am exploring bakeries. I've spent days in Bologna scouring the city to sample breads, breadsticks and *focacce*. I always return from my travels laden with baked goods.

I like the way dough feels and changes and, of course, how it smells as it bakes. The making of bread is a miraculous process, one I never tire of, and I've made thousands of loaves over the years. Each time is like the first time in some ways; dough is a living thing, never quite the same from one batch to another. I am always learning more, changing my techniques here and there as I am exposed to different ways of working with dough.

There are probably as many different rules about making bread as there are bakers, and they all seem to work, as long as certain principles are observed. The methods I will show you here work for me, and I have tried to explain them so that they will work for you. My goal is to take the mystery out of breadmaking and to provide you with recipes for some truly delicious breads. I hope you become as spoiled as I am. Once you begin making your own, you'll be reluctant to go back to the baker's shop.

Martha Rose Shulman, April 1989

Ingredients

Bread can be only as good as the ingredients that go into it – flours, grains, oils, sweeteners. For a really thorough discussion of ingredients, and also of milling, ovens – in short, everything about bread and what goes into it – Elizabeth David's *English Bread and Yeast Cookery* is essential. Below I describe, in as few words as possible, the basic components of the breads you will find in this book. All the flours used to develop and test the recipes can be obtained from supermarkets and wholefood shops in the UK.

Grains and Flours

Wheat flour

Without wheat flour, bread will not rise. Breads can be made from other grains, but wheat is essential for yeast-risen bread.

Wheat flour is milled from whole wheatberries – small, hard, brown grain kernels that resemble brown rice. The hard, fibrous outer shell of the kernel is called the *bran*. This comprises 13–17 per cent of the weight of the wheatberry, and adds bulk and fibre to flour. The embryo, or sprouting section of wheat, is the *germ*. Wheatgerm comprises 2–3 per cent of the weight of the kernel, and is full of nutrients: good-quality protein, unsaturated fats, vitamins and minerals. It is the most flavourful part of the wheatberry. Because of its high fat content, raw wheatgerm can go rancid very quickly if not refrigerated and wholemeal flours should be kept in a cool, dry place or, preferably, refrigerated. The rest of the kernel is the *endosperm*, which is made up of starch and protein. The protein component is the *gluten*. When dough is kneaded, long strands of gluten are formed; they stretch and expand in the presence of fermenting yeast, and the dough rises. It is the endosperm that remains when the bran and germ are refined or sifted away. Modern roller-milled white flour contains only this part of the grain.

There is some disagreement among bakers over which flours are best for making bread. Commercial bakers rely on flours made from a combination of high-gluten hard wheat from North America and softer European wheat. These flours perform well because of their gluten content, creating dough which expands more than that made from soft wheats; therefore the bakers get more loaves for their money. Most of the flour we buy in supermarkets and wholefood shops is also made from a combination of soft and hard wheats, and is called 'strong' flour, which means that it has a high gluten content. But according to authorities such as Tom Jaine and Elizabeth David, soft wheats have more flavour than hard wheats. French breads, made from soft flours, certainly bear that out (when properly made). Yet many North Americans would disagree about quality. I have one friend in Paris who for years shipped her flour over from America.

The arguments suggest that the strong North American wheat performs better, while softer European wheat is tastier. I myself don't yet have a strong opinion about these flavour differences. I seek out the best domestic flour I can get, whether I'm in America, England or France. The most important thing to me is how it has been milled, stoneground always being unquestionably preferable to roller-milled because the flavourful and most nutritious bits in the germ have not been removed. The best flours in my opinion are stoneground organic flours, which are readily available in wholefood shops.

Stoneground 100 per cent wholemeal flour is flour from which nothing has been removed and to which nothing has been added. The wheat has been crushed between large, flat, slow-moving stones, and the germ and bran remain intact. The process has changed very little since ancient times. If the bag that the wholemeal flour comes in does not specify that it has been stoneground, then it has probably been roller-milled and had the bran and germ added back to it. This kind of flour is not 100 per cent wholemeal, but more like 95 per cent, and it does not have the same sweet flavour or coarse texture as 100 per cent wholemeal flour. The germ will have been overheated and denatured by the high-speed roller-mills.

I find that most 100 per cent wholemeal flour ground in the UK is quite coarse; in fact, some small millers mill their wheat so coarsely that it hardly resembles flour, and in fact doesn't perform like flour: it is more like meal, or bulgur. Flour like this should be used only as an *addition* to, not as the main component of, wholemeal bread. When flour is too grainy the gluten remains trapped in the kernels and the bread won't rise properly. Because of the coarseness of most British

100 per cent wholemeal flour, I normally use it in combination with unbleached white flour or with 85 per cent wholemeal flour.

No matter how coarse or fine, wholemeal flour will always make stickier doughs than white flour because it absorbs less water.

Stoneground 81–85 per cent wholemeal flour is lighter and finer than 100 per cent wholemeal flour, with 81–85 per cent of the kernel present. The wheat is stoneground and then sieved. It has a light-brown colour and a sweet flavour, though not as distinctive as that of 100 per cent wholemeal flour. It can make very fine bread in combination with wholemeal and/or unbleached white flour.

Wholemeal pastry flour is made from soft wheat and is more finely milled than wholemeal flour. Sometimes it is sold as '100 per cent extra-fine stoneground wholemeal flour'. Bread and pastry made from wholemeal pastry flour is lighter, with a finer crumb, than that made from regular wholemeal flour. I use it in combination with unbleached white flour in many of the sweet breads in this book, when I want the flavour of wholemeal flour but not the bulk.

Unbleached white flour is white flour that has not been bleached by chemicals, but by a natural ageing process. The unbleached flour I use for bread is strong plain bread flour, made with a combination of soft and medium-soft wheats and North American hard wheat. Most white flour is milled in high-speed steel roller-mills. The grain is ripped open instead of being crushed, and the germ and bran are sifted out, leaving about 70–73 per cent of the grain – the endosperm, or starch and protein. The small hard granules that remain (semolina) are then pulverised into fine white flour. If the flour is unbleached, it has a slightly off-white colour instead of the snow-white colour of bleached flour. Bread made from unbleached white flour has a richer flavour than that made from bleached.

Stoneground unbleached flour is also available from wholefood shops. It has a greyish colour and a sweeter flavour than roller-milled flour. Stoneground unbleached flour is achieved by milling the grain in a stone mill and extracting or sieving the bran, germ and semolina. Residues of these particles remain, resulting in a superior-tasting flour.

White-flour doughs are much smoother and more elastic than wholemeal, rye or other wholegrain doughs.

Semolina flour This coarse, golden flour is very finely ground semolina, which is ground from durum wheat, the hardest wheat variety. It absorbs much less water than other flours and the doughs made with it are stiff and elastic. One of my favourite breads, from

Sicily, is made with this lovely yellow flour (p. 180) and it is also used to make the best industrial pastas. If you can't find it, use durum flour, or grind up semolina in a blender with some unbleached white flour. Sometimes fairly finely ground semolina is sold in packets as semolina, and this can often be substituted for the flour. I will note when this is possible in my recipes.

Other flours that you will come across in shops include **gluten flour**, a highly refined flour made by refining the gluten out of wheat and combining it with white or wholemeal flour, and **self-raising flour**, which is white or wholemeal flour to which raising agents – bicarbonate of soda and cream of tartar – have been added. Neither of these flours appears in the recipes in this book, and I must admit that I have never used them.

Other flours, grains and meals

Bulgur and cracked wheat Bulgur is cracked wheat that has been parboiled and dried. Both are lovely additions to mixed-grain breads, adding good texture and a sweet, grainy flavour.

Rye flour is milled from whole rye-berries (which resemble wheat-berries). Like wheat flour, it is best when stoneground. It has a rich, earthy flavour and a grainy texture, and it is excellent in sourdough breads. Rye has a lower gluten content than wheat, and this flour must be used in combination with wheat flour. Doughs made from rye flour are quite sticky and often unwieldy, but a proper balance of rye and wheat will result in good elasticity. **Rye flakes** are rolled or flaked rye-berries, resembling oatmeal or oat flakes. I use them in some of my mixed-grain breads (see Chapter 2). They have a sweet, earthy flavour and a chewy texture.

Cornmeal or maize meal is ground from hard corn kernels (called *grano turco* in Italy) and has a grainy texture, a sweet taste and a lovely golden colour. Polenta can be substituted for cornmeal as long as the polenta isn't too coarse; basically they are the same thing. Stoneground yellow cornmeal, or medium to fine polenta, combined with wheat flour make delicious grainy-textured breads. Use cornmeal for dusting baking stones and sheets. Store it in the refrigerator to prevent the natural oils in the kernel from going rancid.

Barleymeal and barley flakes Barley has always been one of Britain's widespread staple grains. Like rye, barley has a low gluten content, so must be mixed with wholemeal or unbleached flour to achieve a good loaf. But it has a delicious, tangy flavour and makes marvellous earthy bread. Barleymeal is used for Welsh and Scottish griddle breads – barley bannocks – and for pancakes. Barley flakes, like oat flakes and rye flakes, make a nutritious and tasty addition to mixed-grain breads (see p. 48).

Oatmeal, oat flakes and oat bran Oats have a sweet cereal flavour, which, together with their chewy texture, makes them a lovely addition to breads. Fine and medium oatmeal or oat flakes are best for breads and muffins. Rolled oats are also good; these are steam-treated oat grains crushed into flakes by mechanical rollers. Oatmeal has a high fat content and should be kept in the refrigerator. Oat bran is a high-fibre bran, differing from wheat bran in that it is soluble whereas wheat bran is not. Some people find it easier to digest than wheat bran, and research has shown that this kind of fibre helps lower blood cholesterol and helps control blood-sugar levels and insulin requirements in diabetics.

Millet, millet meal and millet flakes Millet is a sweet, tasty grain that looks like tiny yellow beads. It can be ground to a coarse meal, which adds texture, yellow colour and flavour to breads. The flakes are lighter than oat, rye or barley flakes, but have the same chewy texture.

Buckwheat flour has a very strong, distinctive flavour, earthy and rather fruity. I add it in small quantities to some breads, and it is essential for *blinis* (Russian yeast-raised pancakes) and for the French crêpes called *galettes au sarrasin* (see the buckwheat crêpes on p. 256).

Chick-pea flour is a high-protein flour made by grinding dried chick peas. It has a marvellous earthy flavour and is the main ingredient in *socca*, a polenta-like Niçoise speciality (p. 253). Store it in the refrigerator to prevent the oils from going rancid.

Soya flour is milled from soya beans and has a very high protein content as well as a high fat content. It can be added in small quantities to breads to increase their protein value. It too should be stored in the refrigerator.

Sesame seeds are tiny, nutty-tasting seeds used in Italian, Middle Eastern and Greek breads as well as for a topping for many of my wholemeal and mixed-grain breads. They should be stored in the refrigerator to prevent the oils from going rancid.

Raising Agents, Sweeteners, Oils and Salt

Yeast When yeast is activated in warm water, it metabolises the sugars in the bread dough, releasing carbon dioxide and alcohol in the process. The long strands of gluten which are created when dough is kneaded stretch as the yeast releases these byproducts, causing the dough to rise.

I use active dried yeast, which I buy either at the supermarket or a wholefood shop. It comes in the form of small, hard beads, or salt-like granules, which must be reactivated by dissolving in warm water. I buy it in small tins. You can also buy it in small packets, but I make so much bread that tins are more economical. Fresh yeast, which you buy in cakes, can be used instead of dried in any of the recipes, substituting ½oz (15g) for 2 teaspoons (¼oz/7–8g) active dried yeast. Store yeast in the refrigerator or freezer: this is important for maintaining freshness, even in dried yeast. Always check the 'use by' date on the tin or packet.

Baking powder and bicarbonate of soda are used to raise quick, moist doughs and batters, where gluten has not been developed. They are fast-acting substances. Bicarbonate of soda reacts with acids in the dough and/or with acids in baking powder which is also added to the mixture, and releases bubbles which cause the dough to rise. Baking powder, which contains baking soda and an acid such as tartaric acid, creates two gaseous reactions, one when the dough is mixed and another when the dough is exposed to high heat (which is why it is called 'double-acting baking powder').

Sourdough has the same characteristics as yeast, but is much slower acting. This is the old-fashioned method of leavening bread: natural yeasts develop when dough is left to ferment for several days. I usually use sourdough in combination with yeast for my sourdough breads (see Chapter 3).

Honey Small amounts of sweetener give yeast a boost. I usually use a mild-flavoured, light-coloured honey, such as acacia or clover. If you use strong honey, even in small amounts (a tablespoon or two), the flavour can be overpowering. I use larger quantities of honey in sweet breads.

Malt extract or malt syrup, usually made from malted barley, is added in very small amounts to some bread doughs to aid the yeast and give the bread a golden crust.

Black treacle gives a dark colour and distinctive flavour to black breads, rye breads, and some mixed-grain breads and muffins.

Oils Some breads call for oil, some do not (see p. 18). I use a very mild-tasting oil, such as sunflower or safflower, unless the recipe specifies melted butter (which should be unsalted), olive oil or walnut oil.

Salt I use sea salt, which has a better flavour than regular salt. Salt is important for the flavour of the bread, and also helps regulate the action of the yeast.

Equipment

Breadmaking does not require too much in the way of equipment.
Most of the items below will be in a working kitchen already.

Kitchen scales You really can't begin without these: they are essential
for measuring flours and other ingredients accurately. I recommend
scales with both metric and imperial measures. Salter makes a very
good set with a useful wide bowl.

Large mixing bowl This can be stainless steel, earthenware, glass,
plastic or ceramic. Earthenware bowls are probably the best for
maintaining temperature, but I have used everything from a plastic tub
to an enamel wash basin with equally good results. The bowl should
hold at least 5 pints (3 litres), preferably more. You should have more
than one bowl for quick breads, for which you must mix liquid and dry
ingredients separately.

Liquid measure for measuring in liquids.

Measuring spoons are essential for these recipes, but if you find
yourself on an island without a set, a level soupspoon will do for a
tablespoon and a teaspoon for a teaspoon.

Large whisk for beating in flours.

Large wooden spoon for folding in ingredients.

Pastry scraper or dough scraper This is essential for turning and
kneading many of these breads, the doughs of which are very sticky. A
traditional dough scraper is a stainless-steel rectangle with a wooden
handle; I prefer a plastic pastry scraper with a curved edge, which is
useful for scraping dough out of a bowl. It works just as well for
kneading, although it is not as effective for cutting the dough.

Banneton A *banneton* is a bowl or basket lined with muslin or
tea-towels in which dough rises, keeping its shape at the same time,
before being transferred to baking stones or sheets (see below). All you
have to do to devise your own is to line a bowl with tea-towels and dust

the towels on the inside with flour. Place the dough in this bowl, and just before baking turn it out on to a hot baking stone or baking sheet.

Baking stone or tiles These porous clay baking stones or tiles are fired at high heat and distribute the heat evenly in your oven, transforming it into something more like a stone bread oven by absorbing the moisture of the dough and giving the breads a harder, thicker crust (though, of course, with some breads you don't want that). I usually keep my round baking stone in the oven even when I'm baking loaves in tins or on baking sheets. Tiles are about the size (5 inches square) and thickness of ordinary wall tiles, and you use at least four together in the oven; stones are 14–15 inches in diameter and about ¼ inch thick. I prefer the large stones to the tiles, because tiles do not always stay close together when you turn the dough on to them. Pre-heat the stones or tiles in the oven for 30 minutes at 400–450°F/200–230°C/gas mark 6–8 and sprinkle them with cornmeal or semolina if baking your loaves directly on the stones or tiles. Baking stones can be obtained in kitchenware shops and some hardware shops.

Shallow tin and/or water spray-bottle A little steam in the hot oven helps to ensure a hard crust, and can be obtained in two ways. I often put an empty cake or pie tin on a shelf near the bottom of the oven while it is heating up, then just before baking I pour a pint of water into it and immediately close the oven door. If you use this method, be sure that your tin isn't too close to the baking tiles or stone, if you are using these, because the sudden rush of steam could cause the clay to crack. The other methods are to spray the loaf with water immediately after putting it into the oven, and repeat the spraying two or three times during the first 10 minutes of baking; or to spray the oven itself immediately before and during baking. I always spray my loaves and the oven, and sometimes use the tin method.

Non-stick baking sheets I use these for some breads, pizzas and *focacce*.

Non-stick loaf tins make a difference when it comes to removing loaves from the tins. Mine measure 9 × 5 × 2¾ inches, and work very well. Earthenware can be used for baking bread, but I have better luck with doughs not sticking to tin. Whether non-stick or not, tin is preferable to other materials because the loaves are less likely to stick and are also closer to the heat. Dough sticks to glass, and glass is a poor heat conductor.

Heavy-duty electric mixer with dough hook This is optional, and expensive, but it really does make a difference with some of the stickier doughs. I recommend either the Kenwood Chef or the Kitchenaid.

Clingfilm is good for covering the bowl while the bread is rising; it creates a constant, warm, gaseous atmosphere for the dough, rather like an incubator. Damp tea-towels can be used instead.

Ovens

While I was writing this book, several people asked me if it was indeed possible to make really good bread in an ordinary home oven. I know that those who have authentic wood-fuelled bread ovens would disagree with me, but I insist that you *can* make delicious bread in a normal oven. It won't have the rich, woody flavour or thick crust of bread baked in an old-fashioned baker's oven, but it will certainly be miles ahead of the bread you find in most shops and bakeries. My purpose in this book is to help you use the materials at your disposal. If the bread you make with them is so good that you want to go further and install a bread oven, then I will have succeeded.

I have used all kinds of ovens for home baking. I tested the recipes in this book in the oven of a tiny gas cooker that wasn't even big enough for my baking stone (which was very disappointing). I've used a convection oven, which is what many French bakers use: it circulates the hot air so that the loaves bake evenly and brown very nicely. I liked it, but not so much that I felt I had to have one. In the end, the most important thing for me is a reliable oven that bakes at the temperature it says it's baking at (or at least is consistently too hot or cool, so that I can gauge the setting correctly). You can create steam with a spray-bottle or a tin of water, stone-like heat with baking stones, as explained on p. 12.

1: How to Make Yeast Bread: Techniques and Basic Recipes

I have made bread and studied breadmaking for years. I have read lots of literature, taken a few courses, worked with French bakers. Each book and baker has a different theory and technique, many of them contradictory. Yet just about all of them seem to work — because, tricky as breadmaking may be for the beginner, only a few things are essential for success.

Yeast-raised bread requires, in its simplest form, five basic steps: mixing up the dough; kneading; shaping the dough into a ball and setting it to rise in a covered bowl; punching down (or deflating) the dough, shaping it and setting it to rise again; and baking.

The basic ingredients have to be good to begin with: the flour not too old and preferably stoneground (see p. 4), the yeast active (not too old), the water not tasting strongly of chlorine and minerals. The liquids and solids must not be too hot or they will kill the yeast; nor should they be too cold, or the action of the yeast will be slowed. The dough must be properly mixed and effectively kneaded to develop the gluten in the flour, the element responsible for the dough's elasticity. The dough must have enough time to rise and develop its full flavour and potential; and the loaves must be properly shaped and baked.

Despite all the breadmaking literature available, I think that there are still some grey areas. Handling dough (certain types in particular) can at first seem awkward and mysterious, and it is difficult to describe such a tactile experience in words. But I'm going to give it a try.

If you are going to make bread, you are going to have to put up with doughy, sticky hands. This, I feel, has not been said before, and in all fairness to you, the baker, it must be made clear. There is a phrase which comes up again and again in recipes and which I think lies at the root of many failed attempts at breadmaking. It is: 'Knead until smooth, silky and elastic.' In my experience dough is hardly ever smooth and silky, and if it does achieve that quality, it doesn't last for long. (Elastic it *must* be, because elasticity is what you are developing in the dough when you knead.) My doughs, more often than not, reach the smooth and silky stage after sufficient kneading, but they quickly become tacky again. If

I kept adding flour to the dough when kneading, just because the surface was a bit tacky, then I would end up with a very heavy loaf. When I use coarse wholemeal flours – especially rye flour – my dough is always sticky and hard to handle, at both the kneading and shaping stages. When I worked at Max Poilane's bakery in Paris, I used so much flour dusting the work surface and the loaves when I shaped them (all eighty at a time) that I would be covered with flour from head to toe when I left the bakery each day. It's just something I have to accept, putting my faith in the fact that well-kneaded, elastic dough will rise no matter how sticky. And rise it does. But when you begin to mix up the dough it is a formless, sticky mass, and can be manipulated easily only with the aid of a plastic or metal pastry scraper. If you are like the French master-baker who taught a very good bread class I took at the Ritz-Escoffier cooking school in Paris, you might be very adept at mixing up the dough and kneading. This man had extremely large hands; he would work the dough very briskly, quickly getting it to a smooth stage where it stuck neither to the kneading surface nor to his hands, and he didn't even have to flour the table. But I and my fellow students, working with the exact same recipes, could never get such an amenable dough, even though some of us were already experienced breadmakers. However, our finished breads were indistinguishable from our teacher's.

I have tried to point out in the recipes in this book what the nature of the dough will be. If it is especially sticky and hard to handle I shall tell you, so that you don't keep adding flour, ending up with a different kind of bread from the one intended. But my advice, before you begin, is: take off your rings; keep a cloth or a plastic bag by the phone so that when it rings during kneading you don't get dough all over it; and have a special sponge with a rough side for rubbing dough off your hands and off the work surface. Dough comes off your hands easily, and the bread you will get will be worth the sticky hands and tacky sponge.

Making Bread By Hand, Step By Step

This is how *I* make bread. It is by no means the only way to do it. Many authorities tell you to warm the flour before beginning, and, indeed, that's a good idea. But I must admit I never do it, and yet my breads work. Flour should definitely not be cold, as that will slow up the yeast action. I add solids to liquids; many people do the reverse, adding liquid to the flour as necessary. The French put their flour on a board, make a well in the centre, and put their yeast, water and salt in the well. They dissolve the yeast in the water with their fingertips, then brush the flour into the water and mix with their fingertips, and when it is all amalgamated they begin to knead. Many breadmakers do something similar in a large bowl, beginning with a fixed amount of flour and varying the amount of liquid. It's sensible, because different kinds of flours absorb different amounts of liquid. But I began making bread the other way, by adding flour to a fixed amount of liquid and varying the amount of flour – and I've always felt more comfortable with this method, so this is the method you'll get from me.

Before You Begin

Consider the size and height of your kneading surface. It should be the size of a large cutting board, at least 14 inches square and preferably larger. Ideally, the surface you knead the dough on should be lower than a cutting surface – about waist or midriff level. This allows you to put more of your weight into kneading, as you lean into the dough. When I began making bread I used to wear platform shoes and stand on a box because I had only an ordinary kitchen worktop. A large plastic, wooden or marble board on a kitchen table is good. If that's not possible, the worktop will do but you may have to stand on your toes while you knead.

Make sure your ingredients are at room temperature or warm. As I have said, many cooks instruct you to warm the flour and/or the bowl in the oven; it's probably a good idea. Also, you might want to put on a record or tape, or turn on the radio: once your hands are doughy it's too late.

Mixing the Dough

The first thing you need to do when you mix up a yeast dough is dissolve the yeast in the liquid, which is usually lukewarm water. Lukewarm is warm but not hot, anywhere from 95–105°F (35–40°C). I usually test by dipping my fingers into it. If it is too hot it will kill the yeast. Many recipe writers have you dissolve the yeast in a small bowl and add this to a larger bowl when you mix up the dough. I see no reason for this. It gives you one more thing to wash, and you lose a little bit of the yeast when you transfer it to the other bowl. I simply dissolve it in the water in the large bowl in which I make the dough. If milk is the liquid called for, I usually dissolve the yeast in a tablespoon or two of water first. It will dissolve more readily in water.

In all my recipes I use active dried yeast (see p. 8). It takes the granules a few minutes to dissolve in lukewarm water, and longer in milk. If you can only obtain fresh yeast (see p. 8), use ½oz (15g) for every 2 teaspoons dried yeast. Crumble fresh yeast into the liquid and dissolve as for dried yeast.

If there is sweetener, such as sugar, honey or treacle, in your bread, add it along with the yeast. The yeast feeds on the sweetener, which gives it some energy. Mix the yeast and liquid together with a whisk or spoon and add the sweetener; wait 5 or 10 minutes, until the liquid is cloudy. You will see the yeast moving like little clouds in the water.

Now stir in oil or melted unsalted butter, if either is called for in the recipe. Opinion differs about whether or not oil should be added to dough. Pure French bread is made with nothing more than flour, water, salt and yeast. But pure French bread dries out in a day (not country breads, but *baguettes* certainly do). The advantage of adding oil is that the bread will last longer, and all breads containing fats freeze well. It will also have a slightly moister texture. Some of my recipes call for oil, some do not. You are free to experiment by leaving it out or adding it wherever you wish. I'm not a purist when it comes to oil, but I respect those who are and I'm sure their reasons for not allowing it are sound.

Salt is added with the flour: it should be mixed up with the flour and not, as many recipes instruct, added to the yeast mixture before flour is added. This is because salt has a traumatic effect on yeast when it comes into direct contact with it. It slows down the yeast's action, which is good in the sense that the dough rises in a more controlled way when there is salt present, but it should be mixed with the flour before being added to the dough. Combine the salt and flour and begin adding to the liquid mixture. Add by large spoonfuls or by cupfuls, folding in after each addition. *Folding* means scooping your spoon under the dough (or liquid batter, which is what it will be until you've added quite a bit of flour) from the middle of the bowl, sliding it to the side of the bowl and turning the batter over itself. Do this by gently flicking your wrist as you bring the spoon up the side of the bowl, ending up with the spoon in the middle of the bowl, pointing down. Each time you add and fold, give the bowl a quarter-turn.

By the time you have added about three-quarters (maybe less) of the flour, the dough will be in a mass – sticky and formless, but in enough of one piece to enable you to scrape it out on to your kneading surface. Which is what you want to do as soon as possible. You will be adding the remaining flour during the kneading process.

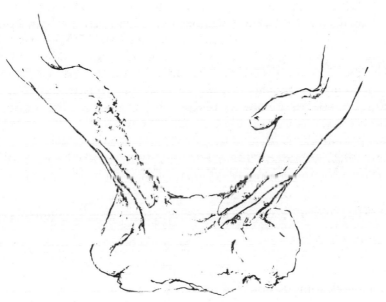

Kneading the Dough

You are kneading the dough for three reasons: to develop the gluten in the flour (these are the long strands of protein which expand as the yeast multiplies, giving the dough its volume and elasticity – see p. 15), to incorporate air into the dough and to generate warmth within the dough, both necessary if the dough is to rise properly. What is actually happening as dough rises is that living yeast is fermenting and turning oxygen and sugars into carbon dioxide and alcohols. The carbon dioxide becomes trapped in the glutenous network of dough, and this is what makes the dough expand and the bread rise.

Before you scrape out the dough, place a generous amount of flour on your kneading surface. Use a pastry scraper (see p. 11) Or your spoon to scrape the dough out of the bowl. Before you begin kneading wait a minute or two to allow the flour to absorb moisture. Roll up your sleeves and flour your hands.

There are several techniques for kneading. I began with just one of them – the 'fold–lean–turn' technique – but now I use them all. I'll begin here with 'fold–lean–turn'.

Using a pastry scraper to facilitate turning the dough, which will be very wet at first, fold the dough in half towards you. With one or both hands (floured, remember), lean into the dough, beginning at the edge where the two folds come together and pressing your weight from the heels of your palms out through your fingertips. Rock forwards on your feet and let your body push your hands into the dough. At first, because the dough is sticky, you should press gingerly or the dough will go all over the place. Now give the dough a quarter-turn to the left or right. Fold the dough in half towards you again and lean into it. The heels of your palms are doing most of the work here (with the help of the rest of your body and of gravity), but the movement ends in the fingertips. Turn the dough again. Fold, lean, turn; fold, lean, turn. The dough will be amorphous and annoyingly sticky at first, but in just a

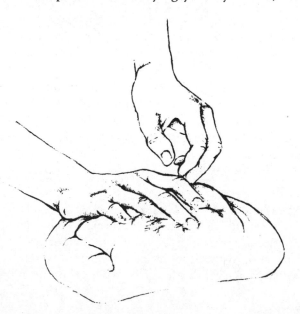

few turns it will begin to stiffen up. Sprinkle flour on to the surface of the dough as necessary to minimise the inevitable sticking, but add most of the flour to the work surface – and add it sparingly. Particularly with wholemeal breads, the flour absorbs the liquid at varying rates, and you want to give it time to do this. If you add too much flour all at once your bread will be too heavy. The dough will be very stiff and hard to handle, and it won't rise. Dough made with white flour begins to get tough, elastic and resistant after about 5 minutes' kneading. Wholemeal flour, which absorbs less liquid, is always a little stickier and less tough than white-flour doughs. Many sourdough breads (see Chapter 3) are hopelessly sticky, sometimes almost like toffee. As the dough toughens up, depending on the quantity you're making, I often find that I'm leaning into the dough several times before turning it, to work it more thoroughly. So the rhythm is fold, lean-lean-lean, turn.

The fold–lean–turn technique is a little slow, and many bakers work more quickly. They are folding, leaning and turning, but it looks and feels a little different. Grab the far side of the dough or scoop it up with a pastry scraper, pull it up and fold the far side over the near side, then with a quick movement slam the dough down on to the work surface, pushing into it with the heel of your palm and quickly give it a quarter-turn. Continue this movement, working briskly and adding flour as necessary, for about 10 minutes, until the dough is elastic and fairly smooth.

You can also grab the entire piece of dough and slap it down on the table, slapping it down, lifting it up as high as your head and slapping it down over and over again. As you lift the dough you will also be stretching it and folding it over itself to incorporate air into the dough. I find that I begin slapping the dough on to my kneading surface after I've been folding and leaning for a while and the dough has become resistant.

Whichever way you knead, try not to tear the dough, as this breaks the strands of gluten that you are working so hard to develop. You can avoid tearing the dough by being gentle when you knead: you don't have to knead violently, just firmly. A steady, peaceful rhythm is best, and can be very relaxing.

Your fingertips and hands will tell you when the dough has been sufficiently kneaded. After you've made bread a few times you'll begin to recognise the point at which dough is ready to rise. It should be bouncy, elastic. As several writers aptly say, 'It should feel as if it had a mind of its own.' It is a living thing, after all, and there is something friendly and lively about properly kneaded dough. It usually takes about 10 minutes' kneading to develop the gluten and get the dough into shape, but this time – and the amount of flour you have to add to your kneading surface – can vary. If it is very humid or hot, the dough may be stickier than it is in dry weather and may take longer to stiffen up. The coarseness of your flour will also affect the texture of the dough: the coarser the flour, the tackier the dough. As I have explained (p. 15), it won't always be smooth, but sometimes it will, which is ideal. Doughs with lots of grains will be dense and slightly tacky on the surface; those with rye flour will be very tacky. White doughs are sometimes tacky if they don't have a lot of flour in them. The way to tell if the dough has been sufficiently kneaded is to shape it into a ball and plunge a few fingers into it. If the dough springs back it is ready to rise. It doesn't necessarily spring back quickly, but it doesn't remain indented and passive. If it doesn't spring back, knead a bit more and add more flour.

Once you have finished kneading and are ready to shape the dough, get it into the bowl quickly, because no matter what the surface of your dough is like, as soon as it sits for a few seconds it will begin to stick to the work surface.

Kneading the dough in an electric mixer

Many heavy-duty electric mixers, such as the Kenwood Chef and the Kitchenaid, come with dough-hook attachments. If you make a lot of bread, these can be very convenient indeed, and whenever they can be used in the recipes I give instructions. When there is more than 2lb (900g) dough I don't use a dough hook, because too much dough strains the motor and the results are not very good. Also, even if you have a machine, it is important to learn to knead by hand in order to familiarise yourself with the way dough should feel. But especially with sticky doughs, electric mixers really can take the trouble out of kneading.

When using an electric mixer, dissolve the yeast in the liquid in the bowl of your mixer, as instructed above, and let it sit for 10 minutes. Add the oil, if used, mix all but about 4oz (115g) of the flour with the salt, and add this all at once to the bowl. Mix together briefly using the mixing attachment, just to amalgamate the ingredients, then change to the dough hook, scraping all the dough that clings to the mixing attachment into the bowl. Knead at low speed (1 on the Kenwood) for 2 minutes, then switch to medium (2 on the Kenwood) and knead for 6–8 minutes. Do not overwork, or the dough will become too hot (as will the machine). The dough should come away from the sides of the bowl and form a ball around the dough hook, which will be working air into the dough and slapping it around to develop the gluten. If the dough continues to adhere to the sides of the bowl, add flour as necessary. After 6–8 minutes, I always use a pastry scraper to scrape the dough out of the bowl on to a floured surface, flour my hands and finish off the kneading by hand, just for about 30–60 seconds. This way I can be sure that the dough has been properly kneaded: contact with the dough is important. But I know plenty of bakers who don't touch the dough after kneading by machine; they just cover it and let it rise, and this seems to work.

Shaping the Dough into a Ball

When the dough has been kneaded sufficiently, shape it into a ball. Do this by folding it over itself, towards you, and turning, without the leaning bit, all the way around. Pinch the seams on the bottom together.

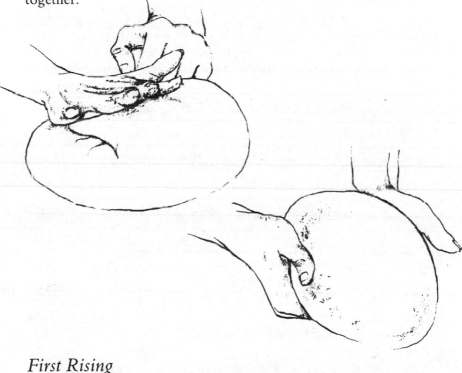

First Rising

Opinion differs about whether or not you should oil the bowl in which the bread is to rise. The most convincing argument I've heard for not oiling is that unabsorbed oil can make holes in the finished loaf. I must admit that I usually do oil my bowl, and have never had holes in my loaves. I oil the bowl so that the surface of the dough doesn't dry out. But if the bowl is properly covered, with clingfilm, this shouldn't happen. So once again, I think oiling the bowl might be a question of habit or taste. It does make it easier to turn out the dough without tearing it when you get around to that step. But if you are a purist, don't. Try it both ways and see which yields the best results for you.

Rinsing out the bowl is another thing about which people have differing opinions. For my sponge-method breads (see Chapter 2) I used never to rinse out the bowl, but now sometimes I do. If there are lots of little bits of dough on the bowl it's a good idea, because if they get into the dough for the loaf they will spoil its texture. Also, it's easier to clean the bowl before the dough hardens.

Anyway, whether you clean and oil your bowl or not, it should be about three times (or at least twice) the volume of the dough, because the dough will double in size during the first rising.

If you have oiled your bowl, place the dough in it, seam side up (i.e. rounded side down) first, then turn the dough over so that the rounded side is up. If you have not oiled the bowl, place the dough in rounded side up. Cover the bowl tightly with clingfilm. This keeps draughts off the dough and helps create a warm incubating atmosphere within the bowl. The dough itself is already warm and is generating heat as the yeast multiplies. It needs to stay warm in order to rise properly. Another reason for covering the dough is so that the surface won't dry out and harden, which would inhibit rising. I also place a tea-towel over the clingfilm to help prevent draughts from reaching the dough, just in case the clingfilm comes loose at the sides, and I instruct you to do so in my recipes.

Set the bowl in a warm spot. If it's a warm day, or if your kitchen is very warm, anywhere will do. When I mix up dough in a ceramic bowl in the summer, I often put it in the sun to rise (not in a stainless-steel bowl, though, as the bowl will become too hot). In winter I often light the oven for a few minutes at a high temperature, then turn it off and let the dough rise in the oven with the door closed. Or I put the bowl on top of a heater, or on top of or next to a radiator. An oven with a pilot light is also a good place. The important thing is for it to be fairly warm and free from draughts.

Allow the dough to rise until it has more or less doubled in volume. This usually takes about 1½–2 hours, depending on the recipe (the sponge-method breads in Chapter 2 have a head start, and require only an hour). *Don't feel as if you have to be a prisoner to your dough.* If you want to go to the cinema, put the dough in the refrigerator to slow the rising. Refrigerated dough can even rise overnight or all day, so you could mix up and knead your dough before going to bed or before going to work, and finish it off later. It will need time to come back to room temperature, but as soon as it does it will perform like normal dough.

Dough can also be frozen. In this case you are putting the yeast to sleep for a while. Like refrigerated dough, once frozen dough comes back to room temperature it will behave normally, although you might have to get it going again with a little kneading.

If you let dough rise too long, the yeast will produce too much carbon dioxide and alcohol, and will suffocate in its own by-products. This is why the dough needs to be punched down and reworked once it has doubled in volume.

Some people find the smell of yeast and rising dough very unappetising. How can rising dough smell so strong and bad when baking bread smells so good? The strong odours come from the carbon dioxide and alcohol produced by the yeast, and is what we call a 'yeasty' smell. This, like sticky hands, is one of the things you'll have to put up with if you're going to make bread. It's worth it.

Punching Down the Dough

When the dough has risen sufficiently, it needs to be deflated, or punched down, to release the gas created by the yeast and to slow down the yeast's action. The dough has doubled in volume, more or less (sometimes this is difficult to discern), and has risen into a soft, spongy mass, with a smooth, usually slightly domed but sometimes billowy or bubbly surface. A good way to tell if the dough is ready for punching down is to wet your finger and stick it gently into the centre of the dough, about ½ inch deep. The dough should feel spongy and the hole should not fill in at all. If it does, the dough needs to rise a little more. If it doesn't, it's time to punch it down and shape the loaves.

Punching down is very satisfying. It isn't really violent, but is called 'punching' because most people deflate the dough by sticking their fist into it, although you can also do this with your fingertips. Sprinkle the surface of the dough with a little flour, and stick your fist or fingertips into the middle of the dough. The dough will sigh and collapse, and you will see how it has transformed into hundreds of little glutenous strands separated by airy bubbles. Punch it, or tap it with the fingers, a few more times in different places to deflate it completely. Don't be hard on the dough: you don't want to tear the strands of gluten, you just want to release the gases. Light doughs will be stickier than dense doughs at this point.

Some recipes call for a second rise in the bowl. In others you will shape the dough before the second rising.

Shaping the Dough

Carefully scrape the dough out of the bowl on to a lightly floured work surface, using a spatula or a pastry scraper and, again, being careful not to tear it. Knead it for a minute or two and shape it into a ball. If you are making more than one loaf, cut the dough into equal-sized pieces, according to the number of loaves or rolls you wish to make, using a metal or plastic pastry scraper, or a sharp knife. If you wish, weigh the pieces to make sure they're equal. Now shape your dough into tight balls (or one tight ball for one large loaf). Do this exactly as you did at the end of kneading, by pulling the edge of the dough up and folding it over itself, turning and folding all the way around. Now cup your hands around the ball, lightly flouring the dough if it is sticky, and gently lift and bounce the dough, turning it inside the dome of your hands, to get a very round, tight ball. Let it rest for 5 minutes.

Round loaves

For round country loaves, making the dough into a ball gives you the shape you will want. After you have let the dough rest for 5 minutes, cup your hands around it again and give it another turn, just to make sure it is nice and tight and smooth. Sometimes round, free-form loaves spread out annoyingly on the baking sheet. The rising alternatives below should help prevent this, but if you continue to have a problem, make a stiffer dough by using more flour than the recipes call for, and reduce the final rising time.

For the second rising, you have a choice of methods. You can let the dough rise upside down in a towel-lined basket called a *banneton* (see p. 11); you can let it rise in the bowl again and then reshape once more; or you can let it rise on a baking sheet.

If using a banneton. Dust a clean, dry tea-towel with flour and line a bowl or basket with it. Form the dough into a ball, dust the surface with flour and place it in the towel-lined bowl or basket, rounded side down. Cover the bowl with another floured tea-towel and set it in a warm spot to rise.

If not using a banneton. Form the dough into a ball and let it rise in an oiled bowl until it has doubled in bulk. Reshape the dough by cupping your hands around it and gently propping it up, without pressing hard enough to deflate it. Move your hands quickly around the edges of the dough. Place it on a baking sheet which has been oiled and sprinkled with cornmeal while you heat the oven. *Or*, shape the dough into a tight ball and let rise directly on an oiled, cornmeal-sprinkled baking sheet. The dough will probably spread out and will have to be reshaped gently before baking, or baked before it spreads out too much.

Pan loaves

While your dough is resting, oil loaf tins, which should measure approximately 8½–9 × 4½ × 3 inches. It is important to oil the tins well so that the finished loaves can be removed easily after baking. I use non-stick tins when I can get them. (See p. 12.)

Press out a ball of dough into a rectangle about 1 inch thick and a little longer than your loaf tin. There are three different ways to form the loaves:

1. Roll the rectangle up tightly, like a sausage. Pinch the edges together firmly along the lengthwise crease. Rock this sausage or log-shape gently on the board to give it a rounded shape. Fold the two short ends in towards the centre and pinch the folds.

2. Make a rectangle as above, and fold it lengthwise like a business letter, folding in one edge to the middle, and the remaining edge over the first fold. Rock this log-shape gently back and forth on the board. Pinch together firmly along the lengthwise crease, and fold in the short ends, as above.

3. Fold the rectangle in half, and pinch together the edges gently, using the heel of your hand. Flatten out the rectangle slightly, fold it over once more, then pinch together the edges of the lengthwise seam. Rock it back and forth on the board to give a rounded log-shape, and fold in the short ends, as above.

Whichever method you have used, now place the loaf, crease side up, in the oiled loaf tin. Gently push it into the tin with the backs of your hands to allow it to be oiled and shaped by the tin. Turn the loaf over so that the smooth side is up, and gently press it into the sides of the tin again. It will spring back, which is a good sign. The dough should fill the tin by about two-thirds or three-quarters (some will fill only by half, depending on the recipe and the size of the tin). Cover the tin loosely with a tea-towel and set it in a warm spot for the dough to rise. It is ready to bake when it rises above the edges of the tin.

Baguettes

Baguette dough is often quite sticky, so work quickly on a lightly floured surface. If there is too much flour, your bread will not have the right kind of surface. Here again, I've used a number of techniques. The first (a French technique) works well:

1. Press or roll the dough into a small rectangle about 1 inch thick. Fold one long side all the way over to the other edge and gently pat the seam together, using the heel of your hand or your fingertips. Now take the dough from the side you have just folded over (which will now be rounded) and fold it over itself again to the other edge of the dough. Pinch or pat the edges together and, placing both hands together at the centre of this log-shape, roll it gently but firmly back and forth under your hands on the work surface while you move your hands away from each other towards the edges of the dough. The dough will stretch out into a long, tight, evenly shaped cylinder as you do this. Fold the short ends under and pinch the seams.

2. You can also fold the rectangle like a business letter. Fold the long edge towards the centre and gently pat the seam together with the heel of your hand or your fingertips. Then fold this rounded piece towards the remaining edge, and pinch or pat together at the seam. Place your hands together in the middle of the log shape and roll it back and forth to stretch it out as above, folding the short ends in and pinching the seams.

3. The dough can also be rolled out into a wider, flatter rectangle and rolled up tightly into a cylinder, folding the ends in and pinching the seams all the way around at the end. The other two methods above, however, result in a more springy dough.

For rising I recommend special *baguette* tins or *bannetons*. You can create a *banneton* for *baguettes* by placing the dough on a generously floured, stiff tea-towel (linen is good) or heavy piece of muslin and making pleats along the edges of the dough, between the *baguettes*. Prop the outside edges of the dough against loaf tins and/or a wall so that it doesn't spread out too much. If you let the loaves rise on baking sheets they will spread out and flatten. If you have *baguette* tins, oil them generously and dust them with cornmeal. *Baguettes* should rise for about 45 minutes, until just about doubled in volume.

Sausage-shape, bloomer or batard

These long, free-form loaves are wider than *baguettes*. They are shaped like pan loaves, but the shaped loaves are then lengthened out like a *baguette*.

Small round rolls

Divide the dough into small, equal-sized pieces and create tight, round balls by cupping your hand over the pieces and rolling them around and around under the dome of your hand on the table (below left). Or shape the balls by pulling one side of the dough over to the opposite side and pinching underneath, then turning the dough and continuing all the way around (below right). Pinch the bottoms together well. Place the rolls on an oiled, cornmeal-dusted baking sheet, or in rows on floured tea-towels, with pleats in between the rows, as for the *baguettes* above.

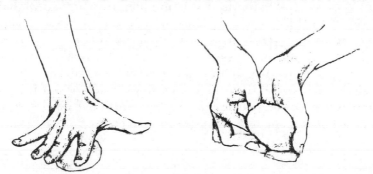

For special shapes like braids and knots, see the specific recipes.

Second Rise

Some breads are brushed at this point with a glaze made from beaten egg, or egg beaten in water, so that the baked loaves will have a very shiny surface. You can also brush them just before baking, but sometimes I find that brushing at this delicate stage causes the loaves to deflate.

The time for the second rise varies with the type of bread and shape of loaf and will be specified in the recipes (see also notes on particular shapes above). It is important to allow the dough to develop its full potential, but it is also very important not to allow it to rise for too long. If it does, it will spread out too much if it is rising on a baking sheet, and it will collapse during baking because there will be too many air bubbles in the dough and not enough structure.

Baking

When you bake the bread, the high heat kills the yeast, stopping its action – but only after one final burst of life, when the dough is exposed to the heat, causing the final, satisfying rise in the oven.

Pre-heat the oven for at least 15 and preferably 30 minutes. The temperature varies with the recipes. Breads baked in loaf tins tend to bake at medium heat (350–375°F/180–190°C/gas mark 4–5). Crusty loaves need a higher heat (400–425°F/200–220°C/gas mark 6–7). Some recipes have you bake the loaves at a very high heat (450–500°F/230–250°C/gas mark 8–10) for the first 10 minutes, then turn down the heat to 350–400°F/180–200°C/gas mark 4–6. I almost always bake the loaves at a steady, fairly high heat (about 400°F/200°C/gas mark 6) with good results. Breads should be baked in the middle or the upper third of the oven. (If you are making two loaves at once, you will usually be able to get them both on a single baking sheet if they are round loaves, or you will be able to fit two loaf tins side by side in the oven, so both will be at the same position in the oven.)

Slashing

Most loaves need to be slashed before baking. The slashes provide escape-hatches for steam, which develops as the loaves bake. Steam develops quickly, and if the slashes weren't there it could cause the loaves to crack or break apart. The best tool for slashing is a sharp razor blade, dipped in water. A sharp knife dipped in water will also work. Slash the loaves just before putting them into the oven, and as they bake the slashes will open up, giving the loaves an attractive appearance.

Several English loaves derive their shape from the way they are slashed. The Coburg (p. 102) is slashed with a cross on the top, and the round loaf opens up into four distinct sections. The bloomer (p. 101) is a sausage-shaped loaf that is slashed several times across the top. A split loaf can be made either by slashing a pan loaf right down the middle, or by squeezing two pieces of dough into the tin side by side.

Achieving a good crust

Breads that are brushed with a glaze should be brushed again halfway through baking to give them a very shiny crust.

Baguettes and country loaves should have a thick, hard crust. This is achieved by the introduction of steam into the oven. You can create steam by placing a baking tin of water in the oven or by spraying the oven or the loaves (see p. 12). See also Chapter 3.

A baking stone or tiles also helps. If you are using these, pre-heat them for 30 minutes in the oven. If baking directly on the stone, dust it with cornmeal or semolina and transfer the dough carefully to the hot stone. Spray, slash and place in the hot oven at once.

Baking times

Baking times vary from recipe to recipe. Rolls usually take about 20 minutes; round country breads generally require 40–50 minutes; pan loaves take 45–60 minutes.

Bread is done when the crust is dark brown (or black for black breads) and hard. The best way to tell is to tap the top or bottom of the bread. It should have a hollow sound. If the bottom seems soft, or it doesn't respond with this hollow sound, bake for a little longer.

Cooling and Storing

Remove bread from tins or baking sheets at once (some quick breads are an exception; see recipes). To remove a loaf from a tin, run a knife around the edge of the tin, then carefully turn it upside down. Tap the bottom of the tin and the loaf should come out easily. Cool bread on racks: it will sweat as it cools and if there is no air circulating underneath it, it will become soggy. Allow the bread to cool for at least an hour, and preferably longer, before slicing. If you cut it too soon it won't develop a proper crumb and won't slice as well as it could.

With the exception of some of the sponge-method breads and loaf breads that do not have hard crusts, breads should never be stored in plastic bags. If you do store bread in plastic, it should be refrigerated after two days to avoid mould forming. I do not keep bread in a breadbin, because they too are warm and humid, again causing mould. For the first couple of days, keep bread in the open air, just covering the cut parts with aluminium foil. Country breads made with wholemeal flours will keep like this for up to a week; after the first couple of days other breads should be wrapped in foil and refrigerated. Except for sourdough country breads, white breads usually dry out in a day or two.

Freezing

Most breads freeze very well, especially if they have oil, butter, milk or eggs in them. Even without added fats, I find that wholemeal breads freeze well. To freeze, wrap the bread tightly in aluminium foil, then seal it in a plastic bag. Frozen bread will be good for up to six months. It takes about two hours to thaw at room temperature, and can be thawed in about 30–45 minutes in a warm oven, wrapped in foil.

Troubleshooting

Here are some things that could go wrong, and possible explanations for them.

The dough didn't rise or the bread was like a rock   This could be due to a number of things:

1. The yeast could have been old; make sure you have not had the yeast beyond the 'use by' date, and always dissolve it in warm water and wait for it to cloud, to avoid wasting all that time and energy if it is not fresh.

2. The water you dissolved the yeast in could have been too hot. Or the dough might have become too hot (sometimes a bowl can get too hot if you put it in too warm a spot).

3. You might have added too much salt.

4. You might have added too much flour. This is the most common reason for dough not rising and loaves being heavy and flat. Even the densest doughs should be pliable. If you add too much flour the dough will not fold easily and it won't have any bounce. It will be dry and hard.

5. You might not have kneaded for long enough. Remember the finger-plunging test (see p. 22).

6. Sometimes the loaf is undersized, or the loaf cracks around the side, because you didn't let the shaped loaf rise long enough before baking.

The finished loaf is squat   Pan loaves baked in a tin that is too big will be squat. Make sure that the shaped dough at least half-fills the tin and that it rises for long enough.

The bread sags and is soggy   This could be because the dough was too liquid (not enough flour) and not sufficiently kneaded.

The bread is slightly soggy   It didn't bake long enough.

The loaf falls flat in the oven and slices have a gooey, uneven texture   The dough rose for too long before baking. If this happens, knead the dough again, reshape it and give it another rise.

Pan loaves are light on the bottom and hard on top   The loaves should be removed from the tins and allowed to brown in the oven for an additional 5 minutes before cooling.

The bread has a deep indentation on the bottom   Either your oven was too hot (in the case of free-form loaves) or you have crammed too much into the loaf tin – or both.

Your free-form loaf spread too much as it was rising or as it baked Your dough was too soft. You can control the spreading either by adding a little more flour, or by baking round loaves in a pastry ring or cake tin.

The crust separates from the top of the bread when you slice it You didn't roll your loaf tight enough when you shaped it, or the dough was too stiff (too much flour). This can also be due to the dough's drying out and crusting over during the final rise, or to over-proving.

The crumb has holes in it and a very chewy texture This is often desirable, especially in French bread and country breads. It is a result of lots of kneading and a long, slow rise. If you don't want this texture (and you won't for many slicing loaves) be careful not to over-knead.

The crumb has holes in it and a coarse texture Sometimes this comes from improper shaping of the loaf. At other times the holes can be due to unabsorbed oil from the bowl, or too much dusting with flour. It can also come from over-proving, which could be due to forgetting the salt or to an underheated oven.

Your bread has doughy, hard lumps in it You didn't mix and knead it properly, and probably added too much flour so that it became very stiff. Remember to add flour very gradually to the dough. Or you incorporated the doughy scraps from the work surface or bowl into the dough.

Your bread is too crumbly This is often due to too much flour and insufficient kneading, or to too many grains, such as wheatgerm, bran, oatmeal, etc. It can also be a result of over-proving or over-kneading.

Your bread tastes bland Did you forget the salt? Did you give the bread enough rising time? If bread is not given sufficient rising time its flavour won't ripen. As a rule, bread is best, and lasts longest, when made with a small amount of yeast and given a long rising time.

Your bread tastes yeasty You used too much yeast, or you let the bread rise for too long.

Your bread goes stale or mouldy very quickly How did you store it? Remember, avoid plastic bags and humid breadbins. Over-yeasted and over-baked bread goes stale quickly. Bread that is too heavy and floury also goes stale very quickly. It is normal, however, for *baguettes* and white loaves to dry out very rapidly.

Basic Recipes

The four recipes that follow are easy to make, basic breads. Two are loaf breads, a white and a wholemeal, and the other two are round, country breads. Make them a few times and get to know how the dough feels. Remember, successful breadmaking is, most of all, a question of touch.

Basic White Loaf

2 SMALL LOAVES

This has a light, moist crumb and a very pleasing flavour. The dough is easy to knead and very elastic.

¾ pint (425ml) lukewarm water
2 teaspoons active dried yeast

1¼–1½ lb (565–680g)
*   unbleached white flour*
2 teaspoons salt

Mixing the dough and kneading

Dissolve the yeast in the water and let it sit for 5–10 minutes.

Mix together 1lb (450g) of the flour and the salt. Gradually stir this into the liquid mixture, a cupful at a time. When you have done this, the dough will be stiff enough to turn out on to your work surface.

Use some of the remaining flour to dust your hands and the work surface, and begin to knead, using a pastry scraper to facilitate folding the dough. Knead for 10–15 minutes, adding flour to the work surface and to your hands as necessary. The dough will become resilient after the first 5 minutes' kneading. By the end of the kneading it should be smooth and elastic. Sprinkle the work surface and your hands with flour and shape the dough into a ball.

Rising, forming the loaf and baking

Place the dough in a bowl and cover tightly with clingfilm and a tea-towel. Allow the dough to rise in a warm spot for 1½–2 hours, until doubled in bulk.

Punch down the dough and allow it to rise again, covered, for another 1½ hours, or until doubled in bulk.

Turn the dough out of the bowl, knead it a couple of times, and shape it into a ball. Cut it into two equal pieces and shape them into balls. Allow the dough to rest for 10 minutes.

Now form loaves. Oil or butter two 8 × 4-inch loaf tins. Place the loaves in the tins, seam side up first, then seam side down. Allow the dough to rise until it rounds up to the edges of the tins and the sides just about reach the top of the edges of the tins.

Meanwhile, pre-heat the oven to 375°F/190°C/gas mark 5. Bake for 50–55 minutes, until the loaves are brown and respond to tapping with a hollow sound.

Remove the loaves from the tins at once and allow them to cool, lying on their sides, on a rack.

Basic Wholemeal Loaf

2 LOAVES

This is a lovely, moist loaf which slices well. The dough is dense, sticky and heavy. At the end of kneading it will be just about smooth – maybe a little tacky – on the surface. This is an excellent basic recipe, which can be modified by substituting different kinds of flour for portions of the wholemeal flour.

1¼ pints (750ml) lukewarm water
2 teaspoons active dried yeast
2 tablespoons mild-flavoured
   honey, or 1 tablespoon malt
   extract
2lb (900g) wholemeal flour

2½ teaspoons salt (you can use up
   to 1 tablespoon if desired)
2 tablespoons sunflower or
   safflower oil
2–3oz (55–85g) extra wholemeal
   or unbleached white flour for
   kneading

Optional

1 egg, beaten with 2 tablespoons
   water, for glaze

2 tablespoons sesame seeds

Mixing the dough and kneading

Dissolve the yeast in the water and let it sit for 5–10 minutes. Stir in the honey or malt extract.

Mix together half the flour and the salt. Gradually stir this mixture into the water, a cupful at a time. Use a whisk to obtain a smooth batter. When this portion of the flour has been added, fold in the oil, then gradually add the remaining flour.

As soon as the dough is stiff enough, place a generous amount of flour on your kneading surface and scrape out the dough. Now begin kneading, using a pastry scraper to facilitate folding the dough, and frequently adding flour to your hands and the work surface.

Knead for 15–20 minutes. The dough will be very sticky at first: you will really need that pastry scraper to turn it, and you will also need a lot of flour on your hands. But it will stiffen up after about 5 minutes. At the end of the kneading, the dough will be dense and elastic, though still tacky on the surface. Sprinkle a little more flour on your work surface, and shape the dough into a ball.

Rising, forming the loaf and baking

Rinse out your bowl and dry it. Lightly oil the bowl and place the dough in it, seam side up first, then seam side down; cover the bowl tightly with clingfilm and a tea-towel. Allow the dough to rise for 1½–2 hours in a warm spot. It should double in size and soften considerably during the rising.

Punch down the dough and allow it to rise again, covered, for 1 hour (this rise can be omitted; loaves will be slightly denser).

Turn the dough out on to a lightly floured work surface, shape it into a ball and cut it in half. Shape the two halves into balls and let them sit for 10 minutes so that the dough relaxes.

Now form the loaves. Oil two 8 × 4-inch loaf tins and place the dough in, upside down first, then right side up. If you are using glaze and topping the loaves with sesame seeds, brush them now with the glaze, sprinkle them with sesame seeds, then brush again with glaze. Cover the loaves with a damp tea-towel and set them in a warm place to rise for 20–45 minutes if this is the third rising, 45–90 minutes if it is the second rising, until the tops curve up above the edges of the tins and the sides reach the tops of the tins.

Meanwhile, pre-heat the oven to 350°F/180°C/gas mark 4. Just before baking, slash the loaves across the top with a razor blade or a sharp knife. Bake for 50–55 minutes, or until the loaves are a nutty-brown colour and respond to tapping with a hollow sound.

Remove them from the oven and take them out of the tins. (To do this it may be necessary to run a knife between the edge of the tin and the loaves.) Cool on racks, laying the bread on its side.

Comments

This dough will vary depending on the coarseness of the flour. If the flour is very coarsely ground, you might want to substitute some unbleached white flour or 85 per cent wholemeal flour for some of the 100 per cent wholemeal – say a quarter of the total amount. It is best to become acquainted with the different brands of wholemeal flour so that you can choose those which aren't too heavy.

White Country Loaf

1 LARGE LOAF

This beautiful crusty bread isn't a country loaf in the traditional sense, in that it doesn't have a sourdough starter like the breads on pp. 65–98. But the large round loaf, baked at high heat in a steamy oven, should have the same hard crust and a denser crumb than the pan bread on p. 35. The dough is altogether unlike wholemeal bread dough: it is resistant and bubbly, and very smooth at the end of kneading; but it will quickly become sticky once it sits for a few minutes.

¾ pint (425ml) lukewarm water
1 teaspoon active dried yeast
1¼–1½lb (565–680g) unbleached
  white flour (up to 2 oz/55g more
  if necessary)

2 teaspoons salt
1oz (30g) rye flour

Mixing the dough and kneading

Dissolve the yeast in the water and let it sit for 5–10 minutes. Whisk in about 12oz (340g) of the unbleached flour and mix until thoroughly blended. Cover with clingfilm and a tea-towel and set in a warm place to rise for 1 hour. The mixture will be bubbly: it is called a sponge.

If kneading the dough by hand. Fold the salt and the rye flour into the sponge. Add another cupful of the unbleached flour to the dough and fold it in. At this point the dough should be stiff enough to turn out on to your work surface. Dust your work surface generously with some of the remaining unbleached flour, and turn out the dough on to it.

Begin to knead, using a pastry scraper to facilitate folding the dough, and frequently adding flour to your hands and the work surface. Knead for 10–15 minutes. The dough will become resilient after the first 5 minutes' kneading. By the end of the kneading it should be smooth and elastic. Sprinkle the work surface and your hands with more flour and shape the dough into a ball.

If using an electric mixer. Combine the salt, rye flour and 8oz (225g) of the remaining unbleached flour. Add to the sponge all at once. Mix together with the mixing attachment, then change to the dough hook. Mix at low speed (1 on a Kenwood) for 2 minutes, then at medium speed (2 on a Kenwood) for 6–8 minutes. Add up to 4oz (115g) more unbleached flour if the dough seems very sticky. Scrape the dough out of the bowl on to a floured work surface, knead it a couple of times and shape it into a ball.

Rising and forming the loaf

Place the dough in a bowl and cover tightly with clingfilm and a tea-towel. Allow the dough to rise in a warm spot for 2–3 hours, until doubled in bulk.

Punch down the dough and turn it out on to the work surface. Knead a couple of times, and shape it into a ball.

If using a banneton. Place the dough upside down in the *banneton* (see p. 11) for the second rising. Let it rise for 1 1½ hours. Half an hour before baking, pre-heat the oven to 400°F/200°C/gas mark 6, with the baking stone (see p. 12), if using, in the oven. If you are not using a baking stone, lightly oil a baking sheet and dust it with cornmeal. Turn out the dough from the *banneton* on to the baking stone or sheet.

If not using a banneton. Place the ball of dough back in the bowl, rounded side up, cover it and let it rise for 1–1½ hours. Pre-heat the oven as above. Reshape the dough and let it rise again for 15 minutes, either on the baking sheet or on a well-dusted board from which you can easily slide the dough on to a baking stone, lightly dusted with cornmeal, when it has risen.

Baking

When the loaf is ready to bake, slash it with a razor blade or a sharp knife. Spray it with water, or use the baking-tin method to obtain steam (see p. 12).

Place the loaf in the pre-heated oven and bake for 45–50 minutes.

Spray the loaf a couple of times during the beginning of the baking, if using that method.

When the bread is dark brown and responds to tapping with a hollow thumping sound, remove it from the oven and cool it on a rack.

Wholemeal Country Loaf

1 LARGE LOAF

Like the preceding recipe, this isn't a country loaf in the traditional sense, in that it doesn't have a sourdough starter like the breads on pp. 65–98. But the large, round loaf, baked at high heat in a steamy oven, should have the same kind of hard country-bread crust and a dense crumb. The dough is dense and sticky, and the bread is hearty.

¾ pint (425ml) lukewarm water
1 teaspoon active dried yeast
1 teaspoon malt extract (optional)
1lb (450g) wholemeal flour
2 teaspoons salt

1 tablespoon sunflower or vegetable oil
1oz (30g) rye flour
4–8oz (115–225g) unbleached white flour for kneading (or use extra wholemeal flour)

Mixing the dough and kneading

Dissolve the yeast in the water and let it sit for 5–10 minutes. Stir in the malt extract, if using. Whisk in about 12oz (340g) of the wholemeal flour and mix until thoroughly blended. Cover with clingfilm and a tea-towel and set the dough in a warm place to rise for 1 hour. The mixture will be bubbly: it is called a sponge.

If kneading the dough by hand. Fold the salt and the oil into the sponge. Fold in the rye flour. Add another cupful of wholemeal flour to the dough and fold it in. At this point the dough should be stiff enough to turn out on to your work surface. Dust your work surface generously with some of the remaining unbleached flour, and turn out the dough.

Begin to knead, using a pastry scraper to facilitate folding the dough, and adding unbleached (or extra wholemeal) flour often to your hands and the work surface. Knead for 10–15 minutes. The dough will become resilient after the first 5 minutes' kneading. By the end of the kneading it should be elastic and somewhat smooth. Sprinkle the work surface and your hands with more flour and shape the dough into a ball.

If using an electric mixer. Combine the remaining wholemeal flour and 4oz (115g) of the unbleached white flour with the salt. Add the oil. Mix together with the mixing attachment, then change to the dough hook. Mix at low speed (1 on a Kenwood) for 2 minutes, then at medium speed (2 on a Kenwood) for 6–8 minutes. If the dough seems very sticky, add up to 4oz (115g) more unbleached white flour. Scrape the dough out of the bowl on to a lightly floured work surface, knead it a few times and shape it into a ball.

Rising and forming the loaf

Place the dough in a bowl and cover it tightly with clingfilm and a tea-towel. Allow it to rise in a warm spot for 2–3 hours, until doubled in bulk

Punch down the dough and turn it out on to the work surface. Knead it a couple of times and shape it into a ball.

If using a banneton. Place the dough upside down in the *banneton* (see p. 11) for the second rising. Let it rise for 1–1½ hours. Half an hour before baking, pre-heat the oven to 400°F/200°C/gas mark 6, with the baking stone (see p. 12), if using, in the oven. If you are not using a baking stone, lightly oil a baking sheet and dust it with cornmeal. Turn the dough from the *banneton* on to the baking stone or sheet.

If not using a banneton. Put the ball of dough back in the bowl, rounded side up, cover it and let it rise for 1–1½ hours. Pre-heat the oven as above. Reshape the dough and let it rise again for 15 minutes, either on the baking sheet or on a well-dusted board from which you can easily slide the dough on to a baking stone, lightly dusted with cornmeal, when it has risen.

Baking

When the loaf is ready to bake, slash it with a razor blade or a sharp knife. Spray it with water or use the baking-tin method to obtain steam (see p. 12).

Place the loaf in the pre-heated oven and bake for 45–50 minutes. Spray a couple of times during the beginning of the baking, if using that method.

When the bread is dark brown and responds to tapping with a hollow thumping sound, remove it from the oven and cool it on a rack.

2: My Favourite Wholemeal Breads: the Sponge Method

One rainy Saturday, back in the early 1970s, I decided I wanted to learn to make bread. I went to my local wholefood shop, bought a book called *The Tassajara Bread Book* by Edward Espe Brown, and the ingredients I would need to make bread. I followed the basic Tassajara recipe for wholemeal bread (the recipe was for four loaves, which was a lot of dough to handle, but I just did what the book said) and the bread came out beautifully. Then I tried the book's oatmeal bread, and then its French bread (which I now know was not really French, but French-*like*). Everything worked. So I began making bread all the time, using the Tassajara method and varying the ingredients. I developed very strong arms (I always made enough dough for four loaves – here the recipes are for two) and a very good reputation for my baking.

The reason I had such good luck with bread from the beginning has a lot to do with the Tassajara method, which was not invented by Edward Espe Brown but which he explained in a very clear and sensible way. The method he uses is called the 'sponge' method, and it works extremely well for wholegrain loaves. Using this technique, you mix together the liquid and the yeast, the sweeteners and half the flour, and let this sit in a warm place for an hour before adding the salt (which inhibits the yeast) and the remaining ingredients, and kneading. During this time the yeast begins to work, forming lots of bubbles and long strands of gluten through the dough. As Mr Brown says: 'Gluten is formed when the sponge stretches in rising, which would otherwise be the product of *your* labor in kneading. This added elasticity makes the remaining ingredients more easily incorporated and kneading more easily accomplished.'

The sponge method is particularly good for my dense-grain breads. The extra rising time gives the bread a lovely, moist texture and results in a relatively light loaf (considering the weight of the ingredients). Mr Brown is absolutely right when he says that the remaining ingredients can be more easily incorporated when added to a sponge, and kneading is more easily accomplished. The resulting loaves are dense without being as heavy as bricks. The crumb is not too close, and the loaves are very moist, with a sweet, grainy flavour. These hearty, nutritious breads have a soft crust and make very nice toast. They also last for a week if refrigerated in plastic bags after a few days (although not advised for keeping most breads, plastic bags are suitable for these sponge-method types because they do not .ave thick, hard crusts which would soften in plastic). If I had to live i.y bread alone, these are the ones I would choose.

Basic Wholemeal Sponge Recipe and Technique

2 LOAVES

Sponge breads take longer to make than other loaves because of the extra rising at the beginning and another before the loaves are formed (there are four risings in all). They don't really require more work, just more time – about 5 hours from start to finish. But don't feel that you have to stick around the house for the whole period. If you have to go out for longer than the required rising time, you can let the dough rise in the refrigerator (see p. 24). And even if you leave it in its usual rising place and it rises for an extra 30 minutes or even an extra hour, it won't have an adverse effect on the bread. The only way, really, that you can mess up one of these loaves is if you add too much flour. And if you're willing to let your hands get sticky, and if you follow these recipes, that shouldn't happen.

I find that I have better luck with my sponge breads if I do the kneading by hand. One of the reasons is that electric mixers don't deal very well with quantities of flour, or flour and grains, greater than 2lb (900g), and these breads weigh about 2lb (900g) each. Also, they are very dense, and I think they require human contact to ensure that too much flour isn't added and that they are properly kneaded to develop maximum gluten. You can try halving the quantities in these recipes and using an electric mixer if you wish, but I recommend that you master kneading the breads.

For the sponge

1¼ pints (750ml) lukewarm water
1 tablespoon active dried yeast
2 tablespoons mild-flavoured honey

2 tablespoons black treacle (or use
   all honey)
8oz (225g) unbleached white flour
8oz (225g) wholemeal flour

For the dough

4 tablespoons safflower oil
1 tablespoon salt

1lb (450g) wholemeal flour, plus
   4–6oz (115–170g) extra for
   kneading

For the topping

1 egg, beaten with 2 tablespoons
   water, for glaze

2 tablespoons sesame seeds
   (optional)

Mixing the sponge

Dissolve the yeast in the warm water in a large bowl and let it sit for 5–10 minutes. Mix in the honey and treacle and stir to dissolve. Use water from the bowl to rinse the measuring spoons. Gradually stir in the unbleached and wholemeal flours, a cupful at a time, mixing well with a large whisk or a large wooden spoon. The mixture will gradually develop a mud-like consistency.

When all the flour has been added, whisk 100 times, changing direction every now and then. This really won't take too long. Make sure you stir the mixture up from the bottom and scrape the sides of the bowl. There should be no lumps when you finish; if there are, stir for a little while longer.

Cover the bowl with clingfilm and a tea-towel and set it in a warm place for 1 hour. The mixture will be bubbly and you will actually be able to see it expanding.

Mixing the dough and kneading

Pour the oil on to the sponge and sprinkle on the salt. Incorporate by scooping the sponge from the bottom and folding it over with a large wooden spoon, giving the bowl a quarter-turn, folding again, and so on until you can no longer see the oil. Do not stir it in, because this tears the dough, reducing the elasticity that results from the sponge.

Now begin folding in the 1lb (450g) wholemeal flour. Sprinkle it on to the dough a cupful at a time, and fold it in in the same way that you folded in the oil and salt, giving the bowl a quarter-turn after each fold. Each cupful should take about four turns to be incorporated.

After you have added about half the flour, the dough should begin to come away from the sides of the bowl and have some semblance of a lump, though a sticky, formless one. As soon as you see that the dough will stay more or less in one piece, it is time to scrape it out on to your kneading surface. Place the next cup of flour on your board or table, spread it around, and scrape out the dough on to it.

To knead, flour your hands and use a pastry scraper to facilitate folding. Fold the mass of dough in half towards you. Because it will be very wet at first, just pat it together at the beginning and give it a quarter-turn. Continue to fold the dough over and gently press it together, adding flour to the kneading surface, to the surface of the dough and to your hands as needed. After a few turns the dough will begin to stiffen up so that you can put more elbow into it and build up a kneading rhythm. After about 3–5 minutes, add flour only to the kneading surface and not to the surface of your dough. As you continue to knead, the dough will become stiff, elastic and resistant – harder to fold and press together. Knead for at least 10 minutes.

At the end of kneading the dough will be stiff, dense and elastic. The surface may be a bit tacky and should spring back when you press it with your finger. Shape it into a ball by folding the dough towards you and giving it a quarter-turn, four times, without kneading. Pinch the folds together at the bottom.

Rinse out the bowl, dry and oil it. Place the dough in it seam side up first, then seam side down. Cover it again with clingfilm and a tea-towel and let the dough rise in a warm spot for an hour. It should just about double in bulk.

Punching down and third rise

Punch down by gently pushing your fist into the puffed-up dough. Do this several times. The dough will sigh and collapse. Cover it again and let it rise for 45–60 minutes. It will puff up and double in bulk again, but it will be much lighter than after the previous rise. (This rise can be omitted if you are very short on time. The loaves will be slightly more dense. If you omit this rise, punch down the dough and go on to the next step.)

Forming the loaves, fourth rise and baking

Turn out the dough on to a lightly floured work surface. Knead it a couple of times and shape it into a ball. Using a sharp knife, cut it into two equal-sized pieces, shape these into balls and let the dough rest for 5 minutes. Meanwhile, oil two 8 × 4-inch loaf tins.

Shape the dough into loaves in the same way as the basic loaves on p. 26, by pressing out the dough into a rectangle and rolling it up lengthwise into a log shape, or by folding it like a business letter. Pinch the edges together firmly along the lengthwise crease, fold the short ends over towards the centre and pinch the folds. Place the loaves in the oiled tins, seam side up first, and press them out towards the edges of the tins with the backs of your fingers. Then turn the loaves so that the smooth side is up. Brush with the glaze, sprinkle with sesame seeds if you wish, and brush again with glaze so that the seeds adhere. The loaves should occupy about two-thirds to three-quarters of the volume of the tins.

Set the tins in a warm spot while you pre-heat the oven to 350°F/ 180°C/gas mark 4.

When the dough has risen above the edges of the tins – this usually takes about 15–25 minutes (longer if you omitted the third rise) – they are ready to bake. Using a very sharp knife or a razor blade, make three ½-inch-deep slashes across each loaf and place them on a middle shelf in the pre-heated oven. Bake for 50–60 minutes. Halfway through the baking, brush the loaves again with the glaze. The bread is done when it is golden-brown and responds to tapping with a hollow thumping sound.

Remove the loaves from the tins and let them cool on a rack. When they are completely cool, put them in plastic bags, or wrap them in foil and plastic bags to freeze. After about three days the bread should be stored in the refrigerator to prevent its spoiling.

Mixed-Grain Bread

2 LOAVES

This is my favourite sponge-method bread. I've been working with it for about eighteen years now, and one version or another is in every one of my cookbooks.

The bread is dense, cakey, slightly sweet and grainy, chewy and wholesome. When you eat it you experience a range of textures and a sweet variation of flavours from the different grains. The only problem I sometimes have with this bread is that it can crumble; I haven't worked out why sometimes it crumbles and sometimes it doesn't. The only inconvenience this might pose is that sandwiches packed in a lunchbox might fall apart; and when you slice it up for a dinner party some of the pieces might not look too neat. But since it's a rather rustic bread anyway this shouldn't matter.

You can vary the grains in the bread, substituting one kind of flake for another – for example, use wheat or rye instead of oats, cornmeal for ground millet, chick-pea flour for soya flour.

This bread takes about 5 hours from start to finish, but the dough can be refrigerated after you knead it or punch it down, so you needn't feel tied to the house for all that time. The dough is dense and heavy, but not difficult to work with.

For the sponge

1¼ pints (750ml) lukewarm water
1 tablespoon active dried yeast
2 tablespoons mild-flavoured honey

2 tablespoons black treacle
8oz (225g) unbleached white flour
8oz (225g) wholemeal flour

For the dough

4 tablespoons safflower oil
1 tablespoon salt
3oz (85g) porridge oats
3oz (85g) barley flakes
4½oz (130g) bulgur or cracked
   wheat

6oz (170g) millet, ground to a
   flour in a blender, or 4oz (115g)
   cornmeal
3oz (85g) soya flour or chick-pea
   flour
12oz (340g) wholemeal flour, as
   necessary

For the topping

1 egg, beaten with 2 tablespoons
   water, for glaze

2 tablespoons sesame seeds

Mixing the sponge

Dissolve the yeast in the warm water in a large bowl. Mix in the honey and treacle. Whisk in the unbleached and wholemeal flours, a cupful at a time. When all the flour has been added, whisk 100 times, changing direction every now and then. This really won't take too long. The sponge should have the consistency of thick mud. Cover it and set it in a warm place for an hour, until bubbly.

Mixing the dough and kneading

Fold the oil, then the salt into the sponge, using a large wooden spoon and turning the bowl between folds. Fold in the grains, one at a time.

Now begin folding in the wholemeal flour. After you have added about two-thirds, the dough should hold together in a sticky mass. Place a large handful of flour on your kneading surface and scrape out the dough. Flour your hands and begin kneading. At first you will have to treat the dough gingerly, as it is sticky, and you will have to keep flouring your hands, but after a few minutes it will begin to stiffen and will become easier to work with. Knead, adding more flour as necessary, for 10–15 minutes. The dough will be dense, but should become stiff and elastic as you knead. The surface will be slightly tacky.

Shape the dough into a ball. Oil the bowl, place the dough in the bowl, seam side up first, then seam side down. Cover it and let it rise in a warm spot for an hour.

Forming the loaves and baking

Punch down the dough. At this point you can let it rise once more in the bowl, or let it rise in the tins. The extra rise will make a lighter loaf. Cover it and let it rise for 45–60 minutes in a warm place.

Turn the dough out on to a lightly floured work surface. Knead it a couple of times and divide it in two. Form two loaves and place them in buttered or oiled loaf tins, seam side up first, then seam side down. Brush the loaves lightly with the glaze, sprinkle with sesame seeds and brush again. Cover them and let them rise until the tops of the loaves rise above the edge of the tins: this will take anywhere from 20–45 minutes, depending on the weather and the stage at which you shaped the loaves.

Meanwhile, pre-heat the oven to 350°F/180°C/gas mark 4. Slash the loaves across the top in three places and bake them on a middle shelf for 50–60 minutes. Halfway through the baking, brush the loaves again with the glaze. The bread is done when it is golden-brown and responds to tapping with a hollow thumping sound. Remove the loaves from the tins and cool them on a rack.

Cornmeal and Millet Bread

2 LOAVES

This lovely, slightly golden-coloured bread is a lot like my mixed-grain bread (p. 48), but more crumbly. It has a rich flavour and grainy texture. The dough is dense and somewhat sticky.

For the sponge

1¼ pints (750ml) lukewarm water
1 tablespoon active dried yeast
3 tablespoons mild-flavoured honey

8oz (225g) unbleached white flour
8oz (225g) wholemeal flour

For the dough

4 tablespoons safflower oil or
   melted butter
1 scant tablespoon salt
3oz (85g) porridge oats

8oz (225g) ground millet
5oz (140g) cornmeal
8–12oz (225–340g) wholemeal
   flour, as necessary

For the topping

1 egg, beaten with 1 tablespoon
   water, for glaze

sesame seeds

Mixing the sponge

In a large bowl dissolve the yeast in the water and stir in the honey. Stir in the unbleached and wholemeal flours, a cupful at a time, and whisk the mixture until smooth, about 100 times, changing direction every now and then. Cover with clingfilm or a damp tea-towel and set in a warm place to rise for an hour.

Mixing the dough and kneading

Fold in the oil or butter and the salt, then the oats, ground millet and cornmeal. Begin folding in the wholemeal flour, a cupful at a time, and as soon as you can turn out the dough, scrape it out on to a floured kneading surface. Knead the dough, adding flour as necessary, for 10 minutes or until it is stiff and elastic.

Oil your bowl, shape the dough into a ball and place it in the bowl, seam side up first, then seam side down. Cover the bowl and let the dough rise for 1½ hours.

Forming the loaves and baking

Punch down the dough and turn it out on to a floured surface. Knead for a minute or two, then divide it in half and form two loaves. Place the loaves in oiled loaf tins, seam side up first, then seam side down. Cover with a damp tea-towel or an oiled sheet of clingfilm and let the dough rise in a warm spot for an hour, or until the loaves rise above the edges of the tins. During the last 15 minutes of the rising, pre-heat the oven to 350°F/180°C/gas mark 4.

Gently brush the loaves with the glaze. Sprinkle with sesame seeds, brush again with glaze and slash the tops with a razor blade or a sharp knife. Bake for 50–60 minutes, brushing again with the glaze halfway through the baking. The loaves are done when they are golden-brown and respond to tapping with a hollow thumping sound. Remove them from the tins and cool them on a rack.

Rye Oatmeal Bread

2 LOAVES

This bread is similar in texture to mixed grain bread (p 48) – moist and cakey. The rye and caraway give it an unmistakable savoury flavour. The dough, like the mixed-grain dough, is dense with grains. Like all rye-bread doughs, this one is sticky. And since rye flour doesn't have the same kind of gluten as wheat flour, the bread is somewhat heavier than all-wheat bread.

For the sponge

1 pint (570ml) lukewarm water
1 tablespoon active dried yeast
¼ pint (140ml) lukewarm coffee
  (or use all water)

2 tablespoons mild-flavoured honey
4 tablespoons black treacle
8oz (225g) unbleached white flour
8oz (225g) wholemeal flour

For the dough

4 tablespoons safflower oil
1 scant tablespoon salt
2–3 tablespoons caraway seeds
   (to taste)
3oz (85g) porridge oats

3oz (85g) rye flakes (if
   unavailable, use additional
   porridge oats)
8oz (425g) rye flour
up to 10oz (285g) wholemeal
   flour, as necessary

For the topping

1 egg, beaten with 2 tablespoons
   water or coffee, for glaze

2 tablespoons caraway seeds
   (optional)

Mixing the sponge

Dissolve the yeast in the warm water in a large bowl. Mix in the coffee and treacle. Whisk in the unbleached and wholemeal flours, a cupful at a time. When all the flour has been added, whisk 100 times, changing direction every now and then. This really won't take too long. The sponge should have the consistency of thick mud. Cover it and set it in a warm place for an hour, until bubbly.

Mixing the dough and kneading

Fold the oil, then the salt and caraway seeds into the sponge, using a large wooden spoon and turning the bowl between folds. Fold in the oats and rye flakes, one at a time, and the rye flour.

Now begin folding in the wholemeal flour. After about one-third has been added, the dough should hold together in a sticky mass. Place a generous amount of flour on your kneading surface and scrape out the dough. Flour your hands and begin kneading. At first you will have to treat the dough gingerly, as it is sticky, and you will have to keep flouring your hands, but after a few minutes the dough will begin to stiffen and will become easier to work with. Knead, adding more flour as necessary, for 10–15 minutes. The dough will be dense, but should become stiff and elastic as you knead. The surface will be slightly tacky. Shape it into a ball.

Oil the bowl, place the dough in the bowl, seam side up first, then seam side down. Cover the bowl and let the dough rise in a warm spot for an hour.

Forming the loaves and baking

Punch down the dough. At this point you can let it rise once more in the bowl or let it rise in the tins. The extra rise will make a lighter loaf. Cover the dough and let it rise for 45–60 minutes in a warm place.

Turn out the dough on to a lightly floured work surface. Knead it a couple of times and divide it in two. Form two loaves and place them in buttered or oiled loaf tins, seam side up first, then seam side down. Brush the loaves lightly with the glaze, sprinkle with caraway seeds if using, and brush again. Cover the loaves and let them rise until the tops rise above the edge of the tins. This will take anywhere from 20–45 minutes, depending on the weather and the stage at which you shaped the loaves.

Meanwhile, pre-heat the oven to 350°F/180°C/gas mark 4. Slash the loaves across the top in three places and bake them on a middle shelf for 50–60 minutes. Halfway through the baking, brush them again with the glaze. The bread is done when it is golden-brown and responds to tapping with a hollow thumping sound. Remove the loaves from the tins and cool them on a rack.

Rye Oatmeal Bread with Anise and Raisins

2 LOAVES

This bread is the same dough as the rye oatmeal bread above, with anise and raisins added. It is delicious for breakfast and with tea.

Follow the recipe for rye oatmeal bread, but replace the caraway seeds with 2 tablespoons crushed anise seeds. Instead of 3oz (85g) porridge oats and 3oz (85g) rye flakes, use 6oz (170g) porridge oats. Fold 6oz (170g) raisins into the dough along with the porridge oats and rye flour.

Wholemeal Bread with Oat Bran and Oat Germ

2 LOAVES

Oat bran is a recent discovery, and is sold in wholefood shops, often mixed with oat germ. See the note on oats and health on p. 7.

When I discovered packaged oat bran and oat germ in my local wholefood shop, I brought some home and worked it into a bread very similar to my mixed-grain bread (p. 48). The bread is dense and delicious.

For the sponge

1¼ pints (750ml) lukewarm water
1 tablespoon active dried yeast
2 tablespoons mild-flavoured honey

2 tablespoons black treacle
8oz (225g) unbleached white flour
8oz (225g) wholemeal flour

For the dough

4 tablespoons safflower or
*   sunflower oil*
1 tablespoon salt
8oz (225g) oat bran and oat germ

12oz (340g) coarsely ground
*   wholemeal flour, plus up to 2oz*
*   (55g) extra for kneading, as*
*   necessary*

For the topping

1 egg, beaten with 2 tablespoons
*   water, for glaze*

2 tablespoons sesame seeds

Mixing the sponge

Dissolve the yeast in the warm water in a large bowl. Mix in the honey and treacle. Whisk in the unbleached and wholemeal flours, a cupful at a time. When all the flour has been added, whisk 100 times, changing direction every now and then. This really won't take too long. The sponge should have the consistency of thick mud. Cover it and set it in a warm place for an hour, until bubbly.

Mixing the dough and kneading

Fold the oil, then the salt into the dough, using a large wooden spoon and turning the bowl between folds. Fold in the oat bran and oat germ.

Now begin folding in the wholemeal flour. After you have added about two-thirds the dough should hold together in a sticky mass. Place a large handful of flour on your kneading surface and scrape out the dough. Flour your hands and begin kneading. At first you will have to treat the dough gingerly, as it is sticky, and you will have to keep flouring your hands, but after a few minutes the dough will begin to stiffen and will become easier to work with. Knead, adding more flour as necessary, for 10–15 minutes. The dough will be dense, but should become stiff and elastic as you knead. The surface will be slightly tacky. Shape it into a ball.

Oil the bowl, place the dough in the bowl, seam side up first, then seam side down. Cover the bowl and let the dough rise in a warm spot for an hour.

Forming the loaves and baking

Punch down the dough. At this point you can let it rise once more in the bowl, or let it rise in the tins. The extra rise will make a lighter loaf. Cover the dough and let it rise for 45–60 minutes in a warm place.

Turn the dough out on to a lightly floured work surface. Knead it a couple of times and divide it in two. Form two loaves and place them in buttered or oiled loaf tins, seam side up first, then seam side down. Brush the loaves lightly with the glaze, sprinkle with sesame seeds and brush again with glaze. Cover them and let them rise until the tops rise above the edge of the tins. This will take anywhere from 20–45 minutes, depending on the weather and the stage at which you shaped the loaves.

Meanwhile, pre-heat the oven to 350°F/180°C/gas mark 4. Slash the loaves across the top in three places and bake on a middle shelf for 50–60 minutes. Halfway through the baking, brush them again with the glaze. The bread is done when it is golden-brown and responds to tapping with a hollow thumping sound. Remove the loaves from the tins and cool them on a rack.

Buckwheat and Wholemeal Bread

2 LOAVES

This is a rich, earthy, slightly sour bread. The dough is dense, pliable and somewhat sticky.

For the sponge

¾ pint (425ml) lukewarm water
1 tablespoon active dried yeast
2 tablespoons mild-flavoured honey
1 tablespoon black treacle

½ pint (285ml) low-fat natural
  yoghurt
8oz (225g) unbleached white flour
8oz (225g) wholemeal flour

For the dough

4 tablespoons safflower or
  sunflower oil
1 tablespoon salt
6oz (170g) buckwheat flour
3oz (85g) semolina or cracked
  wheat

12oz (340g) wholemeal flour, plus
  up to 3oz (85g) extra for
  kneading
1 egg, beaten, for glaze

Mixing the sponge

Dissolve the yeast in the lukewarm water and add the honey and treacle. Stir in the yoghurt, then the unbleached and wholemeal flours, a cupful at a time. When all the flour has been added, stir 100 times, changing direction every now and then. Cover with clingfilm and a tea-towel and set in a warm place to rise for an hour, when the sponge should be bubbly.

Mixing the dough and kneading

Fold in the oil. Mix together the salt and buckwheat flour and fold in, along with the semolina or cracked wheat. Begin folding in the wholemeal flour. As soon as you can (see p. 18), scrape the dough out of the bowl on to a floured work surface.

Flour your hands and begin to knead. Knead for 10 minutes, or until the dough is stiff and elastic, adding flour as necessary. The dough will remain a bit tacky. Shape it into a ball and oil your bowl. Place the dough in the bowl, seam side up first, then seam side down. Cover the bowl and place it in a warm spot for the dough to rise for 1½ hours, until doubled in bulk.

Forming the loaves and baking

Punch down the dough and turn it out on to a lightly floured work surface. Knead it a few times, then divide it in two and form two loaves. Place them in buttered or oiled loaf tins and cover them with a tea-towel. Let them rise for an hour, or until the tops rise above the edges of the tins.

About 15 minutes before the end of the rising time, pre-heat the oven to 375°F/190°C/gas mark 5. Gently brush the tops of the loaves with the beaten egg, slash with a razor blade or sharp knife, and bake on a middle shelf for 50–60 minutes, until the loaves are golden-brown and respond to tapping with a hollow thumping sound. Remove them from the tins and cool them on a rack.

Oatmeal Bread

2 LOAVES

This rich, moist bread made with cooked porridge oats is one of my favourites. The dough is sticky and dense.

For the sponge

4oz (115g) porridge oats or flaked oats
1 pint (570ml) boiling water
4fl. oz (120ml) lukewarm water

1 tablespoon active dried yeast
3 tablespoons mild-flavoured honey
4oz (115g) unbleached white flour
8oz (225g) wholemeal flour

For the dough

4 tablespoons safflower or sunflower oil
1 tablespoon salt
1¼lb (565g) wholemeal flour, plus up to 4oz (115g) for kneading

1 egg, beaten, for glaze
1 tablespoon sesame seeds for topping

The night before

Place the porridge oats in a bowl and pour on the boiling water. Cover and let sit overnight.

Mixing the sponge

On the day you wish to bake, dissolve the yeast in the lukewarm water and let it sit for 10 minutes. Stir in the porridge oats and their liquid, and add the honey.

Gradually whisk in the unbleached and wholemeal flours, a cupful at a time, and stir 100 times, changing direction every now and then. Cover with clingfilm and a tea-towel and set in a warm spot to rise for an hour, by which time the mixture should be bubbly.

Mixing the dough and kneading

Fold the oil and the salt into the sponge. Fold in the wholemeal flour, a cupful at a time, and when the dough is stiff enough, scrape it out on to a floured work surface and begin to knead, flouring your hands and adding small amounts of wholemeal flour as necessary. Knead for 10 minutes. The dough will stiffen up but will remain tacky.

Shape the dough into a ball, clean and oil your bowl and place the dough in it, seam side up first, then seam side down. Cover the bowl and set it in a warm spot for the dough to rise for 1–1½ hours, until doubled in bulk.

Forming the loaves and baking

Punch down the dough and let it rise again for 45 minutes. Turn the dough out on to a lightly floured work surface. Shape it into a ball and divide it into two equal pieces.

Oil two loaf tins, shape the dough into loaves and place them in the tins, seam side up first, then seam side down. Brush them with the beaten egg, sprinkle with sesame seeds, then brush again with the beaten egg. Cover them with tea-towels and set them in a warm place to rise until the loaves rise above the edges of the tins.

Meanwhile, pre-heat the oven to 375°F/190°C/gas mark 5. When the dough is ready, slash the loaves three times with a razor blade or a sharp knife, and place them in the oven. Bake for 50 minutes, brushing again with glaze halfway through. The bread is done when it is golden-brown and responds to tapping with a hollow sound. Remove the loaves from the tins and cool them on a rack.

Note

Leftover cooked porridge or hot cereal makes a terrific addition to any wholemeal bread. You will have to reduce the liquid correspondingly, depending on how much you add to the dough.

Sesame-grain Bread

2 LOAVES

This bread is rich and special, crunchy and fragrant with sesame seeds and grains. Like the mixed-grain bread (p. 48) it takes about 5 hours from start to finish, but the dough can be refrigerated after you knead it or punch it down, so you needn't feel tied to the house for all that time. The dough is dense and heavy, the bread slightly lighter than mixed-grain bread. It slices well.

For the sponge

1¼ pints (750ml) lukewarm water
1 tablespoon active dried yeast
2 tablespoons mild-flavoured honey

2 tablespoons black treacle
8oz (225g) unbleached white flour
8oz (225g) wholemeal flour

For the dough

4 tablespoons safflower oil
1 tablespoon salt
3oz (85g) porridge oats
5oz (140g) cornmeal

4oz (115g) sesame seeds
up to 12oz (340g) wholemeal
*   flour, as necessary*

For the topping

1 egg, beaten with 2 tablespoons
*   water, for glaze*

2 tablespoons sesame seeds

Mixing the sponge

Dissolve the yeast in the warm water in a large bowl. Mix in the honey and treacle. Whisk in the unbleached and wholemeal flour, a cupful at a time. When all the flour has been added, whisk 100 times, changing direction every now and then. This really won't take too long. The sponge should have the consistency of thick mud. Cover it and set it in a warm place for an hour, until bubbly.

Meanwhile, put the sesame seeds in a mortar, or a food processor fitted with the steel blade, and pound or process until the seeds are just cracked. Do not over-process or you will get sesame butter.

Mixing the dough and kneading

Fold the oil, then the salt into the dough, using a large wooden spoon and turning the bowl between folds. Fold in the oats and the cornmeal, then fold in the sesame seeds.

Now begin folding in the wholemeal flour. After you have added about two-thirds, the dough should hold together in a sticky mass. Place a generous handful of flour on your kneading surface and scrape out the dough. Flour your hands and begin kneading. At first you will have to treat the dough gingerly, as it is sticky, and you will have to keep flouring your hands, but after a few minutes the dough will begin to stiffen and will become easier to work with. Knead, adding more flour as necessary, for 10–15 minutes. The dough will be dense, but should become stiff and elastic as you knead. The surface will be slightly tacky. Shape it into a ball.

Oil the bowl, place the dough in the bowl, seam side up first, then seam side down. Cover the bowl and let the dough rise in a warm spot for an hour.

Forming the loaves and baking

Punch down the dough. At this point you can let it rise once more in the bowl, or let it rise in the tins. The extra rise will make a lighter loaf. Cover the dough and let it rise for 45–60 minutes in a warm place.

Turn out the dough on to a lightly floured work surface. Knead it a couple of times and divide it in two. Form two loaves and place them in buttered or oiled loaf tins, seam side up first, then seam side down. Brush the loaves lightly with the glaze, sprinkle with sesame seeds and brush again. Cover them and let them rise until the tops of the loaves rise above the edge of the tins. This will take anywhere from 20–45 minutes, depending on the weather and the stage at which you shaped the loaves.

Meanwhile, pre-heat the oven to 350°F/180°C/gas mark 4. Slash the loaves across the top in three places and bake them on a middle shelf for 50–60 minutes. Halfway through the baking, brush them again with the glaze. The bread is done when it is golden-brown and responds to tapping with a hollow thumping sound. Remove the loaves from the tins and cool them on a rack.

High-protein Bread

2 LOAVES

This is a hearty bread, dense and heavy. It is also very tasty. Make sure that you don't add too much flour to the dough, even if it is sticky.

For the sponge

¾ pint (425ml) lukewarm milk
4oz (115g) porridge oats
2 tablespoons mild-flavoured honey
8fl. oz (225ml) lukewarm water

1 tablespoon active dried yeast
2 tablespoons black treacle
8oz (225g) unbleached white flour
4oz (115g) wholemeal flour

For the dough

2 eggs
4 tablespoons safflower oil
1 tablespoon salt
2oz (55g) wheatgerm
3oz (85g) barley flakes

3oz (85g) bulgur or cracked wheat
6oz (170g) soya flour or chick-pea
  flour
8oz (225g) wholemeal flour, as
  necessary

For the topping

1 egg, beaten with 2 tablespoons
  water, for glaze

2 tablespoons sesame seeds

Mixing the sponge

Bring the milk to a simmer and stir in the porridge oats and honey. Cook, stirring, until the mixture begins to thicken. Remove from the heat and cool to lukewarm. (Alternatively, pour the milk over the porridge oats the night before you wish to bake, and refrigerate. Add the honey, heat to lukewarm and proceed with the recipe.)

Dissolve the yeast in the warm water in a large bowl. Mix in the treacle. Whisk in the cooled milk and oats, then the unbleached and wholemeal flours, a cupful at a time. When all the flour has been added, whisk 100 times, changing direction every now and then. This really won't take too long. The sponge should have the consistency of thick mud. Cover it and set it in a warm place for an hour, until bubbly.

Mixing the dough and kneading

Beat the eggs and fold them into the sponge, then fold in the oil and salt, using a large wooden spoon and turning the bowl between folds.

Fold in the wheatgerm, barley flakes, bulgur or cracked wheat and soya or chick-pea flour, one at a time.

Now begin folding in the wholemeal flour. After you have added about two-thirds, the dough should hold together in a sticky mass. Place a large handful of flour on your kneading surface and scrape out the dough. Flour your hands and begin kneading. At first you will have to treat the dough gingerly, as it is sticky, and you will have to keep flouring your hands, but after a few minutes the dough will begin to stiffen and will become easier to work with. Knead, adding more flour as necessary, for 10–15 minutes. The dough will be dense and heavy, but should become stiff and elastic as you knead. The surface will be slightly tacky. Shape it into a ball.

Oil the bowl, place the dough in the bowl, seam side up first, then seam side down. Cover the bowl and let the dough rise in a warm spot for an hour.

Forming the loaves and baking

Punch down the dough. At this point you can let it rise once more in the bowl, or let it rise in the tins. The extra rise will make a lighter loaf. Cover it and let it rise for 45–60 minutes in a warm place.

Turn the dough out on to a lightly floured work surface. Knead it a couple of times and divide it in two. Form two loaves and place them in buttered or oiled loaf tins, seam side up first, then seam side down. Brush the loaves lightly with the glaze, sprinkle with sesame seeds and brush again with glaze. Cover them and let them rise until the tops of the loaves rise above the edge of the tins. This will take anywhere from 20–45 minutes, depending on the weather and the stage at which you shaped the loaves.

Meanwhile, pre-heat the oven to 350°F/180°C/gas mark 4. Slash the loaves across the top in three places and bake on a middle shelf for 50–60 minutes. Halfway through the baking, brush them again with the glaze. The bread is done when it is golden-brown and responds to tapping with a hollow thumping sound. Remove the loaves from the tins and cool them on a rack.

Sprouted Wheatberry Bread

2 LOAVES

When whole wheatberries have sprouted they become sweet and chewy. Added to bread, they make a moist, chewy, sweet-tasting loaf. Whole wheatberries can be bought in wholefood shops.

To sprout wheatberries: soak 6oz (170g) whole wheatberries in ¾ pint (425ml) water overnight, or for at least 10 hours. Drain and spread the berries in a bowl, a sprouting box or a clay plant-dish. Cover with a plate and place in a cool place. Water and drain them twice a day for two days. The berries will grow short white sprouts and will then be ready to use. (NB 6oz (170g) wheatberries will yield about 12oz (340g) sprouts.)

For the sponge

1¼ pints (750ml) lukewarm water
1 tablespoon active dried yeast
2–3 tablespoons mild-flavoured
 honey (to taste)

8oz (225g) unbleached white flour
8oz (225g) wholemeal flour

For the dough

4 tablespoons safflower oil
1 tablespoon salt
about 12oz (340g) sprouted
 wheatberries, chopped in a food
 processor

1½lb (680g) wholemeal flour, as
 necessary
up to 2oz (55g) unbleached white
 flour for kneading, if necessary

For the topping

1 egg, beaten with 2 tablespoons
 water, for glaze

2 tablespoons sesame seeds

Mixing the sponge

Dissolve the yeast in the warm water in a large bowl. Mix in the honey. Whisk in the unbleached and wholemeal flours, a cupful at a time. When all the flour has been added, whisk 100 times, changing direction every now and then. This really won't take too long. The sponge should have the consistency of thick mud. Cover it and set it in a warm place for an hour, until bubbly.

Mixing the dough and kneading

Fold the oil, then the salt into the sponge, using a large wooden spoon and turning the bowl between folds. Fold in the chopped wheatberries.

Now begin folding in the wholemeal flour. After you have added about two-thirds, the dough should hold together in a sticky mass. Place a large handful of flour on your kneading surface and scrape out the dough. Flour your hands and begin kneading. At first you will have to treat the dough gingerly, as it is sticky, and you will have to keep flouring your hands, but after a few minutes the dough will begin to stiffen and will become easier to work with. Knead, adding more flour as necessary, for 10–15 minutes. The dough will be dense, but should become stiff and elastic as you knead. The surface will be slightly tacky. Shape it into a ball.

Oil the bowl, place the dough in the bowl, seam side up first, then seam side down. Cover it and let it rise in a warm spot for an hour.

Forming the loaves and baking

Punch down the dough. At this point you can let it rise once more in the bowl, or let it rise in the tins. The extra rise will make a lighter loaf. Cover the bowl and let the dough rise for 45–60 minutes in a warm place.

Turn out the dough on to a lightly floured work surface. Knead it a couple of times and divide it in two. Form two loaves and place them in buttered or oiled loaf tins, seam side up first, then seam side down. Brush the loaves lightly with the glaze, sprinkle with sesame seeds and brush again with glaze. Cover them and let them rise until the tops of the loaves rise above the edge of the tins. This will take anywhere from 20–45 minutes, depending on the weather and the stage at which you shaped the loaves.

Meanwhile, pre-heat the oven to 350°F/180°C/gas mark 4. Slash the loaves across the top in three places and bake them on a middle shelf for 50–60 minutes. Halfway through the baking, brush them again with the glaze. The bread is done when it is golden-brown and responds to tapping with a hollow thumping sound. Remove the loaves from the tins and cool them on a rack.

3: Pains de Campagne: Sourdough Country Breads

There are probably as many different sourdough starters and techniques for breads made with this kind of leaven as there are countries. Sourdough, called *chef* or *levain* in France, *biga* in Italy, and simply 'sourdough starter' in the United States, is a fermented bit of dough that leavens bread while imparting an earthy, acidic flavour. Some sourdoughs are begun with the help of a little yeast; others are merely flour and water, left to ferment and develop yeasts over a few days. Even after years of working with these flour-and-water leavens, I still find them miraculous, awe-inspiring. How can flour and water turn into something that makes such wonderful bread? They are replenished either by keeping a piece of the bread dough from each batch of bread, or by adding flour and water to your starter each time you use it.

I got hooked on sourdough country breads in France, where I find them consistently superior to the ever-deteriorating *baguette*. There I made my first *chef*, which has travelled far and wide with me over the years. Every once in a while I forget to retain a bit of dough from a batch of bread and have to begin my starter all over again. Each one is slightly different from the one before, and they change with each batch of bread – but they are always powerful and pungent. The *chef* is very hearty; it can lie neglected in the refrigerator for a few weeks, as mine has done when I've gone off and forgotten to freeze it, but it always comes back to life after a batch or two of bread. It also freezes very well.

My wholemeal *pain de campagne* is a household staple; rarely do I serve a dinner without it. Sometimes I vary the flours, or add things like walnuts, olives or sun-dried tomatoes, but the technique for making it stays the same. In this chapter I have concentrated on the *chef*-based country breads, because this is the sourdough I always work with and like best. However, I have also included a recipe for an American starter, which contains yeast and is more liquidy. Other starters are made from potatoes, others from beer.

Most sourdough breads have great staying power (the exception are *baguettes*, which go hard after a day). They can last for up to a week if kept in fairly cool place. I just cover the cut surface with foil to prevent it from going hard. You do lose the very hard texture of the crust, but it is still quite tasty, and the bread stays moist.

General Techniques for Sourdough Country Breads

The recipes in this chapter are almost all for great round loaves (or two smaller loaves) containing about 1½lb (680g) flour, 8oz (225g) starter and ¾ pint (425ml) water. The texture of the doughs is very different from that of the breads in Chapter 2. Generally these doughs are not as bulky and dense, but they are much stickier and they can be unwieldy. Especially when rye flour is added, to make these breads you have to accept the fact that you will get dough all over your hands. If you have an electric mixer with a dough hook, you'll really appreciate its help with the recipes in this chapter.

One of the nice things about sourdough breads is that they are very easy to mix up and require relatively little rising time. There are only two rises involved, one after mixing up the dough and kneading, the other after removing some of the starter and shaping the loaf. The breads are baked at high heat in a moist oven.

Mixing the Dough and Kneading

Dissolve the yeast in the liquid in a large bowl or in the bowl of your electric mixer and let it sit for 10 minutes. If you are kneading the dough by hand, add any oil called for in the recipe, mix together the flour(s) and salt and fold them in, a cupful at a time. As soon as the dough is stiff enough, scrape it out on to your kneading surface. Knead, adding unbleached white flour as necessary, for 10 minutes. The dough will be extremely sticky and unwieldy, especially for the first 5 minutes. Use a pastry scraper to help you fold the dough and see my additional instructions for kneading on p. 19. When the dough is stiff and resilient, but not necessarily smooth, shape it into a ball and place it in the bowl (some recipes call for the bowl to be oiled).

If you are using an electric mixer, combine the flour(s) and salt, and add all at once to the bowl along with the oil. Mix together with the mixing attachment, then change to the dough hook. Mix at low speed (1 on a Kenwood) for 2 minutes, then at medium speed (2 on a Kenwood) for 6–8 minutes. If the dough seems very wet and sticky, sprinkle in up to 2oz (55g) unbleached white flour. Scrape out the dough on to a lightly floured surface and knead it a few times by hand, using a pastry scraper if necessary to help turn the dough. Shape it into a ball and place it in the bowl.

Cover the bowl with clingfilm and a tea-towel, and set it in a warm place to rise for 1½ hours, or until the dough has doubled in size.

Punching Down, Forming the Loaves and Second Rising

Sprinkle some flour over the top of the dough and punch it down a few times. It will have puffed up considerably if it is a yeasted dough and will sigh when you punch it. Turn it out on to your floured work surface. Remove about 8oz (225g) of this dough and place it in a large jar, crock or bowl with a cover to use as a starter for your next loaf. Let it sit for an hour or so before refrigerating.

Shape the remaining dough into a ball, or into two balls. Make sure the balls are very tight. To do this, pull the dough from one side all the way over itself to the other, give it a quarter-turn, and continue to do this all the way around (see p. 23). Pinch together the seams at the bottom, cup your hands around the dough and gingerly turn it around, bouncing it lightly on the surface to form a ball. Again, it will be sticky and unwieldy. Keep your hands floured and use a pastry scraper if necessary.

For the next rising, you can use a *banneton* (see p. 11). The only problem I sometimes have with this is that this type of dough is so moist that it sticks to the tea-towel and tears when you remove the towel. Flouring both the dough and the tea-towel *very* heavily helps prevent this. I have also made a kind of *banneton* without a tea-towel, using a *very* heavily oiled and cornmeal-dusted bowl instead. If you use a *banneton*, form the dough into a tight ball and place it upside down in the *banneton*. Cover it loosely with a flour-dusted tea-towel and let the dough rise until doubled in bulk, which will take anywhere from 45 minutes to 2 hours, depending on the recipe.

If you are not using a *banneton*, shape the dough into a tight ball, place it in an oiled bowl, and let it rise as above. Reshape the dough gently (it will be sticky again, so oil or flour your hands) and place it on a baking sheet which has been oiled and sprinkled with cornmeal. Let it rise while you pre-heat the oven. It will spread out quickly.

Note

Even after all these years, I still often find when I turn out the dough that the top has stuck to the bowl or *banneton*. If this happens, scrape it off and place it back on top of the rest of the dough, which will by now have sunk. Don't slash the dough before baking – it's already slashed. Your bread will be rather flat, but it will still be good.

Baking

If you are using a baking stone (see p. 12), pre-heat it in the oven for 30 minutes and dust it with cornmeal. If you are using a baking sheet, brush it with oil and sprinkle it with cornmeal. Pre-heat the oven to 400°F/200°C/gas mark 6.

If you have used a *banneton*, turn the dough out gently on to the baking sheet or hot baking stone. If the loaves have risen on baking sheets and have spread out too much, gently bolster up the sides with floured or oiled hands. Slash the loaves with a sharp razor blade or very sharp knife dipped in water, making an X or several criss-crosses across the top, or making a kind of square, crossing the sides.

To achieve a really hard crust, create steam using the baking-tin method (see p. 12) and also spray the loaf or loaves with water just before putting them into the oven (see also p. 12). If you don't use the baking-tin method, spray the oven a couple of times during the first 10 minutes of baking.

Bake one large loaf for 40–50 minutes, smaller loaves for about 35–40 minutes, until the bread is dark brown and responds to tapping with a hollow sound. Remove it from the heat and cool it on a rack.

Note

When you turn out the bread from the *banneton* on to the baking stone or sheet, it may spread out quite a bit and look very flat. It will rise up considerably in the hot oven, but even so your first loaves may look rather flat. However, you will see that the breads still have a lovely crumb, texture and taste. Cut long slices and cut these into pieces, or cut the bread in half or into quarters and slice those. *Pain de campagne* is often sold in large quarters in France. This is also a good way to freeze the bread to keep it fresh if you don't have a large bread-eating family.

Storing

Don't store these crusty country loaves in a breadbin. The crust will soften because of the moisture. Just keep the cut side covered with foil. To freeze, add a tablespoon of oil to the given recipe if no oil is called for, and when the bread is cool wrap it tightly in foil and seal it in a plastic bag.

Chef – French Sourdough Starter

This is the starter I have been using over the years for my sourdough breads. It is based on Patricia Wells's version of the starter, or *chef*, used by the famous French baker Lionel Poilane. Unlike most sourdough starters, the *chef* isn't runny, but is more like a spongy dough. You keep it going by saving about 8oz (225g) of dough every time you make country bread. As a result, my *chef* is always changing, because I tend to vary the flours I use in my breads. Most of the breads in this chapter rely on a *chef* that originated with this recipe. It freezes well, travels well and is very hearty.

The first day

3fl. oz (90ml) water

4oz (115g) flour, 85 per cent wholemeal or unbleached white, or a combination

Stir together the water and flour until smooth. Cover with a damp tea-towel and let it sit at room temperature for 72 hours. The dough will form a crust on the top and turn a greyish colour, which is normal. If you keep wetting the tea-towel it will reduce the drying. The dough will rise slightly and take on an acidic aroma.

After 72 hours

4fl. oz (120ml) lukewarm water

6oz (170g) flour, 85 per cent wholemeal or unbleached white, or a combination

Add the water to the starter and blend together. If the crust which the dough has formed is like cardboard, peel it off and discard it. (I find that this happens if the flour I work with is very coarse, but with 85 per cent wholemeal, or unbleached white, it doesn't happen.) Add the flour and stir to blend it in. Transfer the dough to a floured work surface and knead it into a smooth ball.

Return the dough to the bowl, cover it with a damp tea-towel and let it sit in a warm place for 24–48 hours. Again, a crust may form on the top. If it is like cardboard or wood, peel it off and discard it before proceeding with a bread recipe.

Note

The recipes that follow call for 8oz (225g) *chef*. If you are using fresh starter for the first time, use all the quantity made here.

Pain de Campagne

1 LARGE OR 2 SMALL LOAVES

This is the closest bread in this chapter to a really traditional French *pain de campagne*. Bakers in France are required by law to use 5 per cent rye flour in their country breads. I tend to use a tiny bit more than 5 per cent rye flour, and sometimes add a small amount of semolina flour; but this is optional. This very sticky dough yields a chewy, resilient, slightly sour loaf with a thick, hard crust.

¾ pint (425ml) lukewarm water
2½ teaspoons active dried yeast
8oz (225g) chef (see p. 69)
2oz (55g) rye flour

2oz (55g) semolina flour (optional; replace with 2oz (55g) extra unbleached white flour if not using)
1¼lb (565g) unbleached white flour, as necessary
2½ teaspoons salt

Mixing the dough and kneading

Dissolve the yeast in the water in a large bowl or in the bowl of your electric mixer and let it sit for 10 minutes. Stir in the sourdough starter. Mix together well.

If kneading the dough by hand. Stir the rye flour and semolina flour into the liquids. Combine 1lb (450g) of the unbleached white flour and the salt and gradually fold into the liquids. By the time you have added this amount of flour, you should be able to knead the dough. Flour your work surface and scrape out the dough. Using a pastry scraper to help fold the dough, knead for 10–15 minutes, adding flour to the surface and to your hands as necessary. The dough will be very sticky. Shape it into a ball.

If using an electric mixer. Add the rye flour and the semolina flour to the liquids. Combine the unbleached white flour and the salt. Add all at once to the liquid mixture. Mix together briefly using the mixing attachment until everything is amalgamated, then scrape the dough off the mixing attachment and change to the dough hook. Knead at a low speed (1 on a Kenwood) for 2 minutes, then at medium speed (2 on a Kenwood) for 8 minutes. Turn out the dough on to a floured surface, knead it a few times and shape it into a ball.

Rising and forming the loaf

Clean the bowl, oil it if desired, return the dough to it and cover it with clingfilm and a tea-towel. Let the dough rise in a warm spot for 1½–2 hours, until doubled in bulk.

Flour your hands and wrists and punch down the dough. Knead it for 2–3 minutes on a lightly floured surface, using a pastry scraper to make it easier to manipulate the sticky dough. Remove a heaped cupful (about 8oz/225g) of the dough and place it in a bowl to use for your next loaf of bread, covering it and refrigerating it after a few hours if you will not be using it again within a day.

Shape the dough into a ball or into two balls.

If using a banneton. Dust the surface of the ball of dough with flour and place it in the *banneton* (see p. 11), rounded side down. (Or use a 3-pint (1.75-litre) bowl, oiled *very* generously and dusted with cornmeal (see p. 24).) Cover it with a tea-towel and let the dough rise in a warm spot for 1½ hours, until doubled in bulk. You can also let the dough rise in the refrigerator for several hours or overnight. Just before baking, turn out the dough on to an oiled baking sheet or, preferably, a pre-heated baking stone (see p. 12) dusted with cornmeal.

If not using a banneton. Dust the surface of the ball of dough with flour and let it rise in an oiled bowl for about 1½ hours, until doubled in bulk. Reshape the dough gently and place it on a baking sheet which has been oiled and sprinkled with cornmeal. Let the dough rise for about 15 minutes while you pre-heat the oven.

Baking

Pre-heat the oven to 400°F/200°C/gas mark 6. Slash the loaf with a razor blade or sharp knife just before baking. Create steam using the baking-tin method and spray the loaf with water (see p. 12). Spray the oven twice more during the first 10 minutes of baking. Bake for 45 minutes, until the bread is brown and responds to tapping with a hollow thumping sound. Remove it from the heat and cool it on a rack.

Wholemeal Pain de Campagne 1

1 LARGE LOAF

Pain de campagne is a mainstay in my home. It has a tart, earthy flavour and a very hard crust. The bread is chewy and dense, and has great staying power.

Sometimes I use all wholemeal flour, as in this recipe, and at other times I combine different quantities of 100 per cent and 85 per cent wholemeal, wholemeal and unbleached white, or wholemeal and other flours, such as buckwheat or rye. This version is rich tasting and dense. It keeps for a week. The dough is sticky – but then all these country bread doughs are.

¾ pint (425ml) lukewarm water, or 10fl. oz (285ml) lukewarm water plus 5fl. oz (140ml) coffee
2½ teaspoons active dried yeast
8oz (225g) chef (see p. 69)

1 tablespoon black treacle (optional)
2½ teaspoons salt
1¼lb (565g) 100 per cent wholemeal flour, plus 4–6oz (115–170g) extra for kneading, as necessary

Mixing the dough and kneading

Dissolve the yeast in the water in a large bowl or in the bowl of your electric mixer and let it sit for 10 minutes. Stir in the sourdough starter, the coffee (if using) and the optional treacle. Mix together well.

If kneading the dough by hand. Combine the 1¼lb (565g) flour and salt. Gradually fold into the liquids. By the time you have added 1lb (450g) you should be able to knead. Flour your work surface and scrape out the dough. Using a pastry scraper to help fold the dough, knead for 10–15 minutes, adding flour to the surface and to your hands as necessary. Shape the dough into a ball.

If using an electric mixer. Combine the 1¼lb (565g) flour and the salt and add all at once to the liquid mixture. Mix together briefly using the mixing attachment until everything is amalgamated, then scrape the dough off the mixing attachment and change to the dough hook. Knead at low speed (1 on a Kenwood) for 2 minutes, then at medium speed (2 on a Kenwood) for 8 minutes, adding up to 4oz (115g) of flour if the dough seems very liquid (it should be sticky). Turn out the dough on to a floured surface, knead it a few times and shape it into a ball.

Rising and forming the loaf

Clean your bowl, return the dough to it and cover it with clingfilm and a tea-towel. Let the dough rise in a warm spot for 1½–2 hours, until doubled in bulk.

Flour your hands and wrists, and punch down the dough. Knead for 2–3 minutes on a lightly floured surface, using a pastry scraper to make it easier to manipulate the sticky dough. Remove a heaped cupful (about 8oz/225g) of the dough and place it in a bowl to use for your next loaf of bread, covering it and refrigerating after a few hours if you will not be using it again within a day.

If using a banneton. Form the dough into a ball, dust the surface with flour and place it in the *banneton* (see p. 11), rounded side down. (Or use a 3-pint (1.75-litre) bowl, oiled *very* generously and dusted with cornmeal (see p. 24).) Cover with a tea-towel and let the dough rise in a warm spot for 1½–2 hours, until almost doubled in bulk. You can also let the dough rise in the refrigerator for several hours or overnight. Just before baking, turn out the dough on to an oiled baking sheet or, preferably, a pre-heated baking stone (see p. 12) dusted with cornmeal.

If not using a banneton. Form the dough into a ball and let it rise in an oiled bowl for about 1½ hours, until doubled in bulk. Reshape the dough gently and place it on a baking sheet which has been oiled and sprinkled with cornmeal. Let the dough rise for about 20 minutes while you pre-heat the oven.

Baking

Pre-heat the oven to 400°F/200°C/gas mark 6. Slash the loaf with a razor blade or sharp knife just before baking. Create steam using the baking-tin method (see p. 12) and spray the loaf with water (see p. 12). Spray the oven twice more during the first ten minutes of baking. Bake for 45 minutes, until the bread is brown and responds to tapping with a hollow thumping sound. Remove it from the heat and cool it on a rack.

Wholemeal Pain de Campagne 2

1 LARGE LOAF

This version, almost all wholemeal, has the same sour taste as the 100 per cent wholemeal version on p. 72, but with a lighter texture and an airier crumb. The dough is sticky and a little more elastic than the other wholemeal version.

¾ pint (425ml) lukewarm water
2 teaspoons active dried yeast
8oz (225g) chef (see p. 69)
1lb (450g) 85 per cent wholemeal
  flour

2½ teaspoons salt
up to 8oz (225g) unbleached white
  flour, as necessary

Mixing the dough and kneading

Dissolve the yeast in the water in a large bowl or in the bowl of your electric mixer and let it sit for 10 minutes. Stir in the *chef* and combine thoroughly.

If kneading the dough by hand. Combine the 85 per cent wholemeal flour and the salt, and gradually fold into the liquid mixture. By the time you have added it all, you should be able to knead the dough. Add a generous amount of unbleached flour to your work surface and scrape out the dough. Using a pastry scraper to help fold the dough, knead for 10–15 minutes, adding unbleached white flour as necessary. Shape the dough into a ball.

If using an electric mixer. Combine the 85 per cent wholemeal flour, the unbleached flour and the salt and add to the liquids. Mix together briefly using the mixing attachment until everything is amalgamated, then scrape the dough off the mixing attachment and change to the dough hook. Knead at low speed (1 on a Kenwood) for 2 minutes, then at medium speed (2 on a Kenwood) for 6–8 minutes. The dough will be sticky. Scrape it out of the bowl on to a floured kneading surface, knead it a few times and shape it into a ball.

Rising and forming the loaf

Cover the dough with clingfilm and a tea-towel and let it rise in a warm spot for 1½–2 hours, until doubled in bulk.

Flour your hands and wrists, and punch down the dough. Knead for 2–3 minutes on a lightly floured surface, using a pastry scraper to make it easier. Remove a heaped cupful (about 8oz/225g) of the dough and place it in a bowl to use for your next loaf of bread, covering it and refrigerating after a few hours if you will not be using it again within a day.

If using a banneton. Form the dough into a ball, dust the surface with flour and place in the *banneton* (see p. 11), rounded side down. (Or use a 3-pint (1.75-litre) bowl, oiled *very* generously and dusted with cornmeal (see p. 24).) Cover with a tea-towel and let the dough rise in a warm spot for 1½–2 hours, until almost doubled in bulk. You can also let it rise in the refrigerator for several hours or overnight. Just before baking, turn out the dough on to an oiled baking sheet or, preferably, on to a pre-heated baking stone (see p. 12) dusted with cornmeal.

If not using a banneton. Form the dough into a ball and let it rise in an oiled bowl for about 1½ hours, until doubled in bulk. Reshape the dough gently and place it on a baking sheet which has been oiled and sprinkled with cornmeal. Let it rise again for about 20 minutes while you pre-heat the oven.

Baking

Pre-heat the oven to 400°F/200°C/gas mark 6. Slash the loaf with a razor blade or sharp knife just before baking. Create steam by using the baking-tin method (see p. 12) and spray the loaf with water (see p. 12). Bake for 45 minutes, until the bread is brown and responds to tapping with a hollow thumping sound. Remove it from the heat and cool it on a rack.

Wholemeal Pain de Campagne 3

1 LARGE LOAF

This is just another fine-tuning of the basic *pain de campagne* on p. 70. It is slightly lighter, with the combination of 100 per cent and 85 per cent wholemeal flour. These variations do make a difference; the dough is less dense than the 100 per cent wholemeal dough and a little easier to work with.

Use the recipe for wholemeal *pain de campagne* on p. 72. Substitute 12oz (340g) coarse 100 per cent wholemeal flour and 12oz (340g) 85 per cent wholemeal flour for all the wholemeal flour in the dough, and proceed with the recipe.

Wholemeal Pain de Campagne with Raisins

1 LARGE LOAF

I love the contrasting flavours of the sweet raisins and the sour bread here. It's one of my favourites, especially nice for breakfast or tea.

Follow the recipe for wholemeal *pain de campagne* on p. 72, but substitute 6oz (170g) rye flour for 6oz (170g) of the wholemeal flour.

When forming the loaf, knead in 12oz (340g) raisins or currants. Proceed with the recipe.

White Pain de Campagne

1 LARGE LOAF

Since my starter is always a combination of mostly wholemeal flours, my *pain de campagne* made with unbleached white flour isn't quite white, but has little flecks of grain in it. The bread has a moist, spongy texture and a hard country crust. Naturally, it's lighter than the other breads in this section.

Follow the instructions for the wholemeal *pain de campagne* (p. 72), substituting unbleached white flour for the wholemeal flour.

I have also made this bread with slightly different quantities of flour and water. For a somewhat smaller loaf, use:

12fl. oz (340ml) lukewarm water
2 teaspoons active dried yeast
½ teaspoon sugar
8oz (225g) chef (see p. 69)

2 teaspoons salt
1¼lb (565g) unbleached white
flour

Follow the instructions for the wholemeal *pain de campagne* on p. 72.

Sourdough Baguettes

2 LOAVES

This is less dense than the round *pain de campagne* (p. 70). It doesn't have such good staying power, because of the shape of the loaves.

8fl. oz (225ml) lukewarm water
2 teaspoons active dried yeast
1 teaspoon malt extract
1 tablespoon safflower oil
4fl. oz (120ml) chef (see p. 69)

2 teaspoons salt
8oz (225g) wholemeal flour
3–6oz (85–170g) unbleached
  white flour, as necessary

Mixing the dough and kneading

Dissolve the yeast in the lukewarm water in a large bowl. Stir in the malt extract and the oil. Stir in the *chef*.

If kneading the dough by hand. Mix together the wholemeal flour and the salt and stir in gradually. Place 2oz (55g) of the unbleached flour on your kneading surface and scrape out the dough. Begin to knead, adding flour as necessary. Knead for 10 minutes. Shape the dough into a ball. (It should be slightly sticky.)

If using an electric mixer. Combine the wholemeal flour, salt and 4oz (115g) of the unbleached flour and add to the liquid mixture. Mix together with the mixing attachment, then scrape the dough off the mixing attachment and change to the dough hook. Knead at low speed (1 on a Kenwood) for 2 minutes, then at medium speed (2 on a Kenwood) for 6–8 minutes. Scrape out the dough on to a floured work surface, knead it a few times by hand and shape it into a ball.

Rising, forming the baguettes and baking

Wash out and oil your bowl. Place the dough in the bowl, seam side up first, then seam side down. Cover the bowl with clingfilm and a tea-towel and set it in a warm spot for the dough to rise for 2 hours, until doubled in bulk.

Punch down the dough and turn it out on to a lightly floured surface. Remove a cupful of dough and place it in a bowl to use for your next loaf of bread. Knead it for a few minutes, then divide it in half. Shape the dough into two long, slender *baguette*-shaped loaves, about 2 inches in diameter (see p. 27).

Oil *baguette* tins and dust them with cornmeal. Place the loaves in the tins, cover them and let the dough rise for about an hour, until doubled in bulk. Towards the end of the rising time, pre-heat the oven to 400°F/200°C/gas mark 6. Create steam by using the baking-tin method (see p. 12). Slash the loaves on the diagonal three or four times, place them in the oven and bake for 30–35 minutes, until they are brown and respond to tapping with a hollow thumping sound. Remove the bread from the tins and cool it on a rack.

Note

You can make *baguettes* with any of the sourdough recipes in this chapter; most of the recipes make more dough than this one does, so you might want to shape some of the dough into a small round loaf and the rest into *baguettes*.

Italian Country Loaf

1 LARGE LOAF

This is another hearty, crusty country loaf. The bread, made with a combination of wholemeal and unbleached white flours, calls for less yeast than the other sourdough breads in this chapter and consequently has a longer rising time. It makes a moist loaf with a rich, nutty flavour, which slices very nicely. The dough is dense, smooth and elastic.

¾ pint (425ml) lukewarm water
1 teaspoon active dried yeast
1 teaspoon malt extract
8oz (225g) chef (see p. 69)
2 heaped teaspoons salt

12oz (340g) wholemeal flour,
  preferably finely ground
8oz (225g) unbleached white flour,
  as necessary

Mixing the dough and kneading

Dissolve the yeast in the water and let it sit for 5–10 minutes. Stir in the malt extract and the *chef*.

If kneading the dough by hand. Combine the wholemeal flour and salt, and gradually stir into the liquid mixture. Fold in 4oz (115g) of the unbleached flour, then place a generous handful of the remaining unbleached flour on your work surface. Scrape out the dough and begin to knead, using a pastry scraper to help turn the dough and flouring your hands and the work surface often. Knead for 10–15 minutes, until the dough is stiff, elastic and somewhat smooth on the surface.

If using an electric mixer. Combine the wholemeal flour, 4oz (115g) of the unbleached flour and the salt. Add to the liquids all at once. Mix together with the mixing attachment, then change to the dough hook and knead for 2 minutes at low speed (1 on a Kenwood) and 8 minutes at medium speed (2 on a Kenwood), adding additional flour if the dough seems very sticky. Finish kneading by hand on a floured work surface for about 2 minutes.

Rising and forming the loaf

Shape the dough into a ball. Rinse out your bowl and oil it with olive oil. Place the dough in it, seam side up first, then seam side down. Cover the bowl with clingfilm and a tea-towel and let the dough rise for 3–4 hours in a warm spot, until doubled in size.

Punch the dough down, remove 8oz (225g) of the dough to use as a starter for your next loaf, covering it and refrigerating after a few hours if you will not be using it again within a day.

Shape the remaining dough into a ball.

If using a banneton. Sprinkle the dough generously with flour and place it in the *banneton* (see p. 11), rounded side down. Sprinkle it again with flour and cover it with a tea-towel. (Or use a 3-pint (1.75-litre) bowl, *very* generously oiled and dusted with cornmeal (see p. 24).) Let the dough rise for 1–2 hours in a warm spot, until doubled in bulk. Towards the end of the rising, pre-heat the oven to 400°F/200°C/gas mark 6, with the baking stone in the oven if you are using one. Just before baking, turn out the dough on to an oiled baking sheet, or on to the pre-heated baking stone dusted with cornmeal.

If not using a banneton. Let the dough rise again in the bowl until almost doubled in bulk. Pre-heat the oven as above, and reshape the dough, gently easing it into a ball shape. Place it on an oiled baking sheet sprinkled with cornmeal and let it rise for 15–20 minutes while the oven is heating.

Baking

Slash the dough just before baking. Spray the dough and the oven with water just before you put it in the oven to create stream, or use the baking-tin method (see p. 12). Bake for 45–55 minutes, until the bread is dark brown and responds to tapping with a hollow sound. Remove it from the heat and cool it on a rack.

Country Bread with Cornmeal and Oats

1 LOAF

This bread is dense, hearty and delicious, with a thick, hard crust, a yellowish colour and a close crumb.

¾ pint (425ml) lukewarm water
2½ teaspoons active dried yeast
8oz (225g) chef (see p. 69)
4oz (115g) rolled or flaked oats

6oz (170g) cornmeal
2½ teaspoons salt
1lb (450g) unbleached white flour

Mixing the dough and kneading

Dissolve the yeast in the water and let it sit for 10 minutes. Stir in the *chef* and combine thoroughly.

If kneading the dough by hand. Stir in the oats, cornmeal and salt. Gradually fold the unbleached flour into the liquid mixture. By the time you have added about 8–12oz (225–340g) you should be able to knead the dough. Add a generous amount of unbleached flour to your work surface and scrape out the dough. Using a pastry scraper to help fold the dough, knead for 10–15 minutes, adding unbleached white flour as necessary. Shape the dough into a ball.

If using an electric mixer. Combine the oats, cornmeal and salt and add them to the liquids. Add 8oz (225g) unbleached flour and mix together briefly, using the mixing attachment, until everything is amalgamated. Then scrape the dough off the mixing attachment and change to the dough hook. Knead at low speed (1 on a Kenwood) for 2 minutes, then at medium speed (2 on a Kenwood) for 8 minutes, adding up to 8oz (225g) of unbleached flour if the dough seems very liquid (it will be sticky in any case). Scrape out the dough on to a floured kneading surface, knead it a few times by hand and shape it into a ball.

Rising and forming the loaf

Clean the bowl and place the dough in it. Cover the bowl with clingfilm and a tea-towel and let the dough rise in a warm spot for 1½–2 hours, until doubled in bulk.

Flour your hands and wrists, and punch down the dough. Knead it for 2–3 minutes on a lightly floured surface, using a pastry scraper to help you manipulate the dough. Remove a heaped cupful (about

8oz/225g) of the dough and place it in a bowl to use for your next loaf of bread, covering it and refrigerating after a few hours if you will not be using it again within a day.

If using a banneton. Form the dough into a ball, dust the surface with flour and place it in the *banneton* (see p. 11), rounded side down. (Or use a 3-pint (1.75-litre) bowl, oiled *very* generously and dusted with cornmeal (see p. 24).) Cover it with a tea-towel and let the dough rise in a warm spot for 1½–2 hours, until almost doubled in bulk. You can also let the dough rise in the refrigerator for several hours or overnight. Just before baking, turn out the dough on to an oiled baking sheet, or preferably a pre-heated baking stone (see p. 12) dusted with cornmeal.

If not using a banneton. Form the dough into a ball and let it rise in an oiled bowl for about 1½ hours, until doubled in bulk. Reshape the dough gently and place it on a baking sheet which has been oiled and sprinkled with cornmeal. Let it rise for about 20 minutes while you pre-heat the oven.

Baking

Pre-heat the oven to 400°F/200°C/gas mark 6. Slash the loaf with a razor blade or sharp knife just before baking. Create steam by using the baking-tin method (see p. 12) and spray the loaf with water (see p. 12). Bake for 45 minutes, until the bread is brown and responds to tapping with a hollow thumping sound. Remove it from the heat and cool it on a rack.

Wholemeal and Buckwheat Sourdough Bread

1 LARGE LOAF

A little bit of buckwheat flour added to the dough gives this bread a distinctive earthy flavour. Buckwheat flour has a strong taste, so you don't need much. This dough is dense (but not as dense as the 100 per cent wholemeal dough in the recipe on p. 72) and is quite sticky. The bread is hearty.

¾ pint (425ml) lukewarm water
2 teaspoons active dried yeast
8oz (225g) chef (see p. 69)
1lb (450g) 100 per cent wholemeal
   flour

2oz (55g) buckwheat flour
2½ teaspoons salt
4–6oz (115–170g) unbleached
   white flour

Mixing the dough and kneading

Dissolve the yeast in the water and let it sit for 10 minutes. Stir in the *chef* and combine thoroughly.

If kneading the dough by hand. Combine the 100 per cent wholemeal flour, the buckwheat flour and the salt, and gradually fold into the liquid mixture. By the time you have added it all you should be able to knead the dough. Add a generous amount of unbleached flour to your work surface and scrape out the dough. Using a pastry scraper to help fold the dough, knead for 10–15 minutes, adding unbleached flour as necessary. Shape the dough into a ball.

If using an electric mixer. Combine the 100 per cent wholemeal flour, the buckwheat flour and the salt and add to the liquids. Mix together briefly using the mixing attachment until everything is amalgamated, then scrape the dough off the mixing attachment and change to the dough hook. Knead at low speed (1 on a Kenwood) for 2 minutes, then at medium speed (2 on a Kenwood) for 6–8 minutes, adding up to 6oz (170g) of unbleached flour if the dough seems very liquid (it will be sticky in any case). Scrape out the dough on to a floured surface, knead it a few times and shape it into a ball.

Rising and forming the loaf

Clean and oil your bowl and place the dough in it, seam side up first, then seam side down. Cover the bowl and let the dough rise in a warm spot for 2 hours, until doubled in bulk.

Flour your hands and wrists, and punch down the dough. Knead for 2–3 minutes on a lightly floured surface, using a pastry scraper to make it easier. Remove a heaped cupful (about 8oz/225g) of the dough and place it in a bowl to use for your next loaf of bread, covering it and refrigerating after a few hours if you will not be using it again within a day.

If using a banneton. Form the dough into a ball, dust the surface with flour and place in the *banneton* (see p. 11), rounded side down. (Or use a 3-pint (1.75-litre) bowl, *very* generously oiled and dusted with cornmeal (see p. 24).) Cover with a tea-towel and let the dough rise in a warm spot for 1½–2 hours, until almost doubled in bulk. You can also let the dough rise in the refrigerator for several hours or overnight. Just before baking, turn out the dough on to an oiled baking sheet or, preferably, a pre-heated baking stone (see p. 12) dusted with corn-meal.

If not using a banneton. Form the dough into a ball and let it rise in an oiled bowl for about 1½ hours, until doubled in bulk. Reshape the dough gently and place it on a baking sheet which has been oiled and sprinkled with cornmeal. Let it rise for about 20 minutes while you pre-heat the oven.

Baking

Pre-heat the oven to 400°F/200°C/gas mark 6. Slash the loaf with a razor blade or sharp knife shortly before baking. Create steam by using the baking-tin method (see p. 12) and spray the loaf with water (see p. 12). Bake for 45 minutes, until the bread is brown and responds to tapping with a hollow thumping sound. Remove it from the heat and cool it on a rack.

Sourdough Bran Bread

1 LARGE LOAF

This high-fibre bread has a very chewy texture and a moist, tender crumb. It has the deep, rich taste of the other wholemeal country breads in this chapter. This is a sticky dough and is best kneaded in the bowl or in an electric mixer.

¾ pint (425ml) lukewarm water
2½ teaspoons active dried yeast
1 tablespoon black treacle
  (optional)
8oz (225g) chef (see p. 69)
4oz (115g) bran

4oz (115g) 100 per cent wholemeal
  flour, fine or coarse
12oz (340g) 85 per cent wholemeal
  flour
up to 2oz (55g) unbleached white
  flour for kneading
2½ teaspoons salt

Mixing the dough and kneading

Dissolve the yeast in the lukewarm water in a large bowl, or in the bowl of your electric mixer, and let it sit for 10 minutes. Stir in the optional treacle and the *chef*.

If kneading the dough by hand. Mix together the bran, flours and salt, and fold into the liquids, a cupful at a time. Knead in the bowl, or, as soon as you can, scrape the dough out on to your kneading surface. Knead, adding unbleached white flour as necessary, for 10 minutes. Shape the dough into a ball.

If using an electric mixer. Combine the bran, flours and salt, and add all at once to the bowl. Mix together with the mixing attachment, then change to the dough hook. Mix at low speed (1 on a Kenwood) for 2 minutes, then at medium speed (2 on a Kenwood) for 6–8 minutes. If the dough seems very wet and sticky, sprinkle in up to 2oz (55g) unbleached white flour. Scrape out the dough on to a lightly floured surface and knead it for a minute or so by hand. Shape it into a ball.

Rising and forming the loaf

Clean and oil your bowl and place the dough in it, seam side up first, then seam side down. Cover the bowl with clingfilm and a tea-towel, set it in a warm place and let the dough rise for 1½ hours, or until it has doubled in size.

Punch down the dough and turn it out on to your work surface. Remove a heaped cupful (about 8 oz/225 g) of the dough and place it in a bowl to use for your next loaf of bread, covering it and refrigerating after a few hours. Shape it into a tight, round loaf.

If using a banneton. Dust the surface of the dough with flour and place it in the *banneton* (see p. 11), rounded side down. (Or use a 3-pint (1.75-litre) bowl, *very* generously oiled and dusted with cornmeal (see p. 24).) Cover it with a tea-towel and let the dough rise in a warm spot for 45–60 minutes, until almost doubled in bulk. You can also let it rise in the refrigerator for several hours or overnight. Just before baking, turn out the dough on to an oiled baking sheet or, preferably, a pre-heated baking stone (see p. 12) dusted with cornmeal.

If not using a banneton. Let the dough rise in an oiled bowl, or right side up on a baking sheet which you have oiled and dusted with cornmeal, for 45–60 minutes, until almost doubled in bulk. Reshape the dough gently and, if you have used a bowl, place it on a baking sheet to rise again for 20 minutes while you pre-heat the oven.

Baking

Pre-heat the oven to 400°F/200°C/gas mark 6. Slash the loaf with a sharp knife or a razor blade just before baking. Create steam by using the baking-tin method (see p. 12) and spray the loaf and the oven with water (see p. 12). Bake for 45 minutes, spraying twice more during the first 10 minutes. The bread is done when it is brown and responds to tapping with a hollow thumping sound. Remove it from the heat and cool it on a rack.

Walnut Bread

1 LARGE OR 2 SMALLER LOAVES

One of my favourite French breads is this country bread with walnuts. It is usually a fairly dark (for France) bread, made with wholemeal flour, and sometimes it's a *pain de campagne*. My version below uses the same dough as the recipe on p. 70, with walnuts added. You could also use the dough for the wholemeal *pain de campagne* on p. 72, without the sourdough starter. Whichever dough you use, you will love the nutty flavour and texture of this bread. It goes especially well with cheese.

¾ *pint (425ml) lukewarm water*
2 teaspoons active dried yeast
1 tablespoon walnut oil (optional)
8oz (225g) chef (see p. 69)

1lb (425g) 100 per cent or 85 per
  cent wholemeal flour (to taste)
2½ teaspoons salt
8oz (225g) unbleached white flour
8oz (225g) shelled walnuts

Mixing the dough and kneading

Dissolve the yeast in the water in a large bowl or in the bowl of your electric mixer and let it sit for 10 minutes. Stir in the walnut oil and the *chef* and combine thoroughly.

If kneading the dough by hand. Combine the wholemeal flour and the salt, and gradually fold into the liquid mixture. By the time you have added it all you should be able to knead the dough. Put a generous amount of unbleached flour on to your work surface and scrape out the dough. Using a pastry scraper to help fold the dough, knead for 10–15 minutes, adding unbleached flour as necessary. Shape the dough into a ball.

If using an electric mixer. Combine the flours and the salt and add to the liquids. Mix together briefly, using the mixing attachment until everything is amalgamated, then scrape the dough off the mixing attachment and change to the dough hook. Knead at low speed (1 on a Kenwood) for 2 minutes, then at medium speed (2 on a Kenwood) for 6–8 minutes. Scrape the dough out of the bowl on to a floured surface, knead it a few times and shape it into a ball.

Rising and forming the loaf

Clean and oil your bowl and place the dough in it, seam side up first, then seam side down. Cover the bowl with clingfilm and a tea-towel and let the dough rise in a warm spot for 1½–2 hours, until doubled in bulk.

Flour your hands and wrists, and punch down the dough. Knead for 2–3 minutes on a lightly floured surface, using a pastry scraper to make it easier. Remove a heaped cupful (about 8oz/225g) of the dough and place it in a bowl to use for your next loaf of bread, covering it and refrigerating after a few hours if you will not be using it again within a day.

Press out the dough and sprinkle the walnuts over the surface. Fold the dough over and knead it for a couple of minutes, until the walnuts are evenly distributed through the dough.

Form the dough into a ball, or two balls for smaller loaves.

If using a banneton. Dust the surface of the dough with flour and place it in the *banneton* (see p. 11), rounded side down, or use a 3-pint (1.75-litre) bowl, *very* generously oiled and dusted with cornmeal (see p. 24).) Cover it with a tea-towel and let it rise in a warm spot for 45–60 minutes, until almost doubled in bulk. You can also let the dough rise in the refrigerator for several hours or overnight. Just before baking, turn out the dough on to an oiled baking sheet or, preferably, a pre-heated baking stone (see p. 12) dusted with cornmeal.

If not using a banneton. Let the dough rise in an oiled bowl or on oiled, cornmeal-dusted baking sheets for about 45–60 minutes, until almost doubled in bulk. Reshape the dough gently and, if you have used a bowl, place it on a baking sheet which has been oiled and sprinkled with cornmeal. Let it rise for about 20 minutes while you pre-heat the oven.

Baking

Pre-heat the oven to 400°F/200°C/gas mark 6. Slash the loaf or loaves with a razor blade or sharp knife shortly before baking. Create steam by using the baking-tin method (see p. 12) and spray the loaf with water (see p. 12). Bake for 45 minutes, until the bread is brown and responds to tapping with a hollow thumping sound. Remove it from the heat and cool it on a rack.

Sourdough Country Bread with Sun-dried Tomatoes

1 LARGE OR 2 SMALL LOAVES

This is a lovely, savoury country loaf brimming with sun-dried tomatoes, which perfume the entire bread. Try to find sun-dried tomatoes that have not been heavily salted. Fratelli Camisa in London makes its own, marinated in olive oil with herbs. They are very sweet and not at all salty.

¾ pint (225ml) lukewarm water
2½ teaspoons active dried yeast
8oz (225g) chef (see p. 69)
4oz (115g) 85 per cent wholemeal
  flour
2 oz (55g) semolina flour (if
  available; or use cornmeal)

1¼lb (565g) unbleached white
  flour, as necessary
2½ teaspoons salt
8oz (225g) sun-dried tomatoes
  (preferably marinated in olive oil
  and drained), chopped

Mixing the dough and kneading

Dissolve the yeast in the water in a large bowl or in the bowl of your electric mixer and let it sit for 10 minutes. Stir in the sourdough starter and mix together well.

If kneading the dough by hand. Combine the 85 per cent wholemeal flour, the semolina flour, 1lb (450g) of the unbleached white flour and the salt. Gradually fold into the liquids. By the time you have added 1lb (450g) you should be able to knead the dough. Flour your work surface and scrape out the dough. Using a pastry scraper to help fold the dough, knead for 10–15 minutes, adding flour to the surface and to your hands as necessary. Shape the dough into a ball.

If using an electric mixer. Combine the 85 per cent wholemeal flour, the semolina flour, 1lb (450g) of the unbleached flour and the salt. Add all at once to the liquid mixture. Mix together briefly using the mixing attachment until everything is amalgamated, then scrape the dough off the mixing attachment and change to the dough hook. Knead at low speed (1 on a Kenwood) for 2 minutes, then at medium speed (2 on a Kenwood) for 8 minutes, adding up to 4oz (115g) of unbleached flour if the dough seems very liquid (it should be sticky). Turn it out on to a floured surface, knead it a few times and shape it into a ball.

Rising and forming the loaf

Clean the bowl, return the dough to it and cover it with clingfilm and a tea-towel. Let the dough rise in a warm spot for 1½–2 hours, until doubled in bulk.

Flour your hands and wrists, and punch down the dough. Knead for 2–3 minutes on a lightly floured surface, using a pastry scraper to make it easier to manipulate the sticky dough. Remove a heaped cupful (about 8oz/225g) of the starter and place it in a bowl to use for your next loaf of bread, covering it and refrigerating after a few hours if you will not be using it again within a day.

Form the dough into a ball, or into two balls. Press out the dough and spread the sun-dried tomatoes over the surface. Fold the dough over and knead until the tomatoes are evenly distributed through the dough (divide the tomatoes in half for two loaves).

Form the dough into one or two balls.

If using a banneton. Dust the surface of the dough with flour and place it in the *banneton* (see p. 11), rounded side down. (Or use a 3-pint (1.75-litre) bowl, *very* generously oiled and dusted with cornmeal (see p. 24).) Cover with a tea-towel and let the dough rise in a warm spot for an hour, until almost doubled in bulk. You can also let the dough rise in the refrigerator for several hours or overnight. Just before baking, turn out the dough on to an oiled baking sheet or, preferably, on to a pre-heated baking stone (see p. 12) dusted with cornmeal.

If not using a banneton. Let the dough rise in an oiled bowl for about an hour, until almost doubled in bulk. Reshape the dough gently and place it on a baking sheet which has been oiled and sprinkled with cornmeal. Let it rise for about 15–20 minutes while you pre-heat the oven.

Baking

Pre-heat the oven to 400°F/200°C/gas mark 6. Slash the loaf or loaves with a razor blade or sharp knife just before baking. Create steam by using the baking-tin method (see p. 12) and spray the loaf with water (see p. 12). Spray the oven twice more during the first 10 minutes of baking. Bake for 45 minutes, until the bread is brown and responds to tapping with a hollow thumping sound. Remove it from the heat and cool it on a rack.

Note

You could also use the recipes for the country loaves on pp. 70–5 for this bread, adding 8oz (225g) sun-dried tomatoes to the dough when you form the loaves.

No-yeast Sourdough Country Bread

1 LARGE LOAF

Many bakers add no yeast to their country bread, because the starter itself gives enough leaven. Whether or not you get good bread without using yeast depends on the strength of your starter. If you bake bread often, the *chef* will be powerful. But if it sits for more than five days it loses some of its strength. I have found that my wholemeal breads can become too heavy and sour without the addition of yeast. However, if I have recently made bread, especially a yeast bread, my *chef* is terrific for lighter breads, made with all unbleached flour or a combination of flours, but predominantly unbleached white. (You can use 100 per cent wholemeal flour, but the bread will be heavy and dense.)

12fl. oz (350ml) lukewarm water
8oz (225g) chef (see p. 69)
2 scant teaspoons salt

1¼lb (565g) unbleached white flour, a combination of unbleached white flour and 85 per cent wholemeal flour, or all 85 per cent wholemeal flour (for a denser loaf)
up to 1oz (30g) additional flour for kneading

Mixing the dough and kneading

Combine the *chef* and the water in a large bowl or in the bowl of your electric mixer. Whisk together until the starter is thoroughly dissolved.

If mixing the dough by hand. Combine the flour and salt, and gradually fold into the liquid. By the time you have added 1lb (450g) you should be able to knead the dough. Flour your work surface and scrape out the dough. Using a pastry scraper to help fold the dough, knead for 10–15 minutes, adding flour as necessary. Shape the dough into a ball.

If using an electric mixer. Combine the flour and salt and add to the liquids all at once. Mix together briefly using the mixing attachment until everything is amalgamated, then scrape the dough off the mixing attachment and change to the dough hook. Knead at low speed (1 on a Kenwood) for 2 minutes, then at medium speed (2 on a Kenwood) for 8 minutes, adding up to 1oz (30g) of flour if the dough seems very liquid (it will be slightly sticky). Scrape out the dough on to a floured work surface, knead it a few times and shape it into a ball.

Rising and forming the loaf

Clean and dry your bowl, place the dough in it and cover it with clingfilm and a tea-towel. Let the dough rise in a warm spot for 1½–2 hours.

Flour your hands and wrists, and punch down the dough. Knead it for 2–3 minutes on a lightly floured surface, using a pastry scraper to make it easier. Remove a heaped cupful (about 8oz/225g) of the dough and place it in a bowl to use for your next loaf of bread, covering it and refrigerating after a few hours if you will not be using it again within a day.

Form the dough into a tight, round loaf.

If using a banneton. Dust the surface of the dough with flour and place it in the *banneton* (see p. 11), rounded side down. (Or use a 3-pint (1.75-litre) bowl, *very* generously oiled and dusted with cornmeal (see p. 24).) Cover it with a tea-towel and let the dough rise in a warm spot for 8–12 hours, until almost doubled in bulk. Just before baking, turn out the dough on to an oiled baking sheet or, preferably, on to a pre-heated baking stone (see p. 12) dusted with cornmeal.

If not using a banneton. Let the dough rise in an oiled bowl for about 8–12 hours, until almost doubled in bulk. Reshape the dough gently and place it on a baking sheet which has been oiled and sprinkled with cornmeal. Let it rise for about 15–20 minutes while you pre-heat the oven.

Baking

Pre-heat the oven to 400°F/200°C/gas mark 6. Slash the loaf with a razor blade or a sharp knife. Create steam by using the baking-tin method (see p. 12) and spray the loaf with water (see p. 12). Spray the oven twice more during the first 10 minutes of baking. Bake for 45 minutes, until the bread is brown and responds to tapping with a hollow thumping sound. Remove it from the heat and cool it on a rack.

Note: what to do if the dough sticks to the banneton or bowl

This often happens because of the long rising. See p. 67.

Country Bread with Olives

1 VERY LARGE LOAF OR 2 SMALLER LOAVES

This olive bread is slightly less acidic than the sourdough breads on pp. 65–90, made with the *chef*. The dough is slightly lighter and there's a lot of it. It can be sticky and unwieldy, but it is worth struggling with it, because the resulting bread is unbeatable. You could also make olive bread using the other sourdough recipes in this chapter, however. Just add the olives when you form the loaves, as instructed here.

This is a three-day bread: you mix the starter on the first day, the sponge on the second and the dough on the third.

For the starter

1 scant tablespoon active dried yeast
8fl. oz (225ml) lukewarm water

4oz (115g) wholemeal flour

For the sponge

¾ pint (425ml) lukewarm water

12oz (340g) 100 per cent or 85 per cent wholemeal flour

For the dough

1 tablespoon olive oil
1 scant tablespoon salt
12oz (340g) 100 per cent or 85 per cent wholemeal flour

8–12oz (225–340g) unbleached white flour, as necessary
8oz (225g) Provençal or Greek olives, stoned and halved or roughly chopped

Day 1: mixing the starter

Two days before you wish to bake, dissolve the yeast in the 8fl. oz (225ml) water in a bowl and stir in the 4oz (115g) wholemeal flour. Mix thoroughly, cover with clingfilm and set in a draught-free place for 24 hours.

Day 2: mixing the sponge

Stir the ¾ pint (425ml) water into the starter. Whisk in the 12oz (340g) wholemeal flour, a cupful at a time. Mix well, cover again and set in a draught-free place for another 24 hours.

Day 3: mixing the dough, kneading, rising and baking

If kneading the dough by hand. Stir the olive oil into the sponge. Mix together the wholemeal flour and the salt and gradually fold into the sponge. By the time you've added all the wholemeal flour you should be able to scrape the dough out on to a floured surface. Place 2–4oz (55–115g) unbleached flour on your kneading surface and knead, flouring your hands often and adding more unbleached flour to the surface, for 10 minutes, or until the dough is elastic. It will be sticky, and it will help if you use a pastry scraper to turn the dough. Shape it into a ball.

If using an electric mixer. Add the olive oil to the sponge. Mix together the wholemeal flour, the salt and 6oz (170g) of the unbleached flour. Add to the dough all at once. Mix together using the mixing attachment, then scrape the dough off the mixing attachment and change to the dough hook. Knead at low speed (1 on a Kenwood) for 2 minutes, then at medium speed (2 on a Kenwood) for 6–8 minutes, adding unbleached white flour if the dough is very sticky. Scrape the dough out of the bowl on to a floured work surface. Knead it a few times and shape it into a ball.

Clean and oil your bowl and place the dough in it, seam side up first, then seam side down. Cover the bowl and let the dough rise in a warm place for 1½ hours, until doubled in bulk.

Punch the dough down and turn it out on to a lightly floured board. Spread the olives over the surface, fold the dough in half, then knead for a couple of minutes, until the olives are evenly distributed through the dough. Divide the dough in half if you are making two loaves and shape it into balls, or shape it into one large ball. Work quickly and keep your hands well floured; the dough will be sticky.

If using a banneton. Dust the surface of the dough with flour and place it in the *banneton* (see p. 11), rounded side down. (Or use a 3-pint (1.75-litre) bowl, *very* generously oiled and dusted with cornmeal (see p. 24).) Cover it with a towel and let the dough rise in a warm spot for 1½–2 hours, until almost doubled in bulk. You can also let the dough rise in the refrigerator for several hours or overnight. Just before baking, turn out the dough on to an oiled baking sheet or, preferably, a pre-heated baking stone (see p. 12) dusted with cornmeal.

If not using a banneton. Let the dough rise in an oiled bowl for about 1½ hours, until almost doubled in bulk. Reshape the dough gently and place it on a baking sheet which has been oiled and sprinkled with cornmeal. Let it rise for about 20 minutes while you pre-heat the oven.

Pre-heat the oven to 400°F/200°C/gas mark 6. Slash the loaf or loaves with a razor blade or sharp knife shortly before baking. Create steam using the baking-tin method (see p. 12) and spray the loaf with water (see p. 12). Bake for 50–60 minutes, until the bread is brown and responds to tapping with a hollow thumping sound. Remove it from the heat and cool it on a rack.

Country Rye Bread with Raisins

2 LARGE OR 3 SMALLER LOAVES

This rye raisin bread is less acidic than many of the previous recipes. It takes 2½–3 days from start to finish to make. If you begin the starter in the afternoon or evening, you will mix up the sponge the following evening and finish the bread the following day. If you mix the starter in the morning, you will mix the sponge the following morning and finish the bread that night. Like all rye breads, this dough can be sticky and unwieldy.

For the starter

8fl. oz (225ml) lukewarm water
1 teaspoon active dried yeast

4oz (115g) rye flour

For the sponge

10fl. oz (285ml) lukewarm water
2 tablespoons black treacle

4oz (115g) unbleached white flour
6oz (170g) rye flour

For the dough

4fl. oz (120ml) lukewarm water
1 tablespoon salt
4oz (115g) wholemeal flour
8oz (225g) rye flour
4oz (115g) unbleached white flour,
as necessary

1lb (450g) raisins or currants
1 egg yolk, beaten with 1
tablespoon water or milk, for
glaze (optional)

Day 1: mixing the starter

In a small bowl, dissolve the yeast in the 8fl. oz (225ml) water and whisk in the 4oz (115g) rye flour. Combine well, cover with clingfilm and set in a draught-free spot to rise for 24 hours.

Day 2: mixing the sponge

Stir down the starter and scrape it out into a large bowl. Whisk in the 10fl. oz (285ml) water, treacle, the unbleached flour and the 6oz (170g) rye flour. Blend well, cover with clingfilm and set the bowl in a draught-free place for 12 hours.

Day 3: mixing the dough, kneading, rising and baking

If kneading the dough by hand. Fold the remaining water, the salt, the wholemeal flour and 4oz (115g) of the rye flour into the dough. Fold in the remaining rye flour half a cupful at a time, until the dough can be turned out of the bowl in more or less one piece. Place about 2oz (55g) unbleached flour on your kneading surface and scrape out the dough, which will be very sticky. Flour your hands well. If the dough is too sticky to handle, use a pastry scraper instead of your hands to fold the dough for kneading. Knead for about 10 minutes, adding unbleached flour by the handful as necessary. After about 5 minutes the dough should give up some of its stickiness and become easier to work with.

If using an electric mixer. Stir the remaining water into the sponge. Mix together the wholemeal flour, the rye flour and salt, and add to the mixture all at once. Mix together using the mixing attachment, then scrape the dough off the mixing attachment and change to the dough hook. Knead at low speed (1 on a Kenwood) for 2 minutes, then at medium speed (2 on a Kenwood) for 6–8 minutes, adding extra unbleached flour if the dough is very sticky. Scrape the dough out of the bowl on to a floured work surface. The dough will be very sticky.

Shape the dough into a ball and place it in an oiled bowl, seam side up first, then seam side down. Cover the bowl with clingfilm and set it in a warm place for the dough to rise for an hour.

Punch down the dough and turn it out on to a well-floured work surface. Press it out to a 1-inch thickness and spread the raisins or currants over the surface. Fold the dough over and knead several times, until the fruit is evenly distributed.

Divide the dough into three equal pieces (for rolls, see note below). Shape these into round balls and place them on a large, oiled baking sheet. Cover with greaseproof paper or a tea-towel and set in a warm place to rise for 30 minutes. Meanwhile, pre-heat the oven to 400°F/200°C/gas mark 6.

Uncover the loaves and, using a razor blade or a thin, sharp knife, make two intersecting Xs across the top, so that eight intersecting lines radiate out from the centre like a star. Brush with the optional glaze and bake for 45–50 minutes, turning the baking sheet around and brushing once more with the glaze halfway through baking. When the bottom crust responds to tapping with a hollow thump, remove the bread from the oven and cool it on racks.

Note

For rolls, divide the dough into 2oz (55g) pieces and roll them into balls. Place them on oiled baking sheets, cover them with greaseproof paper and let them rise for about an hour, until doubled in size. Pre-heat the oven for about 20 minutes before baking.

Brush the rolls with glaze, if using, and slash an X across the top of each. Bake for 25–30 minutes, turning the baking sheets around and brushing the rolls again halfway through baking. Cool the rolls on racks or eat while still warm.

Liquid Sourdough Starter

1½ PINTS (850ML)

This starter is easy to mix up. Unlike the *chef* on p. 69, you replenish it not by keeping a piece of the dough, but by adding more water and flour to it every time you use it. It isn't quite as acidic as the *chef*. It makes a nice addition to pancakes and scones, as well as to sourdough breads.

¾ pint (425ml) lukewarm water
1 tablespoon active dried yeast

2 teaspoons sugar or mild-flavoured
  honey
8oz (225g) unbleached white flour

Dissolve the yeast in the water in an earthenware bowl and stir in the sugar or honey. Stir in the flour and mix well. Cover and leave to sit at room temperature for 5 days, stirring the mixture once or twice a day. Pour into a wide-mouthed jar or crock, cover and refrigerate.

When you use this starter, replenish it by adding 4fl. oz (120ml) water and 4oz (115g) unbleached flour.

Sourdough French Bread

4 *BAGUETTES* OR 18–24 ROLLS

This is an authentic hard-crusted French loaf. The dough is sticky and a bit hard to handle, but it's worth the trouble when those crusty, slightly sour loaves come out of the oven. They go stale very quickly and do not freeze well.

2 teaspoons active dried yeast
8fl. oz (225ml) lukewarm water
½ teaspoon mild-flavoured honey
  or malt extract
4fl. oz (120ml) sourdough starter
  (see p. 96)

1 tablespoon safflower oil or
  softened unsalted butter
  (optional)
1½ teaspoons salt
4oz (115g) wholemeal flour
1lb (450g) unbleached white flour

Mixing the dough and kneading

Dissolve the yeast in the lukewarm water in a large bowl, or in the bowl of your electric mixer, add the honey or malt extract and let it sit for 10 minutes. Stir in the sourdough starter and the optional safflower oil or butter.

If kneading the dough by hand. Mix together the wholemeal flour and salt and fold into the liquid, then fold in about three-quarters of the unbleached flour. As soon as you can, scrape out the dough on to your kneading surface. Knead, adding unbleached flour as necessary, for 10 minutes.

If using an electric mixer. Combine the flours and salt, and add all at once to the liquid. Mix together with the mixing attachment, then scrape the dough off the mixing attachment and change to the dough hook. Mix at low speed (1 on a Kenwood) for 2 minutes, then at medium speed (2 on a Kenwood) for 6–8 minutes. If the dough seems very wet and sticky, sprinkle in up to 2oz (55g) unbleached white flour. Scrape out the dough on to a lightly floured surface and knead for a minute or so by hand. Shape the dough into a ball.

Clean and oil your bowl, and place the dough in it, seam side up first, then seam side down. Cover the bowl with clingfilm and a tea-towel, and set it in a warm place to let the dough rise for 1½ hours, or until it has doubled in size.

Punch down the dough and turn it out on to your work surface. Knead it for a few minutes, adding flour as necessary. The dough will be very sticky. Cut it into four equal pieces for *baguettes*, or into 18–24 pieces for rolls. Shape them into balls (as you do this cover the shaped balls loosely with clingfilm to prevent the dough drying out while you shape the remaining balls) then shape *baguettes* (see p. 27) or rolls. (For knotted rolls, shape the dough into thin *baguette*-type cylinders, about 6–8 inches long, and tie in loose knots, as in the illustration below.) Place in oiled, cornmeal-dusted *baguette* pans or on baking sheets.

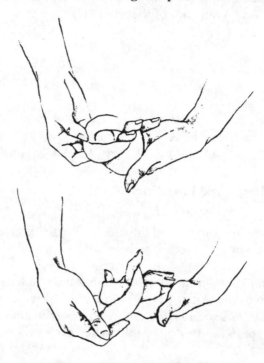

Cover the dough loosely with a tea-towel and set it in a warm spot to rise for 40–50 minutes. Meanwhile, pre-heat the oven to 400°F/200°C/ gas mark 6.

Slash the *baguettes* with a razor or a sharp knife (no need to slash knotted rolls) and spray them with water (see p. 12). Spray the oven, place the baking sheets on two shelves in the mid–upper part of the oven and bake for 30–40 minutes, switching the position of the baking sheets halfway through and spraying twice more during the first 10 minutes.

When the bread is golden and hard, remove it from the oven and cool it on a rack.

4: English Breads, Scones, Tea Cakes and Pancakes

When I came to England I couldn't wait to have my first English tea; I imagined tea trolleys overflowing with scones, thick cream and jam, toasted crumpets, cakes and sandwiches. I wanted to taste all those wonderful-sounding foods I had read about in books, beginning with nursery rhymes when I was a child.

I went searching for the imagined tea. I often found a good tea, with scones (I have eaten many a good one and probably more bad ones – they are a real weakness of mine), dainty sandwiches and sometimes toast; but the sweet pastries I found at most teas were sugary cakes, really more like French pastry than English. Where were the crumpets and buns, currant breads and Sally Lunns, lardy cakes and tea bracks? I can't seem to find these traditional breads and cakes anywhere.

My original idea for these pages was to roam around the British Isles, find bakers who were making these breads and learn from them. But as I began to sniff around for the bakers, it became apparent that I was going to have to look long and hard. It's not that a good British baker is hard to find; but one who is making a variety of traditional breads is. The best professional bakers today tend to turn out excellent granary loaves, soda breads, wholemeal loaves, occasionally some good French bread. But good cottage loaves and bloomers? Barm brack, Chelsea buns, tea brack and saffron bread? When I do find these breads they are disappointing; the yeast breads are often made from tasteless flour and go stale quickly, the buns are sugary and bland, and the tea breads are chemically raised and lifeless when they should be yeast-raised and full of flavour.

I am sure that the place to find well-made English breads is in people's homes, in the countryside. So many of the breads here evoke regions, towns, places: country kitchens equipped with heavy iron griddles (or girdles) and wood-fired ovens, farms where oats and barley are staples and are transformed into luscious, healthy pancakes, bannocks and baps. Some of the breads, like the rich lardy cakes, were festival breads, made for the fairs at harvest time. Saffron bread would never have become a tradition in Cornwall and Devon if saffron had not been cultivated there. Chelsea buns were made at a famous Chelsea tea house, and Bath buns did originally come from Bath. Cornish splits (hot plain buns split open) were a vehicle for the rich Cornish clotted cream and tasty jam.

The farmhouse kitchens might not be accessible to you, but you can acquaint yourself with the breads – and develop a weakness for them – by making them in your own kitchen, as I have done. As I researched and tested recipes for this chapter (thanks to Elizabeth David, Elisabeth Luard and Jane Grigson I had no trouble in finding recipes), I ended up with my own versions. I've seen so many variations on these breads that I don't feel as if the rules are hard and fast, as long as the basic ingredients are there. I often take the liberty of using some wholemeal flour (usually 85 per cent as opposed to 100 per cent) in doughs that may traditionally be made entirely with white flour, if I find that wholemeal flour renders the breads tastier. I also often reduce the excessive amounts of fat and sugar that many traditional recipes call for.

The recipes collected in this chapter are by no means exhaustive. I have tried to bring together the breads with the most popular tradition – those that one still finds today in the British Isles – and the breads, pancakes and scones I have found too delicious to leave out. I only wish that they were still as popular as ever – that a rich yeasted pancake or a good scone was not so hard to find. Luckily, they are easy to make.

Yeasted Loaves and Soda Breads

Some of the breads in this section – the bloomer, Coburg and cottage loaf – are named for their shape rather than for the ingredients in the dough. There are conflicting theories and guesses about the origins of their names (discussed in detail by Elizabeth David in *English Bread and Yeast Cookery*). Others are traditional breads containing specific ingredients – barley, grains, soda, saffron. These breads are easier to find in the UK than many of the tea breads in this chapter. But good ones? Once you make them yourself you'll be spoiled.

Bloomer Loaves

2 LOAVES

The bloomer, like the Coburg (p. 102) and the cottage loaf (p. 102), is a specific shape rather than a type of dough. I usually make these breads with sourdough, using the recipes on pp. 65–98, but you could also use the dough for the country breads on pp. 38–40. I also like the country mixture below, which substitutes milk for half of the water. The dough should be stiff enough to hold its shape when you form the loaves.

2 teaspoons active dried yeast	8oz (225g) chef (see p. 69)
8fl. oz (225ml) lukewarm water	1lb (450g) wholemeal flour
7fl. oz (200ml) lukewarm milk	4–8oz (115–225g) unbleached
1 teaspoon malt extract	white flour

Dissolve the yeast in the water and add the milk and the malt extract. Follow the instructions on p. 70 for making the dough up to the end of the first rise.

Punch down the dough and turn it out on to your work surface. Knead it for a few minutes, then divide it into two equal portions. Shape each portion into a ball, cover with clingfilm and let them sit for 5 minutes.

Now shape each piece into a long, sausage-shaped loaf by rolling up the dough like a pan loaf (see p. 27), then rolling the cylinder between your hands and the table until it is 10–12 inches long. Fold the short ends under and pinch the seams. Place on an oiled and cornmeal-dusted baking sheet, cover loosely with a tea-towel and let the dough rise for 20 minutes.

Meanwhile, pre-heat the oven to 450°F/230°C/gas mark 8. Slash the loaves across about six times and wait for the slashes to begin to open out. Spray the loaves and the oven with water (see p. 12) and place in the hot oven. After 10 minutes turn the heat down to 400°F/200°C/gas mark 6, spray the oven again, and bake for another 20–30 minutes, until the loaves are brown and hollow sounding when tapped. Remove them from the heat and cool them on a rack.

Coburg Loaf

1 LARGE LOAF

A Coburg is a large, round loaf slashed with a deep cross that opens out into four distinct pieces as the bread bakes. Any of the country breads on pp. 38–41 or the sourdough breads on pp. 65–98, as well as the dough used in the cottage loaf below, will work for this.

Follow the recipes up to the point where you slash the dough just before baking. The oven should be hot. With a sharp knife or razor blade, make a long slash, about ½ inch deep, right across the middle of the top, from one side to the other. Then make cuts on either side, from the edge of the loaf at a 90° angle right up to the first slash. Spray the loaf and the oven with water (see p. 12). As soon as the slashes begin to open out (within a minute, usually), place the dough in the oven. Bake the bread as directed in the particular recipe, spraying the oven a few times during the first 10 minutes. Cool it on a rack.

Cottage Loaf

1 LARGE LOAF

This is a loaf with a top-knot. I learned to make it from Elizabeth David's *English Bread and Yeast Cookery*. The important things to remember when you make this bread are to have a dough that isn't too flimsy, and not to let the dough over-prove on the second rising, or the loaf won't retain its shape.

1 scant pint (570ml) lukewarm
  water
2½ teaspoons active dried yeast
1½lb (680g) unbleached white
  flour, plus extra for kneading

8oz (225g) 85 per cent wholemeal
  flour
1 tablespoon salt

Mixing the dough and kneading

Dissolve the yeast in the lukewarm water in a large bowl or in the bowl of your electric mixer, and let it sit for 10 minutes.

If kneading the bread by hand. Mix together the flours and salt, and fold them into the liquid a cupful at a time. As soon as you can, scrape out the dough on to your kneading surface. Knead, adding unbleached white flour as necessary, for 10 minutes. The dough should be stiff and elastic. Shape it into a ball and place it in the bowl.

If using an electric mixer. Combine the flours and salt and add them all at once to the liquid. Mix together with the mixing attachment, then change to the dough hook. Mix at low speed (1 on a Kenwood) for 2 minutes, then at medium speed (2 on a Kenwood) for 6–8 minutes. If the dough seems very wet and sticky, sprinkle in up to 2oz (55g) unbleached flour. Scrape out the dough on to a lightly floured surface and knead it for a minute or so by hand. Shape it into a ball and place it in the bowl.

Rising, forming the loaf and baking

Cover the bowl with clingfilm and a tea-towel, and set it in a warm place to let the dough rise for 1½ hours, or until it has doubled in size.

Punch down the dough and turn it out on to your work surface. Shape it into a ball. Weigh the dough and cut it into two unequal pieces, one weighing one-third of the total weight. Shape these pieces into tight balls and place the larger one on an oiled and cornmeal-dusted baking sheet, with the rounded side up, and the smaller one in a bowl, with the rounded side down. Cover both pieces with clingfilm and set in a warm spot to rise for 40 minutes. You do not want to finish the second rise, or the dough will collapse when you assemble the bread.

After about 40 minutes, flatten the top of the larger (bottom) piece slightly and slash it with an X across the middle, about 1½ inches wide. Now slightly flatten the bottom – the seam side – of the top-knot and gently place it on top of the bottom piece (see below). The loaves should not merge into one piece but should remain distinct. If they do merge, they have proved for too long.

Cover the dough with a tea-towel and let it rest for about 10 minutes to recover its shape. Do not leave it for too long or it will spread and lose its shape. If the dough is too slack and begins to collapse as soon as you assemble the two pieces, put it into the oven straight away.

Uncover the dough, place it in the lower part of the oven and turn the oven on to 450°F/230°C/gas mark 8. The dough will prove as the oven warms up and as it gets hot it will begin to bake. Bake for 40 minutes, or until the bread is golden-brown and hollow sounding when tapped. (Elizabeth David suggests that you put a bowl over it after 30 minutes, but this seems unduly complicated to me.) Cool it on a rack.

Note

If your oven is already hot, bake the bread at 400°F/200°C/gas mark 6.

Granary Loaves

2 LOAVES

Granary loaves are really not much different from the mixed-grain bread on p. 48 – at least mine aren't. They are wholemeal loaves that contain a mixture of grains. Sometimes they are free-form; others are baked in loaf tins. Most of those that I see in shops don't appeal to me because the grains are too coarse and they hurt my teeth. The recipe below is an adaptation of my mixed-grain bread, and I think it would be recognised in the UK as a granary loaf.

For the sponge

1¼ pints (750ml) lukewarm water
1 tablespoon active dried yeast
2 tablespoons mild-flavoured honey

2 tablespoons black treacle
8oz (225g) unbleached white flour
8oz (225g) wholemeal flour

For the dough

4 tablespoons safflower oil
1 tablespoon salt
3oz (85g) porridge oats
3oz (85g) rye flakes

*4½oz (130g) coarsely ground or
    cracked wheat*
4oz (115g) rye flour
*12oz (340g) wholemeal flour, as
    necessary*

For the topping

*1 egg, beaten with 2 tablespoons
    water, for glaze*

*3 tablespoons medium or fine oat
    flakes*

Mixing the sponge

Dissolve the yeast in the warm water in a large bowl. Mix in the honey and treacle. Whisk in the unbleached and wholemeal flours, a cupful at a time. When it has all been added, whisk 100 times, changing direction every now and then. This really won't take too long. The sponge should have the consistency of thick mud. Cover it and set it in a warm place for an hour, until bubbly.

Mixing the dough and kneading

Fold the oil, then the salt into the sponge, using a large wooden spoon and turning the bowl between folds. Fold in the grains one at a time, then the rye flour.

Now begin folding in the wholemeal flour. After you have added about two-thirds, the dough should hold together in a sticky mass. Place a large handful of flour on your kneading surface and scrape out the dough. Flour your hands and begin kneading. At first you will have to treat the dough gingerly, as it is sticky, and you will have to keep flouring your hands, but after a few minutes the dough will begin to stiffen and will become easier to work with. Knead, adding more flour as necessary, for 10–15 minutes. The dough will be dense, but should become stiff and elastic as you knead. The surface will be slightly tacky. Shape it into a ball.

Oil the bowl, place the dough in the bowl, seam side up first, then seam side down. Cover the bowl and let the dough rise in a warm spot for an hour.

Forming the loaves and baking

Punch down the dough. At this point you can let it rise once more in the bowl, or let it rise in the tins. The extra rise will make a lighter loaf. Cover it and let it rise for 45–60 minutes in a warm place.

Turn the dough out on to a lightly floured work surface. Knead it a couple of times and divide it in two. Form two loaves and place them in buttered or oiled loaf tins, seam side up first, then seam side down. Brush the loaves lightly with the glaze and sprinkle with the oat flakes. Cover them and let them rise until the tops rise above the edge of the tins. This will take anywhere from 20–45 minutes, depending on the weather and the stage at which you shaped the loaves.

Meanwhile, pre-heat the oven to 350°F/180°C/gas mark 4. Slash the loaves across the top in three places and bake on a middle shelf for 50–60 minutes. Halfway through baking, brush the tops again with glaze. The bread is done when it is golden-brown and responds to tapping with a hollow thumping sound. Remove it from the tins and cool it on a rack.

Barley Bread

2 LOAVES

Barley meal, which can be purchased in wholefood shops, gives this bread a malty, earthy flavour. It is very much like the wholemeal loaf on p. 44 and made in the same way. The dough is similar too: dense, sticky and moderately heavy. At the end of kneading it will be just about smooth, maybe a little tacky, on the surface. The bread has a beautiful texture and toasts very nicely.

2 teaspoons active dried yeast
1¼ pints (750ml) lukewarm water
2 tablespoons mild-flavoured honey
*   or 1 tablespoon malt extract*
2fl. oz (60ml) buttermilk
8oz (225g) barley flour
1lb (450g) 100 per cent wholemeal
*   or 85 per cent wholemeal flour*
1 tablespoon salt

2 tablespoons sunflower or
*   safflower oil*
8oz (225g) unbleached white flour,
*   plus 2–3oz (55–85g) extra for*
*   kneading*
1 egg, beaten with 2 tablespoons
*   water, for glaze*
2 tablespoons sesame seeds

Mixing the dough and kneading

Dissolve the yeast in the water and let it sit for 5–10 minutes. Stir in the honey or malt extract and the buttermilk.

Mix together the barley flour, half the wholemeal flour and the salt. Gradually stir this mixture into the liquid, a cupful at a time. Use a whisk to obtain a smooth batter. When this portion of the flour has been added, fold in the oil and begin adding the remaining wholemeal and the unbleached flour, a cupful at a time. As soon as you can, scrape the dough out of the bowl on to a kneading surface dusted generously with flour.

Now begin kneading, using a pastry scraper to facilitate folding the dough and knead for about 15 minutes, frequently flouring your hands and the work surface with flour. The dough will be very sticky at first, but will stiffen up after about 5 minutes. At the end of the kneading, the dough will be stiff, dense and elastic. Sprinkle a little flour on your work surface and shape the dough into a ball.

Rising, forming the loaves and baking

Rinse out your bowl and dry it. Lightly oil the bowl and place the dough in it, seam side up first, then seam side down. Cover the bowl tightly with clingfilm and a tea-towel. Allow the dough to rise for 1½–2 hours in a warm spot. It should double in size and soften considerably during the rising.

Punch the dough down and allow it to rise again, covered, for an hour (this rise can be omitted, the loaves will be slightly denser). Turn out the dough on to a lightly floured work surface, shape it into a ball and cut it in half. Shape the two halves into balls and let them sit for 10 minutes so that the dough relaxes.

Now form the loaves. Oil two 8 × 4-inch baking tins and place the loaves in, upside down first, then right side up. Brush them with the glaze, sprinkle with sesame seeds, and brush again with the glaze. Cover them with a damp tea-towel and set them in a warm place to rise for 20–45 minutes if this is the third rising, 45–90 minutes if this is the second rising, until the tops curve up above the edges of the tins and the sides reach the tops of the tins.

Meanwhile, pre-heat the oven to 350°F/180°C/gas mark 4. Just before baking, slash the loaves across the tops with a razor blade or a sharp knife. Bake for 50–55 minutes, or until the loaves are a nut-brown colour and respond to tapping with a hollow sound. Remove the bread from the oven and take it out of the tins. It may be necessary to run a knife between the sides of the tins and the loaves. Cool it on racks, laying the bread on its side.

Dark Malted Bread with Dried Fruit

1 LOAF

Dark and spicy, this sweet bread makes a good tea or breakfast bread. It toasts nicely.

1½ teaspoons active dried yeast
8fl. oz (225ml) lukewarm water
4fl. oz (120ml) lukewarm
  Guinness
2 tablespoons malt extract
1 tablespoon black treacle
12oz (340g) 100 per cent or 85 per
  cent wholemeal flour
1½ teaspoons salt
1 teaspoon mixed spice (optional)

2 tablespoons sunflower or
  safflower oil
4oz (115g) unbleached white flour,
  plus up to 2oz (55g) extra for
  kneading
3oz (85g) currants
3oz (85g) raisins or sultanas
1 egg, beaten with 2 tablespoons
  water, for glaze

Mixing the dough and kneading

Dissolve the yeast in the water and let it sit for 5–10 minutes. Stir in the Guinness, the malt and the treacle.

If kneading the dough by hand. Mix together half the wholemeal flour, the salt and the optional spice. Gradually stir this mixture into the liquid, a cupful at a time. Use a whisk to obtain a smooth batter. When this portion of the flour has been added, fold in the oil, and begin adding the remaining wholemeal and the unbleached flour, a cupful at a time. As soon as you can, scrape the dough out of the bowl on to a kneading surface dusted generously with flour.

Now begin kneading, using a pastry scraper to facilitate folding the dough, and knead for about 15 minutes, frequently dusting your hands and the work surface with flour. The dough will be very sticky at first, but will stiffen up after about 5 minutes. At the end of the kneading, the dough will be stiff, dense and elastic. Sprinkle a little more flour on your work surface, and shape the dough into a ball.

If using an electric mixer. Mix together all but the additional 2oz (55g) unbleached flour for kneading with the salt and the optional spice and add to the liquids. Mix together using the mixing attachment, then scrape the dough off the mixing attachment and change to the dough hook. Knead at low speed (1 on a Kenwood) for 2 minutes, then at medium speed (2 on a Kenwood) for 6–8 minutes, adding extra unbleached flour if the dough is very sticky. Scrape the dough out of the bowl on to a floured work surface. Knead for about a minute, then shape into a ball.

Rising, forming the loaf and baking

Rinse out and dry your bowl. Lightly oil it and place the dough in it, seam side up first, then seam side down. Cover the bowl tightly with clingfilm and a tea-towel. Allow the dough to rise for 1½–2 hours in a warm spot. The dough should double in size and soften considerably during the rising.

Punch the dough down and turn it out on to a lightly floured surface. Add the raisins and currants and knead them into the dough until they are evenly distributed. Shape the dough into a ball and let it rest for 5–10 minutes, then shape it into a loaf.

Oil or butter an 8 × 4-inch baking tin and place the loaf in it, upside down first, then right side up. Brush with the glaze. Cover with a damp tea-towel and set it in a warm place to rise for about 45 minutes, until the top of the loaf curves up above the edges of the tin and the sides reach the top of the tin.

Meanwhile, pre-heat the oven to 375°F/190°C/gas mark 5. Bake for 50–55 minutes, or until the loaf is a nut-brown colour and responds to tapping with a hollow sound. Remove the loaf from the oven and take it out of the tin. It may be necessary to run a knife between the sides of the tin and the loaf. Cool the bread on a rack, laying it on its side.

Wholemeal Baps

8–10 BAPS

Baps are the traditional morning roll of Scotland, and have become a common sandwich roll in England. These wholemeal baps with sesame have a particularly rich, nutty flavour.

2 teaspoons active dried yeast
¼ pint (140ml) lukewarm water
¼ pint (140ml) lukewarm milk
1 teaspoon mild-flavoured honey
2 teaspoons salt

12oz (340g) wholemeal flour
8oz (225g) unbleached white flour
2oz (55g) lard or margarine
milk, for brushing the surfaces
a few tablespoons sesame seeds

Mixing the dough and kneading

Dissolve the yeast in the water and add the milk and honey. Let it sit for 10 minutes.

If kneading the dough by hand. Mix together the flours and salt, then rub in the lard or margarine. Add the liquids and stir together to form a soft dough. Scrape the dough out on to a floured kneading surface. Knead for 10 minutes, adding extra unbleached white flour to the surface and to your hands as necessary. The dough should be fairly sticky.

If using an electric mixer. Combine the flours and salt, and add all at once to the yeast mixture in the bowl of your electric mixer, along with the lard or margarine. Mix together with the mixing attachment, then change to the dough hook. Mix at low speed (1 on a Kenwood) for 2 minutes, then at medium speed (2 on a Kenwood) for 6–8 minutes. If the dough seems very wet and sticky, sprinkle in up to 2oz (55g) unbleached white flour. Scrape out the dough on to a lightly floured surface and knead by hand for a minute or so. Shape into a ball.

Rising, forming the baps and baking

Clean and lightly oil your bowl. Place the dough in it, seam side up first, then seam side down. Cover the bowl with clingfilm and a tea-towel, then set it in a warm place for the dough to rise for 1½ hours, or until it has doubled in size.

Punch down the dough and turn it out on to your work surface. Shape it into a ball and divide it into 8–10 equal pieces, forming tight, round balls. Place them on an oiled and cornmeal-dusted baking sheet, brush with milk and sprinkle with sesame seeds, patting the sesame seeds into the dough.

Cover with a tea-towel and let the dough rise in a warm spot for about 20 minutes, while you pre-heat the oven to 400°F/200°C/gas mark 6. Bake for 15–20 minutes, until the baps are puffed and golden. Cool them on a rack.

Coarse Wholemeal Irish Soda Bread

1 LOAF

It's amazing how easy it is to make a good loaf of bread with no yeast at all. This Irish soda bread has a very dense, highly textured crumb, due to the coarse wholemeal flour I use. A lighter bread can be achieved with finer wholemeal flour, wholemeal pastry flour or 85 per cent wholemeal flour, but this one best resembles the bread my Irish mother-in-law has brought me from Ireland.

12oz (340g) coarse wholemeal flour
4oz (115g) unbleached white flour
2 teaspoons salt
1 level teaspoon bicarbonate of soda
¾ teaspoon baking powder
12–15fl. oz (340–425ml) buttermilk or sour milk

Pre-heat the oven to 375°F/190°C/gas mark 5. Mix together the flours, salt, bicarbonate of soda and baking powder in a large bowl. Blend thoroughly so that the bicarbonate of soda and baking powder are distributed evenly. Add the buttermilk or sour milk and stir together to make a soft but firm dough. If you are using very coarse flour, the dough will be wet.

Knead the dough gently on a floured board for about 3 minutes, until smooth. Form the dough into a round loaf and place it on a well-buttered baking sheet. Cut an X across the top with a sharp knife or blade.

Bake for 35–45 minutes, until the bread is nicely browned and the loaf responds to tapping with a hollow sound. Remove it from the heat and cool it on a rack. Slice it very thin.

Note

Soda bread will not keep for long. Store it in the refrigerator in plastic bags.

White Irish Soda Bread

1 LOAF

Substitute unbleached white flour for the wholemeal flour and proceed as in the above recipe.

Irish Soda Farls

2–3 FARLS

These are small soda breads, much like the bread on p. 111.

1½lb (680g) 85 per cent or 100 per cent wholemeal flour (or use part unbleached white flour, part wholemeal)
2 teaspoons salt
1 tablespoon tartaric acid

1 teaspoon bicarbonate of soda
1oz (30g) unsalted butter, softened
1 pint (570ml) buttermilk or sour milk
1 egg and 3 tablespoons flour, for topping

Pre-heat the oven to 450°F/230°C/gas mark 8. Butter two baking sheets.

Sift together the flour, salt, tartaric acid and bicarbonate of soda. Rub in the butter. (This can be done in a food processor fitted with the steel blade, using the pulse action, or in a mixer.) Stir ¾ pint (425ml) of the buttermilk or sour milk into the flour mixture. Mix together to form a dough with an even consistency. Add more buttermilk if the dough is too dry. Do not over-work.

Transfer the dough to a lightly floured work surface and divide it into two or three pieces. Shape these into rounds and roll them out to a thickness of about 1 inch.

Place the farls on the prepared baking sheets. Slash each one with a large X that divides the round into quarters. Brush with beaten egg, dust with flour and bake for 20–30 minutes, until golden-brown.

Barleymeal Bonnag

2–3 LOAVES

This is another soda bread, made with a combination of barleymeal and wheat flour. It is adapted from an Elizabeth David recipe. Barleymeal has a very pungent flavour; I have reduced the quantity given in the original recipe, but if you still feel that the taste is too strong, substitute some wholemeal or unbleached white flour for some of the barleymeal.

8oz (225g) barleymeal
8oz (225g) unbleached white flour
1 teaspoon salt
1 teaspoon baking powder

1 teaspoon tartaric acid
2oz (55g) margarine or unsalted butter
½ pint (285ml) buttermilk

Pre-heat the oven to 350°F/180°C/gas mark 4. Butter or oil two baking sheets.

Combine the barleymeal, unbleached white flour, salt, baking powder and tartaric acid in a large bowl. Rub in the margarine. (This can also be done in a food processor fitted with the steel blade, using the pulse action, or in a mixer.) Stir the buttermilk into the flour mixture. Mix together well. Transfer the dough to a lightly floured board and divide it into two or three pieces. Shape round loaves and place them on the baking sheets.

Bake in the pre-heated oven for 45–60 minutes, until the loaves are golden brown and respond to tapping with a hollow sound. Remove them from the heat and cool them on racks.

Scones

As I have said, I adore these easy-to-make breads. There are literally hundreds of recipes for scones, and I'm giving you just a smattering here. They can be sweet or savoury, grainy or white. They should always be rich and light, and should melt in your mouth. The secret of making good scones is handling the dough as little as possible, so that the gluten doesn't develop and toughen the dough.

Scones are sometimes baked on a griddle, and you'll find recipes for those later in this chapter.

Wholemeal Scones

12 SCONES

I like wholemeal scones much better than those made with white flour, because of their grainy texture and rich taste. Some wholemeal scones, however, are heavy. But not these: they're as light as can be and irresistible with afternoon tea or for breakfast. They will remain moist for several days.

8oz (225g) wholemeal pastry flour
½ teaspoon bicarbonate of soda
2 teaspoons baking powder
¼ teaspoon salt
1 tablespoon sugar (brown,
   Demerara or white)

3oz (85g) cold unsalted butter, cut
   into small pieces
1 tablespoon mild-flavoured honey
3fl. oz (90 ml) low-fat natural
   yoghurt
3oz (85g) currants

Pre-heat the oven to 400°F/220°C/gas mark 6. Butter two baking sheets.

Sift together the flour, bicarbonate of soda, baking powder, salt and sugar. Rub in the butter until the mixture resembles coarse cornmeal. (This can be done in a food processor fitted with the steel blade, using the pulse action, or in a mixer.) Mix together the honey and yoghurt and stir into the flour mixture along with the currants. Mix together to form a soft dough.

Turn out the dough on to a lightly floured board and gently knead about ten times, just until the ingredients are combined. Press or roll the dough into a rectangle, and cut it into twelve triangular pieces, or use a round scone cutter. Place the scones on the baking sheets and bake for 12–15 minutes, until they begin to brown on the top. Remove them from the heat and cool them on a rack, or serve them warm.

Cream Scones

12 SCONES

These scones are rich, sweet and flaky. You can make them with or without the currants.

8oz (225g) unbleached white flour
½ teaspoon bicarbonate of soda
2 teaspoons baking powder
¼ teaspoon salt
2 tablespoons white sugar

3oz (85g) cold unsalted butter, cut
  into small pieces
4fl. oz (120ml) single or double
  cream
3oz (85g) currants (optional)

Pre-heat the oven to 400°F/200°C/gas mark 6. Butter two baking sheets.

Sift together the flour, bicarbonate of soda, baking powder, salt and sugar. Rub in the butter until the mixture resembles coarse cornmeal. (This can be done in a food processor with the steel blade, using the pulse action, or in a mixer.) Stir in the cream and mix to a soft dough.

Gather up the dough and turn it out on to a lightly floured board. Gently knead it about ten times, just until the ingredients are combined. Press or roll the dough into a rectangle and cut it into twelve triangular pieces, or use a round scone cutter. Place the scones on the baking sheets and bake for 12–15 minutes, until they begin to brown on the top. Remove them from the heat and cool them on a rack, or serve them warm.

Fig and Orange Drop Scones

12–15 SCONES

These scones have a marvellous, crunchy texture and the sweet–tart flavour of figs and orange. This dough is quite moist.

4oz (115g) dried figs
8fl. oz (225ml) orange juice
8oz (225g) wholemeal pastry flour
½ teaspoon bicarbonate of soda
2 teaspoons baking powder
¼ teaspoon salt

1 tablespoon sugar (brown,
  Demerara or white)
3oz (85g) cold unsalted butter, cut
  into small pieces
1 tablespoon mild-flavoured honey
2fl. oz (60ml) low-fat yoghurt

Place the figs in a bowl. Heat the orange juice to a simmer in a saucepan and pour it over the figs. Let them sit for 1–2 hours. Alternatively, you can omit bringing the orange juice to a simmer and soak the figs in it overnight.

Drain and measure out 2fl. oz (60ml) of the orange juice. Chop the figs in a food processor fitted with the steel blade, or use a large, sharp knife. Set aside.

Pre-heat the oven to 400°F/200°C/gas mark 6. Butter two baking sheets.

Sift together the flour, bicarbonate of soda, baking powder, salt and sugar. Rub in the butter until the mixture has the consistency of coarse cornmeal. (This can be done in a food processor fitted with the steel blade, using the pulse action, or in a mixer.) Mix together the honey, yoghurt and the reserved 2fl. oz (60ml) orange juice, and stir into the flour mixture, then stir in the figs.

Drop heaped tablespoons of the batter on to the prepared baking sheets. Bake for 12–15 minutes, until the scones begin to brown on the top. Remove them from the heat and cool them on a rack, or serve them warm.

Buttermilk Drop Scones

ABOUT 15 SCONES

These rich, white, slightly cakey scones are very nice with afternoon tea.

10oz (285g) unbleached white
   flour
1 tablespoon baking powder
½ teaspoon bicarbonate of soda
¾ teaspoon salt
½ teaspoon cinnamon
3 tablespoons white sugar

4oz (115g) cold unsalted butter, cut
   into small pieces
3oz (85g) sultanas, raisins or
   currants
2 large eggs
6fl. oz (180ml) buttermilk

Pre-heat the oven to 425°F/220°C/gas mark 7. Butter two baking sheets.

Sift together the flour, baking powder, bicarbonate of soda, salt, cinnamon and sugar. Rub in the butter until the mixer has the consistency of coarse cornmeal. (This can be done in a food processor fitted with the steel blade, using the pulse action, or in a mixer.) Add the raisins. Beat together the eggs and buttermilk, and stir into the mixture. Stir together to form a smooth dough, but don't over-beat.

Drop heaped tablespoons, or more for large scones, of the batter on to the prepared baking sheets, leaving about 2 inches between each scone. Moisten your fingers and gently press the tops for a flatter scone. Bake for 15 minutes, until the scones are golden. Remove them from the heat and serve them warm.

Stilton Scones

12 SCONES

I developed these scones when I had a lot of Stilton left over after Christmas. They are rich and savoury and make a nice accompaniment to soups and salads.

4oz (115g) unbleached white flour
4oz (115g) wholemeal flour or
   wholemeal pastry flour (or use
   all unbleached white flour)
½ teaspoon salt
2 teaspoons baking powder

½ teaspoon bicarbonate of soda
2oz (55g) unsalted butter
4oz (115g) Stilton, crumbled
1 egg
2 tablespoons milk

Pre-heat the oven to 450°F/230°C/gas mark 8. Butter a baking sheet.

Sift together the flours, salt, baking powder and bicarbonate of soda. Rub in the butter until the mixture has the consistency of coarse cornmeal, then stir in the Stilton. (This can be done in a food processor fitted with the steel blade, using the pulse action, or in a mixer.)

Beat together the egg and milk, and stir into the mixture. Gather up the dough and gently knead it, not working it like bread dough but just pressing it so that it comes together in a cohesive lump: the less you work the dough, the lighter your scones will be. It will be slightly sticky, so flour your hands lightly. Roll the dough out to a thickness of about ¾ inch, and cut it into squares, triangles or rounds.

Place the scones on the prepared baking sheet and bake for 12–15 minutes, until they begin to brown. Serve them warm.

Scotch Pancakes or Drop Scones

10–12 SCONES

These rich cream scones, also called Scotch pancakes, are sweet and very light. Other scone recipes could be baked on a griddle like this, although (like the bannocks below) it's difficult to get them right because the surface often burns before the inside is cooked through. You need a low flame and an evenly heated griddle.

8oz (225g) wholemeal flour or
    unbleached white flour
1 teaspoon baking powder
½ teaspoon bicarbonate of soda

1 tablespoon caster sugar
2oz (55g) unsalted butter, softened
1 egg, beaten
4fl. oz (120ml) double cream

Sift together the flour, baking powder, bicarbonate of soda and sugar. Rub in the butter. (This can be done in a food processor fitted with the steel blade, using the pulse action, or in a mixer.) Add the egg and the cream and mix thoroughly, but don't over-work.

Heat your griddle over a low heat. Drop heaped tablespoons of the batter on to the griddle and cook each scone for about 8 minutes on each side. Remove from the griddle with a spatula, and serve hot.

Barley Bannocks

2 LARGE BANNOCKS

Bannocks are really large, round scones that are cooked on a griddle. In fact, the dough for scones and bannocks can be used interchangeably. Griddle scones and bannocks can be a bit tricky, however: if the griddle is too hot, they will burn on the outside before they are baked through. So keep the heat low, and heat the griddle thoroughly before you place the bannocks on it. These particular bannocks have the sharp, earthy flavour that comes from barley.

4oz (115g) barleymeal
6oz (170g) 85 per cent wholemeal
    flour or unbleached white flour
1 teaspoon tartaric acid
¼ teaspoon salt

1oz (30g) lard or margarine
1oz (30g) unsalted butter, softened
1 teaspoon bicarbonate of soda
4fl. oz (120ml) buttermilk

Sift together the barleymeal, flour, tartaric acid and salt. Rub in the lard or margarine and the butter. (This can be done in a food processor fitted with the steel blade, using the pulse action, or in a mixer.) Dissolve the bicarbonate of soda in the buttermilk, and when the buttermilk begins to bubble add it to the flour mixture. Bring together into a soft, sticky dough, and pat it out on a floured work surface to ½-inch thickness. Cut the dough into two large rounds – larger than a scone but not so large that they are difficult to handle (the dough is delicate and will fall apart easily), and place them on a hot griddle. Cook them on each side for about 8–10 minutes, until the bannocks are brown and baked through. (Use a wide spatula to turn them.) Cool them on a rack, or serve them hot.

Oatmeal Bannocks

2 LARGE BANNOCKS

This dough is delicate, like the dough for the barley bannocks. The bannocks have a rich flavour and chewy texture.

5oz (140g) medium oatmeal
5oz (140g) 85 per cent or 100 per cent wholemeal flour
½ teaspoon salt
1 teaspoon tartaric acid

1oz (30g) lard or margarine
1oz (30g) unsalted butter, softened
¼ pint (140ml) buttermilk
1 teaspoon bicarbonate of soda

Mix together the oatmeal, flour, salt and tartaric acid. Rub in the butter and lard or margarine. (This can be done in a food processor fitted with the steel blade, using the pulse action, or in a mixer.) Dissolve the bicarbonate of soda in the buttermilk and heat gently until it begins to bubble. Add it to the dough. Gather the dough into a ball and pat or roll it out to ½-inch thickness. Continue as for the barley bannocks.

Potato Scones

12 SCONES

These are like mashed-potato pancakes, comforting and delicious. Make sure you use starchy potatoes: waxy potatoes are too gummy.

8oz (225g) starchy potatoes,
  cooked in boiling salted water
  and mashed

½ teaspoon salt
1 tablespoon melted unsalted butter
2oz (55g) unbleached white flour

Mix together all the ingredients, roll out the dough to about ½-inch thickness, dusting your work surface with flour as necessary. Cut the dough into 3-inch rounds and prick them over with a fork.

Heat the griddle over a medium heat and brush it lightly with butter or margarine. Cook the scones on the hot griddle for 3–5 minutes on each side, until nicely browned. Keep each batch warm in the oven while you use up the remaining dough. Serve the scones warm.

Sweet Breads, Buns and Tea Breads

You will find many similarities among these sweet, for the most part fruit-filled, breads and yeast cakes. The Welsh bara brith and the Irish barm brack, for example, are practically identical. Their names reflect the regions from which they come. They have been around for a long time – but unfortunately these are the breads that are most difficult to find today.

Sweet spices are called for in most of these breads. Every recipe seems to vary over quantities and types; I finally settled on the versions that tasted best to me. You can use commercial spice mixes, but I recommend Elizabeth David's spice blend below for a more vivid flavour.

Elizabeth David's Spice Blend

This sweet and spicy mix can be substituted for commercial spice blends in all the recipes in this chapter. It is more pungent than the commercial blends.

1 large nutmeg, grated
1 tablespoon white or black
  peppercorns, or allspice berries
a 6-inch (12cm) cinnamon stick

2 teaspoons (about 30) cloves
1½ teaspoons ground ginger or
  dried ginger root

Combine all the ingredients and grind them to a powder in a spice mill. Store in a well-sealed jar.

Saffron Bread and Saffron Cakes

Between the fourteenth and eighteenth centuries saffron was widely cultivated in England; the people who cultivated it were known as the Crokers of Saffron Walden. It was already a well-established cash crop in the eastern counties of England by the fourteenth century, but because its cultivation is so labour-intensive – it takes 250,000 flowers to produce 1lb (450g) of saffron, which is the dried stamens of the *crocus sativus* flower – it had been abandoned as a profitable crop by the nineteenth century. What a pity! Its legacy are the saffron cakes and breads from Cornwall and Wales (sadly, the authentic cake is difficult to come by now). These recipes come from Elisabeth Luard (below) and Elizabeth David (p. 123), with slight moderations.

Elisabeth Luard's Saffron Bread

1 VERY LARGE LOAF OR 2 SMALLER LOAVES

This shiny-crusted bread has a marvellous pungent flavour and a gorgeous yellow hue – the flavour and colour of saffron. It goes well with fish and meat dishes and also toasts well.

¼–½ teaspoon saffron strands
½ pint (285ml) lukewarm water
¼ pint (140ml) lukewarm milk
2lb (900g) unbleached white flour
1 teaspoon salt

1½ teaspoons active dried yeast (or
1oz/30g fresh)
1 teaspoon white sugar
2 eggs
2oz (55g) unsalted butter, melted
milk or beaten egg, for glaze

Mixing the dough and kneading

Place the saffron in a small bowl and pour on about 3fl. oz (90ml) boiling water. Let it sit for about 10 minutes, then crush the saffron with the back of a spoon, or liquidise it in a blender to release its intense yellow colour and rich flavour.

Combine the flour and salt in a large bowl, or in the bowl of your electric mixer. Dissolve the yeast in 8fl. oz (225ml) of the warm water and let it sit for 5 minutes.

Make a well in the centre of the flour and pour in the yeast mixture. Brush some flour over the top and cover the bowl with clingfilm. Let the dough rise for 20 minutes.

If kneading the dough by hand. Add the saffron liquid to the remaining water and the milk. Beat the eggs and stir them into this mixture, along with the melted butter. Add to the flour mixture and stir to form a soft dough. Add a little more flour if necessary, turn out the dough on to a lightly floured work surface, and knead until it is smooth, firm and uniformly yellow – about 10–15 minutes. The dough will be stiff and elastic. Shape it into a ball.

If using an electric mixer. Add the saffron liquid to the remaining water and the milk. Beat the eggs and stir into this mixture, along with the melted butter. Add this to the flour mixture in the bowl of your electric mixer. Mix together using the mixing attachment, then change to the dough hook. Mix at low speed (1 on a Kenwood) for a couple of minutes, then at medium speed (2 on a Kenwood) for 6–8 minutes, until the dough is smooth and elastic. Turn out the dough on to your work surface and knead for about a minute, then shape it into a ball.

Rising, forming the loaf and baking

Clean and oil or butter your bowl, place the dough in it, cover the bowl with clingfilm and place it in a warm spot for the dough to rise for 1–1½ hours, until doubled in bulk.

Punch down the dough. Knead it again for about 5 minutes on a well-floured surface, then shape it into one large ball or two smaller balls. Set it on a baking sheet and let it rise again, covered lightly with a tea-towel, for about 45 minutes.

Meanwhile, pre-heat the oven to 400°F/200°C/gas mark 6. Brush the top of the loaf lightly with milk or beaten egg and bake for 50–60 minutes for a large loaf, 40–45 minutes for smaller loaves. The bread is done when it is golden-brown and responds to tapping with a hollow thumping sound. Remove it from the heat and cool on a rack.

Cornish Saffron Cake with Fruit

1 LOAF

This sweet saffron cake with dried fruit and spices, based on an Elizabeth David recipe, is less pungent than the savoury bread (p. 120), probably because of the presence of the fruit and spices.

½ teaspoon saffron strands
6fl. oz (180ml) milk
1 teaspoon active dried yeast
2 tablespoons lukewarm water
1lb (450g) unbleached white flour
2oz (55g) white sugar
1 teaspoon salt
¼ teaspoon ground nutmeg

¼ teaspoon ground cinnamon
¼ teaspoon mixed spice
4oz (115g) unsalted butter, softened, or double cream
2oz (55g) sultanas
2oz (55g) currants
2 tablespoons milk and 1 tablespoon sugar, for glaze

Mixing the dough and kneading

Pre-heat the oven to 375°F/180°C/gas mark 5. Place the saffron in an ovenproof dish and put it in the oven for 3 minutes. Meanwhile, bring half the milk to a boil. Remove the saffron from the oven, crumble the strands into a cup and pour the boiling milk over. Let it sit for 10 minutes.

Dissolve the yeast in the lukewarm water. Warm the remaining milk to lukewarm and add it to the yeast mixture. Let it sit for 10 minutes.

If kneading the dough by hand. Combine the flour, sugar, salt and spices in a large bowl. Make a well in the centre and add the yeast mixture, the softened butter or cream and the saffron infusion. Stir together to make a dough, and turn it out on to a lightly floured board. Knead until the dough is firm and elastic – about 10 minutes. Shape it into a ball.

If using an electric mixer. Combine the flour, sugar, salt and spices in the bowl of your electric mixer. Add the yeast mixture, the softened butter or cream and the saffron infusion. Mix together using the mixing attachment, then scrape the dough off the mixing attachment and change to the dough hook. Knead at low speed (1 on a Kenwood) for 2 minutes, then at medium speed (2 on a Kenwood) for 6–8 minutes, adding more unbleached flour if the dough is very sticky. Scrape out the dough on to a floured work surface and finish kneading by hand. Shape the dough into a ball.

Rising, forming the loaf and baking

Clean and oil or butter your bowl and place the dough in it, seam side up first, then seam side down. Cover the bowl with clingfilm and a tea-towel, and let the dough rise in a warm spot for 2 hours or more, until it has doubled in volume.

Punch down the dough. Toss the sultanas and raisins with a little flour and add them to the dough. Work in and knead until they are evenly distributed. Shape the dough into a loaf (see p. 26).

Butter a loaf tin generously and place the dough in it. Gently shape it to fit the tin. Cover lightly with a tea-towel and let the dough rise in a warm spot for 45–60 minutes, until it just about reaches the top of the tin.

Pre-heat the oven to 375°F/190°C/gas mark 5. Bake on a middle shelf for 40–45 minutes, until the cake is golden and sounds hollow when tapped. Remove it from the heat.

Heat the milk and sugar together until the sugar is dissolved, then brush the hot cake at once. Let it cool in the tin for 15 minutes, before turning out. This is best served freshly baked and warm.

Bara Brith

1 LOAF

Bara brith is a spicy fruit bread from Wales, much like the Irish barm brack (p. 128). I've seen many versions of the recipe, calling for different spices, some with egg and some without, some with candied peel and some without. In this recipe and the next, I'm giving you two distinctive versions.

1 teaspoon active dried yeast
2 tablespoons lukewarm water
¼ pint (140ml) lukewarm milk
3oz (85g) unsalted butter, melted
1 egg
2oz (55g) unrefined brown sugar
8oz (225g) unbleached white flour
6–8oz (225g) 85 per cent
  wholemeal flour (or omit the
  unbleached white flour and use
  up to 1lb (450g) 85 per cent
  wholemeal)

1 teaspoon salt
1–2 teaspoons (to taste) mixed
  spice or Elizabeth David's spice
  blend (see p. 121)
3oz (85g) currants
3oz (85g) sultanas, or 6oz (170g)
  dried mixed fruits
1oz candied peel (optional)

Mixing the dough and kneading

Dissolve the yeast in the water in a large mixing bowl or in the bowl of your electric mixer, and stir in the milk. Let it sit for 10 minutes. Stir in the butter, the egg and the sugar.

If kneading the dough by hand. Combine the flours, salt and spice, and gradually stir into the liquids, a cupful at a time. Mix until you have a soft dough. Turn it out on to a lightly floured board and knead for about 10 minutes. The dough will be stiff, elastic and smooth by the end of the kneading.

If using an electric mixer. Combine all but 2oz (55g) of the flour, salt and spice and add all at once to the liquid mixture in the bowl of your mixer. Mix together with the mixing attachment, then change to the dough hook. Mix at low speed (1 on a Kenwood) for 2 minutes, then at medium speed (2 on a Kenwood) for 6–8 minutes. If the dough is very sticky, sprinkle in a little extra flour. Scrape out the dough on to a lightly floured work surface and knead by hand for a minute or so.

Rising, forming the loaf and baking

Oil or butter your bowl. Shape the dough into a ball and place it in the bowl, seam side up first, then seam side down. Cover the bowl with clingfilm and a tea-towel and set it in a warm place for the dough to rise for 1–1½ hours, until doubled in bulk.

Meanwhile combine the dried fruits and optional candied peel and warm them in the oven for about 5–10 minutes.

Punch down the dough and fold in the fruit mixture. Add a little milk if the dough is too stiff. Shape it into a ball and let it rest for 5 minutes, then shape it into a loaf (see p. 26). Butter a loaf tin generously and place the dough in it, seam side up first, then seam side down. Pat the dough so that it fills the tin evenly. Cover it with a tea-towel and set it in a warm place to rise until it reaches the top of the tin – about an hour.

Meanwhile, pre-heat the oven to 400°F/200°C/gas mark 6. Bake the loaf for 30–40 minutes. Cover the top with a piece of foil during the last 10 minutes of cooking if the bread becomes too brown (the fruit on the surface will probably burn, but you can easily pick that off). Allow to cool for 10 minutes in the tin, then turn the loaf out on to a rack to cool further. Serve thinly sliced, with tea.

Bara Brith with Caraway

1 LOAF

I've seen a few recipes for bara brith seasoned with caraway, as I have seen barm brack seasoned with caraway. I like caraway, and think it adds a nice dimension to this bread, but some people insist that the bread should not contain this ingredient. You can choose between this recipe and the preceding one to see which you like better. This dough is fairly sticky, probably because of the treacle and the large measure of butter.

1 teaspoon active dried yeast
  (or ½oz fresh)
2 tablespoons lukewarm water
4 tablespoons white sugar
6fl. oz (180ml) lukewarm milk
1lb (450g) unbleached white flour
1 egg

1 tablespoon black treacle
4oz (115g) unsalted butter, melted
1 teaspoon caraway seeds
1 teaspoon salt
8oz (225g) raisins and currants,
  mixed

Mixing the dough and kneading

Dissolve the yeast and 1 tablespoon of the sugar in the lukewarm water in a large mixing bowl or in the bowl of your electric mixer. Add 4fl. oz (120ml) of the milk. Let it sit for 5 minutes. Sprinkle in 2oz (55g) of the flour and mix well. Cover with clingfilm and set aside for 15 minutes, until the mixture is beginning to bubble.

Beat together the egg and the remaining milk and add to the yeast mixture. Stir in the treacle, the remaining sugar, the butter and the caraway seeds.

If kneading the dough by hand. Mix together the remaining flour and the salt and fold into the mixture, a cupful at a time. As soon as you can, scrape the dough out on to a floured kneading surface. Knead for 10 minutes, adding unbleached white flour as necessary. The dough will be elastic but somewhat sticky.

If using an electric mixer. Combine the remaining flour and salt and add all at once to the bowl. Mix together with the mixing attachment, then change to the dough hook. Mix at low speed (1 on a Kenwood) for 2 minutes, then at medium speed (2 on a Kenwood) for 6–8 minutes. If the dough seems very wet and sticky, sprinkle in up to 2oz (55g) extra unbleached white flour. Scrape out the dough on to a lightly floured surface and knead by hand for a minute or so.

Rising, forming the loaf and baking

Oil or butter your bowl. Shape the dough into a ball and place it in the bowl, seam side up first, then seam side down. Cover the bowl with clingfilm and a tea-towel and set it in a warm spot for the dough to rise for 1½ hours, or until doubled in bulk.

Toss the raisins and currants with a little flour (this prevents them from sinking to the bottom of the loaf). Punch down the dough and work in the raisins and currants. Knead until they are evenly distributed through the dough. Shape the dough into a ball and let it rest for 5 minutes. Then shape it into a loaf (see p. 26).

Butter a loaf tin and place the dough in the tin, seam side up first, then seam side down. Let it rise in a warm spot for 30–40 minutes, until the dough rises above the edges of the tin.

Meanwhile, pre-heat the oven to 350°F/180°C/gas mark 4. Bake for an hour, until the loaf is golden. Let it cool in the tin for 10 minutes, then remove it from the tin and cool it on a rack.

Barm Brack

1 LOAF

Barm brack is Irish tea bread. Like the other fruity tea breads in this chapter, there are many versions. My Irish mother-in-law says that it's always spicy and contains both raisins and currants, and she has never seen one with caraway seeds. I have seen recipes with caraway seeds, some with no fruit, others with just one kind. In the end I have settled on my own recipe, which contains sweet spices, no caraway and a mixture of dried fruits.

For the sponge

1½ teaspoons active dried yeast
2 tablespoons lukewarm water
¼ pint (140ml) warm milk

1 tablespoon white sugar
2oz (55g) unbleached white flour

For the dough

4oz (115g) unsalted butter,
    softened
2 eggs
2oz unrefined brown sugar
    (optional)
14–16oz (395–450g) unbleached
    white flour (or use half 85 per
    cent wholemeal flour)

1 teaspoon salt
2 teaspoons mixed spice, or
    Elizabeth David's spice blend
    (see p. 121)
8oz (225g) dried mixed fruits
    (raisins, currants, sultanas, etc.)

Mixing the dough and kneading

First make the sponge. Dissolve the yeast in the warm water in a large bowl or in the bowl of your electric mixer. Add the milk and 1 tablespoon of sugar. Let it sit for 5 minutes. Whisk in the 2oz (55g) unbleached white flour and mix well. Cover with clingfilm and set in a warm place for 30 minutes.

Beat the eggs, butter and optional sugar into the sponge. Combine the flour, salt and spices.

If kneading the dough by hand. Begin adding the flour to the liquid mixture, a cupful at a time. As soon as you can, scrape out the dough on to a floured work surface and begin to knead. Add flour as necessary and knead for about 10 minutes, until you have a smooth, stiff dough.

If using an electric mixer. Add the flour all at once to the dough. Mix together using the mixing attachment, then scrape the dough off the mixing attachment and change to the dough hook. Knead at low speed

(1 on a Kenwood) for 2 minutes, then at medium speed (2 on a Kenwood) for 6–8 minutes, adding more unbleached white flour if the dough is very sticky. Scrape out the dough on to a floured work surface and knead by hand for a minute or so.

Rising, forming the loaf and baking

Oil or butter your bowl, and shape the dough into a ball. Place it in the bowl and cover with clingfilm and a tea-towel. Let the dough rise for 1–1½ hours, or until doubled in bulk.

Sprinkle the dried fruit with flour. Punch down the dough and add the fruit. Turn the dough out of the bowl and knead for a couple of minutes, until the fruit is evenly distributed through the dough.

Butter a loaf tin or a baking sheet generously. Shape the dough into a loaf (see p. 26) or a round ball, and place it in the tin or on the baking sheet. Cover it loosely with a tea-towel and let it rise for 45–60 minutes.

Meanwhile, pre-heat the oven to 400°F/200°C/gas mark 6. Bake the bread for 35–45 minutes, until it is dark brown and responds to tapping with a hollow sound. Remove it from the oven and allow it to cool in the tin for 10 minutes, then remove it from the tin or baking sheet and cool it on a rack.

Irish Tea Brack

1 LOAF

This is a baking-powder-raised tea bread, much like a barm brack, and very tasty, with lots of fruit and spice.

10oz (285g) dried mixed fruit, chopped
8fl. oz (225ml) boiling black tea
1 egg, beaten
1 tablespoon marmalade
4oz (115g) unrefined brown sugar
12–14oz (340–395g) unbleached white flour

1½ teaspoons mixed spice, or Elizabeth David's spice blend (see p. 121)
2 teaspoons baking powder
½ teaspoon bicarbonate of soda
¼ teaspoon salt

Place the mixed fruit in a bowl. Pour on the hot tea and leave it to soak overnight or for several hours. The next morning (or several hours later) beat in the egg, sugar and marmalade.

Sift together 12oz (340g) of the flour, the mixed spice, baking powder, bicarbonate of soda and salt. Stir into the wet ingredients and mix together well. If the mixture seems very liquid – it should be like a thick batter – add the remaining 2oz (55g) flour.

Pre-heat the oven to 375°F/190°C/gas mark 5. Generously butter a loaf tin or an 8-inch-square baking tin. Pour the batter into the tin and bake on a middle shelf for 1½ hours. Allow the loaf to cool in the tin for 10 minutes, then cool it further on a rack. Serve in thin slices.

Lardy Cakes

12 CAKES

Lardy cakes, which come from the Midlands and the north of England, are absolutely contrary to everything I believe in about eating well. As Elizabeth David so aptly describes them, they are 'oozing with fat, sticky with sugar . . . just about as undesirable, from a dietician's point of view, as anything one can possibly think of. Like every packet of cigarettes, every lardy cake should carry a health warning.' That said, they are such a part of the British tradition – they were special harvest cakes, made only at harvest time and for festivals – that they should have a place in this chapter. I am not what you would call a lard fan, but most authorities insist on it: how could a lardy cake be a lardy cake without lard? I have, however, seen recipes in which margarine can be substituted for lard. This recipe is moderate; others I have come across call for 6oz (170g) lard, or for 4oz (115g) lard and 4oz (115g) butter. So if you want a richer cake, add more fat.

1½ teaspoons active dried yeast
2 tablespoons lukewarm water
4fl. oz (120ml) lukewarm milk
1 tablespoon mild-flavoured honey
  or sugar
1 teaspoon mixed spice, or
  Elizabeth David's spice blend
  (see p. 121)
1 teaspoon salt
1 egg

8oz (225g) unbleached white flour,
  as necessary
2oz (55g) lard (margarine can be
  substituted)
2oz (55g) unsalted butter
2–4oz (55–115g) unrefined brown
  sugar
4–6oz (115–170g) currants (to
  taste)
2oz (55g) mixed peel (optional)

Mixing the dough and kneading

Dissolve the yeast in the lukewarm water. Add the warm milk and the honey or sugar. Let it sit for 5 minutes.

If kneading the dough by hand. Place the unbleached white flour, spice and salt in a large bowl. Make a well in the centre and pour in the milk mixture. Add the egg. Fold in the flour with a large wooden spoon. The dough will be quite wet. Scrape out the dough on to a well-floured surface. Knead, flouring your hands and the work surface, for 5–10 minutes, adding flour as necessary, until the dough is elastic. Shape it into a ball.

If using an electric mixer. Combine the unbleached flour, spice and salt in the bowl of your electric mixer. Add the milk-and-yeast mixture and the egg. Mix together with the mixing attachment, then change to the dough hook. Mix at low speed (1 on a Kenwood) for 2 minutes, then at medium speed (2 on a Kenwood) for 6–8 minutes. If the dough seems very wet and sticky, sprinkle in up to 2oz (55g) more unbleached white flour. Scrape out the dough on to a lightly floured surface and knead by hand for a minute or so. Shape the dough into a ball.

Rising, shaping and baking

Clean and oil your bowl. Place the dough in it, seam side up first, then seam side down. Cover the bowl with clingfilm and a tea-towel and set it in a warm place for the dough to rise for 1½ hours, or until it has doubled in size.

Punch down the dough and knead it for a minute or two on a lightly floured surface. Roll it out into a rectangle measuring about 8 × 10 inches, and ½ inch thick. Have the rectangle facing you on the work surface like a sheet of typing paper. Spread the top two-thirds of the dough with one-third each of the lard and butter, the sugar and the currants and optional peel. Fold the dough in three like a business letter, then give it a quarter-turn. Roll it out with a rolling pin, as you would for puff pastry. Place it in the refrigerator for 5–10 minutes. Now put the dough on your work surface like a sheet of typing paper again, and repeat the turns twice more, chilling the dough slightly between each turn, until you have used up the filling ingredients.

Shape the dough to fit a large square or oblong tin, and set it in a warm spot to rise for 45–60 minutes, or until the dough just about reaches the edges of the tin.

Meanwhile, pre-heat the oven to 400°F/200°C/gas mark 6. Bake for 30–45 minutes, or until the dough is golden. Remove it from the heat and let it cool in the tin for 10 minutes, then remove it and cool it further on a rack. To serve, cut it into squares.

English Currant Bread

1 LOAF

This classic English bread is much like the bara brith (p. 125) and barm brack (p. 128) – spicy and fruity, excellent with tea.

1½ teaspoons active dried yeast
2 tablespoons lukewarm water
¼ pint (140ml) lukewarm milk
1oz (30g) soft brown sugar
2oz (55g) unsalted butter, softened
1 egg
1 teaspoon salt
1½ teaspoons mixed spice, or
   Elizabeth David's spice blend
   (see p. 121)

12oz (340g) unbleached white
   flour, as needed (or use 85 per
   cent wholemeal flour, or half
   wholemeal, half white)
4oz (115g) currants
2 tablespoons milk and 1 tablespoon
   mild-flavoured honey or sugar,
   for glaze

Mixing the dough and kneading

Dissolve the yeast in the lukewarm water and add the warm milk. Let it sit for 5 minutes, then stir in the sugar, softened butter and beaten egg.

If kneading the dough by hand. Place all but 2oz (55g) of the flour in a large bowl and stir in the spice and the salt. Make a well in the centre and pour in the milk mixture. Fold in the flour with a large wooden spoon. Add the currants and fold them in. The dough will be quite wet. Place 2oz (55g) unbleached flour on your work surface and scrape the dough out of the bowl. Knead, flouring your hands and the work surface, for 5–10 minutes, adding flour as necessary, until the dough is elastic. Shape the dough into a ball.

If using an electric mixer. Combine the flour and the salt, and add all at once to the bowl along with the spice and the currants. Mix together with the mixing attachment, then change to the dough hook. Mix at low speed (1 on a Kenwood) for 2 minutes, then at medium speed (2 on a Kenwood) for 6–8 minutes. If the dough seems very wet and sticky, sprinkle in up to 2oz (55g) more unbleached flour. Scrape out the dough on to a lightly floured surface and knead by hand for a minute or so. Shape the dough into a ball.

Rising, forming the loaf and baking

Clean and oil your bowl. Place the dough in it, seam side up first, then seam side down. Cover the bowl with clingfilm and a tea-towel, and set it in a warm place for the dough to rise for 1½ hours, or until it has doubled in size. Meanwhile, generously butter a loaf tin.

Punch down the dough and knead it for a minute or two on a lightly floured surface. Shape it into a loaf (see p. 26) and place it in the prepared tin. Cover it loosely with a tea-towel and let it rise for 30–45 minutes, until it reaches the top of the tin.

Meanwhile, pre-heat the oven to 400°F/200°C/gas mark 6. Bake for 30–40 minutes, until the bread is brown and hollow sounding when tapped.

While the bread is baking, mix together the milk and honey or sugar and heat gently to dissolve the sugar or honey. As soon as you remove the bread from the oven, brush it with this mixture. Remove the loaf from the tin and cool it on a rack.

Sally Lunn

1 CAKE

This is a simple, rich tea cake, much like *brioche*. The name comes from a corruption of the French *soleil et lune* (sun and moon), which was the name of a similar kind of yeast cake popular in the eighteenth century – although some people insist that there was a woman named Sally Lunn in Bath in the eighteenth century who sold the cakes in the street, crying out their name. Sally Lunn cakes are sometimes baked in small muffin tins, sometimes in rings. I like this loaf version.

1 teaspoon active dried yeast
2 tablespoons lukewarm water
1 tablespoon white sugar
4fl. oz (120ml) double cream,
   warm or at room temperature
2 eggs, at room temperature

finely chopped rind of 1 lemon
10–12oz (285–340g) unbleached
   white flour, as necessary
1 teaspoon salt
2 tablespoons milk and 1 tablespoon
   caster sugar, for glaze

Mixing the dough and kneading

Dissolve the yeast in the lukewarm water in a large bowl, or in the bowl of your electric mixer, and let it sit for 10 minutes. Beat in the sugar, cream, eggs and lemon rind.

If kneading the bread by hand. Mix together the flour and salt, and gradually fold into the yeast mixture. As soon as you can, scrape the dough out on to a floured kneading surface. Knead, adding unbleached white flour as necessary, for 10 minutes. The dough will be very sticky and you will need a pastry scraper and generously floured hands to manipulate it. Work very briskly and slap the dough against the work surface rather than folding and leaning.

If using an electric mixer. Combine 10oz (285g) of the flour and the salt, and add all at once to the bowl. Mix together with the mixing attachment, then change to the dough hook. Mix at low speed (1 on a Kenwood) for 2 minutes, then at medium speed (2 on a Kenwood) for 6–8 minutes. If the dough is so wet and sticky that it doesn't adhere to the dough hook, sprinkle in up to 2oz (55g) more unbleached white flour. Scrape out the dough on to a lightly floured surface (the dough will be quite sticky), and knead it a few times by hand.

Rising, forming the cake and baking

Butter a loaf tin generously and dust it with flour. Transfer the dough to the tin and pat it out gently to fill the tin. Cover the tin with a tea-towel and let the dough rise in a warm spot until it just about reaches the edges of the tin.

Towards the end of the rising, pre-heat the oven to 400°F/200°C/gas mark 6. Bake for 20–25 minutes, until the cake is golden and comes away from the sides of the tin.

While it is baking, mix together the milk and caster sugar in a small saucepan and heat to boiling point. As soon as you take the cake from the oven, brush it with the hot glaze. Let the cake cool in the tin for 10 minutes, or until it comes away easily from the sides. Remove it from the tin and cool it further on a rack. The cake can also be eaten warm.

Black Bun

1 VERY LARGE BUN

Black bun, traditionally eaten in Scotland at New Year, is like a Christmas pudding or dense fruit cake in a yeasted pastry shell. I must admit that when I first read Elizabeth David's recipe, I couldn't believe that I would like anything with so much dried fruit in it – nor did I believe her recipe would work. I altered it slightly, reducing the quantities of flour and fruit so that the bun would fit a 12-inch *tarte* tin or cake tin. And when I tasted my beautiful black bun the morning after I made it, I liked it very much indeed. I always have liked mincemeat, and the ingredients are similar. It should be eaten in very thin slices, as it is rich. If you make a large one like this, you can cut it into quarters and give pieces away as presents. One of these will certainly last your family through the Christmas and New Year holidays.

For the dough

2 teaspoons active dried yeast
2 tablespoons lukewarm water
12fl. oz (350ml) lukewarm milk
4oz (115g) unsalted butter,
  softened
6oz (170g) Demerara sugar

½ teaspoon salt
1lb (450g) unbleached white flour
8–12oz (225–340g) 85 per cent
  wholemeal flour, as necessary
1 egg, beaten, for the topping

For the filling

2 eggs
3fl. oz (90ml) black treacle
1½lb (680g) of the above dough
  (or half the weight)
1½lb (680g) currants

1lb (450g) sultanas or dried mixed
  fruit
2 tablespoons mixed spice
7oz (200g) candied peel
4oz (115g) whole blanched
  almonds

Mixing the dough and kneading

Dissolve the yeast in the warm water in the bowl of your electric mixer or in a large bowl. Add the milk. Let it sit for 10 minutes. Add the butter and Demerara sugar and mix together well.

If kneading the dough by hand. Mix together the unbleached flour and salt and stir into the yeast mixture. Begin adding the wholemeal flour and, as soon as you can, turn out the dough on to a floured work surface and knead for 10 minutes, adding flour as necessary.

If using an electric mixer. Add all but 4oz (115g) of the flour to the liquid mixture and mix together with the mixing attachment, then scrape the dough off the mixing attachment and change to the dough hook. Knead at low speed (1 on a Kenwood) for 2 minutes, then at medium speed (2 on a Kenwood) for 6–8 minutes, adding flour if the dough is very sticky. Scrape out the dough on to a floured work surface and knead by hand for a minute or so.

Rising, mixing the filling, forming the bun and baking

Oil or butter your bowl. Shape the dough into a ball and place it in the bowl, seam side up first, then seam side down. Cover the bowl with clingfilm and a tea-towel, and set it in a warm spot for the dough to rise for about 4 hours.

Punch down the dough. Weigh it (it should weigh about 3lb (1.35kg)) and divide it in half.

In a large bowl, or in the bowl of your electric mixer, beat together the eggs and the treacle. Add half the dough, the currants, sultanas or mixed fruit, spice, almonds and candied peel, and mix together thoroughly. This will take quite a while, as the dough is very elastic and won't mix readily with the wet ingredients; but after a while the mixture will become amalgamated. If you are using your hands, prepare for them to get full of treacle and dough, and squeeze the mixture through your fingers to mix. If you are like me, at this point you might find it difficult to believe that this sticky, heavy mess will become a delicious, stiff filling.

Divide the remaining dough into two pieces, one weighing three-quarters of the total weight of the dough, the other weighing one-quarter. Generously butter a 12-inch cake tin or *tarte* tin. Roll out the larger piece of dough thin (about ¼ inch thick), into a large flat circle, large enough to cover the tin with an overhang. Line the tin with the rolled-out pastry and top it with the filling. Wrap the edges of the pastry up over the filling. Roll out the remaining piece of pastry into a 12-inch circle and place it over the top of the filling. It should completely cover the edges of the bottom piece of pastry, overlapping by at least ½ inch (preferably more). Brush the top and the exposed part of the sides of the bun thoroughly with beaten egg. Pierce the bun in several places with a sharp knife.

Pre-heat the oven to 350°F/180°C/gas mark 4. Bake the bun for about 1½ hours, or longer, until it is thoroughly brown and hollow sounding when tapped. Brush it again with beaten egg halfway through baking. If the top gets too brown before the end of the baking, place a piece of foil over the top.

Remove the bun from the heat and allow it to cool for 15 minutes or longer in the tin, then cool it further on a rack. Serve it cut into thin wedges.

Gingerbread

1 LOAF

Gingerbread can be very sweet and cloying, but this one is not. It has the perfect balance of sweet and spice. The bread is moist and delicious. Thin slices go nicely with tea, and thicker portions, topped with whipped cream or yoghurt, make a good dessert. It keeps very well – up to ten days in the refrigerator.

3 eggs
4fl. oz (120ml) black treacle
4oz. (115g) unrefined brown sugar
3oz (85g) unsalted butter, melted
1 teaspoon grated lemon rind
   (optional)
4oz (115g) wholemeal pastry flour
4oz (115g) unbleached white flour

2 heaped teaspoons ground ginger
1 teaspoon cinnamon
½ teaspoon allspice
¼ teaspoon ground nutmeg
¼ teaspoon salt
1 teaspoon bicarbonate of soda
4fl. oz (120ml) low-fat natural
   yoghurt or buttermilk

Pre-heat the oven to 350°F/180°C/gas mark 4. Butter and lightly flour a loaf tin or cake tin.

Beat the eggs until light and frothy. Add the treacle and the sugar and continue to beat at medium speed (2 on a Kenwood) for a minute or two. Beat in the butter and continue to beat at medium speed for a further minute or two. Stir in the optional lemon rind.

Sift together the flours, spices, salt and bicarbonate of soda. Gradually add one cupful to the batter, beating slowly. Add the yoghurt or buttermilk, then the remaining flour. Mix until just blended.

Pour the batter into the prepared tin and bake for about an hour if using a loaf tin, about 45 minutes if using a cake tin, until the gingerbread has shrunk from the sides of the tin and a knife inserted in the centre comes out clean. Remove the loaf from the oven and let it cool for 10 minutes in the tin, then cool it further on a rack. Serve, if you wish, topped with whipped cream or yoghurt.

Hot Cross Buns

2 DOZEN

These hot cross buns are slightly sweet and spicy. Made with half wholemeal flour, half unbleached white, the dough is light and pliable, easy to work after its initial stickiness.

1 tablespoon active dried yeast
2 tablespoons lukewarm water
8fl. oz (225ml) milk
2fl. oz (60ml) mild-flavoured honey
4 tablespoons unsalted butter, melted and cooled
2 eggs, beaten
8oz (225g) wholemeal pastry flour
up to 14oz (395g) unbleached white flour, as necessary

2 teaspoons mixed spice, or Elizabeth David's spice blend (see p. 121)
1 teaspoon sea salt
4oz (115g) currants
1 egg white
2 tablespoons lemon juice and 1 tablespoon mild-flavoured honey or caster sugar, for glaze

Mixing the dough and kneading

Dissolve the yeast in the lukewarm water. Gently heat the milk to lukewarm and add it to the yeast. Let it sit for 5–10 minutes, then stir in the honey, melted butter and beaten eggs.

If kneading the dough by hand. Place the wholemeal pastry flour and 4oz (115g) of the unbleached white flour in a large bowl and stir in the spice and the salt. Make a well in the centre and pour in the milk mixture. Fold in the flour with a large wooden spoon. Add the currants and fold in. The dough will be quite wet. Place 2oz (55g) unbleached white flour on your work surface and scrape the dough out of the bowl. Knead, flouring your hands and the work surface, for 10 minutes, adding flour as necessary, until the dough is elastic. Shape the dough into a ball.

If using an electric mixer. Combine the wholemeal flour and 8oz (225g) of the unbleached flour and the salt, and add all at once to the bowl, along with the spice and the currants. Mix together with the mixing attachment, then change to the dough hook. Mix at low speed (1 on a Kenwood) for 2 minutes, then at medium speed (2 on a Kenwood) for 6–8 minutes. If the dough seems very wet and sticky, sprinkle in up to 4oz (115g) unbleached white flour. Scrape out the dough on to a lightly floured surface and knead by hand for a minute or so. Shape the dough into a ball.

Rising, forming the buns and baking

Clean and oil your bowl. Place the dough in it, seam side up first, then seam side down. Cover the bowl with clingfilm and a tea-towel, and set it in a warm place for the dough to rise for 1½ hours, or until it has doubled in size.

Punch down the dough and knead for a minute or two on a lightly floured surface. Now divide the dough in half, and divide each half into twelve equal pieces. Shape these pieces into tight, round balls. Place them on oiled baking sheets and press them down gently with the bottom of a jar or glass, or with moistened fingers. Cover and let them rise until doubled in volume – about 45–60 minutes.

Meanwhile, pre-heat the oven to 375°F/190°C/gas mark 5. Beat the egg white until frothy and gently brush the tops of the buns. Using a very sharp knife or a razor blade, cut an X across the top of each bun. Bake for 20 minutes, until the buns are lightly browned.

While the buns are baking, mix together the lemon juice and honey or sugar. As soon as you remove the buns from the oven, brush them with the mixture. Cool them on racks. These are marvellous served warm with tea.

Chelsea Buns

18 BUNS

I'm not sure which is more famous – Chelsea buns or the Chelsea Bun House that gave them their name and their reputation. The Bun House, built either at the end of the seventeenth century or early in the eighteenth, was located near Sloane Square on what is now Pimlico Road. It was a combined pastry shop, bakery and tea house, and was at first famous for its hot cross buns, later for the rich buns which bear its name. These are similar to the French *pain aux raisins*, or to the pecan rolls on p. 207. The dough is rich, smooth and easy to work with.

For the sponge

2 teaspoons active dried yeast
2 tablespoons lukewarm water
¼ pint (140ml) warm milk

1 tablespoon sugar
2oz (55g) unbleached white flour

For the dough

14–16oz (395–450g) unbleached
  white flour (or use half 85 per
  cent wholemeal flour)
1 teaspoon salt
1 teaspoon ground cinnamon

2oz (55g) unrefined brown sugar
3oz (85g) unsalted butter, softened
2 eggs
grated rind of 1 lemon or orange
  (optional)

For the filling, topping and glaze

3oz (85g) currants or raisins
3oz (85g) soft brown sugar
2oz (55g) unsalted butter, melted

2oz (55g) caster sugar, for topping
2 tablespoons caster sugar and 2
  tablespoons milk, for glaze

Mixing the sponge

Dissolve the yeast in the lukewarm water and add the warm milk and the sugar. Let it sit for 5 minutes. Whisk in the 2oz (55g) unbleached white flour and mix well. Cover it with clingfilm and set it in a warm place for 30 minutes.

Mixing the dough and kneading

If kneading the dough by hand. Combine the flour, salt, sugar and cinnamon in a large bowl. Rub the butter into the flour and add the eggs and optional lemon or orange rind. Make a well in the centre and stir in the sponge. Turn out the dough on to a floured work surface and, adding flour as necessary, knead until stiff and elastic – about 10 minutes. Shape it into a ball.

If using an electric mixer. In the bowl of your electric mixer, combine the flour, salt, sugar and cinnamon. Add the butter, eggs, optional lemon or orange rind and the sponge. Mix together with the mixing attachment, then change to the dough hook. Mix at low speed (1 on a Kenwood) for 2 minutes, then at medium speed (2 on a Kenwood) for 6–8 minutes, until the dough is stiff and elastic. Scrape the dough out of the bowl and knead for about a minute by hand, then shape it into a ball.

Rising, forming the buns and baking

Oil your bowl and place the dough in it, seam side up first, then seam side down. Cover the bowl with clingfilm and a tea-towel, and set it in a warm spot for the dough to rise for an hour, or until doubled in volume.

Sprinkle the dough with flour and punch it down. Turn it out of the bowl and knead it for a couple of minutes. Divide the dough into two equal portions, then roll each into a rectangle about ½ inch thick. Brush each rectangle with an equal amount of butter and sprinkle with brown sugar and currants.

Fold the rectangles in three, like a letter, and roll them out again into rectangles about 8 × 10 inches. Now roll these rectangles up tightly – lengthwise, like a Swiss roll. Cut each rectangle into slices, 1–2 inches thick, and place the slices on a buttered baking sheet, leaving space in between to allow for rising. Cover lightly with a tea-towel and place in a warm spot to rise until they have just about doubled in volume.

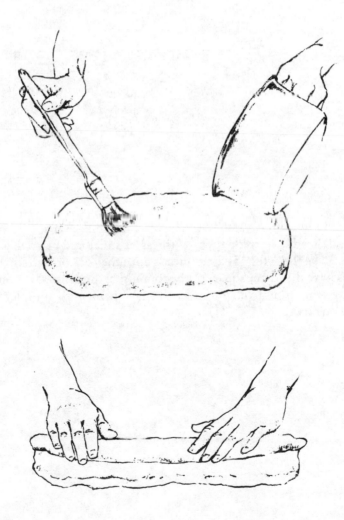

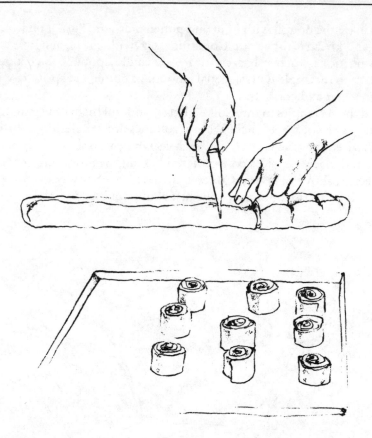

Meanwhile, pre-heat the oven to 425°F/220°C/gas mark 7. When the buns are ready, sprinkle them with caster sugar and place them in the oven. Bake them for 15–20 minutes, until they are brown.

Dissolve the caster sugar for the topping in the milk. As soon as you remove the buns from the oven, brush them with the glaze. Cool them on racks.

Bath Buns

1 DOZEN

These are rich, buttery buns topped with sugar. Authentic Bath buns can be almost as buttery as French *brioche*, but in this recipe I have reduced the butter. Like so many of these traditional breads, the recipe has many versions. The constant ingredient is the coarse sugar crystals sprinkled over the top. Some recipes call for candied peel, some don't. I'm not much of a fan of candied peel, so I've left that optional. The dough is basically the same as that used for the Chelsea buns on p. 139.

For the sponge

2 teaspoons active dried yeast
2 tablespoons lukewarm water
¼ pint (140ml) warm milk

1 tablespoon sugar
2oz (55g) unbleached white flour

For the dough

14–16oz (395–450g) unbleached
   white flour (or use half 85 per
   cent wholemeal flour)
1 teaspoon salt
2oz (55g) white sugar
3oz (85g) unsalted butter, softened

2 eggs
grated rind of 1 lemon or orange
   (optional)
3oz (85g) currants
1oz (30g) candied peel (optional)

For the glaze

2 tablespoons caster sugar
2 tablespoons milk

2 tablespoons sugar crystals

Mixing the dough and kneading

Dissolve the yeast in the lukewarm water, add the warm milk and mix in the sugar. Let it sit for 5 minutes. Whisk in the 2oz (55g) unbleached white flour and mix well. Cover with clingfilm and set in a warm place for 30 minutes.

If kneading the dough by hand. Combine the flour, salt and sugar in a large bowl. Rub the butter into the flour mixture and add the eggs, currants, optional candied peel and lemon or orange rind. Make a well in the centre and stir in the liquid mixture. Turn out the dough on to a floured work surface and, adding flour as necessary, knead until stiff and elastic – about 10 minutes. Shape the dough into a ball.

If using an electric mixer. In the bowl of your electric mixer, combine the flour, salt and sugar. Add the butter, eggs, currants, optional lemon or orange zest and candied peel, and the liquid mixture. Mix together with the mixing attachment, then change to the dough hook. Mix at low speed (1 on a Kenwood) for 2 minutes, then at medium speed (2 on a Kenwood) for 6–8 minutes, until the dough is stiff and elastic. Scrape out the dough and knead for about a minute by hand, then shape it into a ball.

Rising, forming the buns and baking

Clean and oil your bowl and place the dough in it, seam side up first, then seam side down. Cover the bowl with clingfilm and a tea-towel and set it in a warm spot for the dough to rise for 1½–2 hours, or until doubled and puffy.

Butter a baking sheet. Punch down the dough, turn it out on to your work surface, divide it into twelve equal portions. Form balls and place them on the baking sheet. (You can form the buns with a tablespoon on the baking sheet.) Smooth over the top of each bun with a moistened spatula. Cover loosely with a tea-towel and set them in a warm place to rise for 30–45 minutes, until puffed.

Meanwhile, pre-heat the oven to 375°F/190°C/gas mark 5. Bake for 15–20 minutes, until the buns are brown (they will join together – no harm).

While the buns are baking, heat the milk and caster sugar together. When you remove the buns from the oven, brush them with this mixture. Sprinkle the sugar crystals over the buns immediately after brushing with the glaze. Cool the buns on a rack.

Cornish Splits

12 BUNS

I looked all over Cornwall for these, but didn't find any. My recipe is an adaptation of one by Elizabeth David. They are meant to be eaten hot, split in half and topped with thick clotted cream and jam.

2 teaspoons active dried yeast
2 tablespoons lukewarm water
½ pint (285ml) lukewarm milk
1 teaspoon sugar

1lb (450g) unbleached white flour
¾ teaspoon salt
2oz unsalted butter, softened

Mixing the dough and kneading

Dissolve the yeast in the lukewarm water and add the milk and sugar. Let it sit for 10 minutes.

If kneading the dough by hand. Mix together the flour and salt. Rub in the butter. Make a well in the centre and add the milk mixture. Mix together and turn out the dough on to a floured work surface. Knead for 5–10 minutes, until soft and elastic, adding extra unbleached white flour as necessary. The dough will be sticky.

If using an electric mixer. Combine the flour and salt in the bowl of your electric mixer. Add the butter and the milk mixture. Mix together using the mixing attachment, then scrape the dough off the mixing attachment and change to the dough hook. Knead at low speed (1 on a Kenwood) for 2 minutes, then at medium speed (2 on a Kenwood) for 6–8 minutes, adding extra unbleached white flour if the dough is very sticky. Scrape out the dough on to a floured work surface and knead for about a minute by hand.

Rising, forming the rolls and baking

Clean and butter your bowl, and set the dough in it. Cover the bowl with clingfilm and let the dough rise in a warm spot for an hour, or until doubled in size.

Turn the dough out of the bowl and knead again for a few minutes on a lightly floured surface. Butter and lightly flour two baking sheets. Divide the dough into twelve equal pieces and shape them into tight, round buns. Place them on the baking sheets, about 2 inches apart, and let them rise for about 20–30 minutes.

Meanwhile, pre-heat the oven to 400°F/200°C/gas mark 6. Bake for about 15 minutes, until the buns are light brown and hollow sounding when tapped. Serve hot.

Griddle Breads

Many of the recipes that follow are yeasted pancakes made on heavy iron griddles. There is something very satisfying about making these. The batter makes a pleasing hissing sound as it hits the hot griddle, and cooks very quickly. Yeasted pancakes are easy to make. They don't spread out like other batters, and they have a rich, satisfying flavour.

The pancakes were probably developed because the grains that were cultivated – barley, buckwheat, oats – were more satisfactory for this kind of bread than for loaves. Whatever the reason, they are delicious, and also convenient. The batters can be kept for days in the refrigerator, and the finished pancakes can also be kept in sealed plastic bags and reheated in the oven.

Crumpets

ABOUT 20 CRUMPETS

According to Elizabeth David, the probable origin of the word 'crumpet' is the Welsh *crempog*, which means pancake or fritter. 'Tea and crumpets' was an expression I grew up hearing in the United States, but I never knew what a crumpet really was. I expected to find out as soon as I came to England, but, unfortunately, a crumpet is not so easy to find these days – especially a good one. I have still never been served a crumpet at a tea, but I have seen them, and bought them, from Harrods food hall.

Fortunately, these yeasted pancakes, with their funny surface full of holes (meant, I am told, to fill up with lots of the butter you should spread on your hot crumpets) and spongy texture, are easy to make. They are baked on a hot griddle in rings, which you can improvise with empty tuna-fish tins. Take both ends off the tins, wash the tins thoroughly and keep them on hand for crumpets.

1 teaspoon active dried yeast
½ pint (285ml) lukewarm water
½ pint (285ml) lukewarm milk
1 teaspoon sugar
2 tablespoons sunflower or
   vegetable oil

1lb (450g) unbleached white flour,
   preferably half plain, half strong
   unbleached white flour
1½ teaspoons salt (or more, to
   taste)
½ teaspoon bicarbonate of soda
¼ pint (140ml) additional
   lukewarm water

Dissolve the yeast in the ½ pint (285ml) lukewarm water and let it sit for 10 minutes. Add the milk, sugar and oil.

Mix together the flour and salt, and stir into the liquids. Beat vigorously until smooth and somewhat elastic – about 5 minutes.

Cover with clingfilm and let the batter rise in a warm spot for 1½ hours, until bubbly.

Dissolve the bicarbonate of soda in the additional ¼ pint (140ml) lukewarm water. Stir it into the batter and mix well. Cover again and let the batter rise in a warm place for 30 minutes.

Brush your griddle and rings lightly with butter or margarine and heat over a medium heat. When the griddle is hot, ladle the batter into the rings, to the height of about ½ inch. Cook until the tops have formed a thin skin and holes have broken through – this should take about 7–10 minutes. (If holes don't break through, the batter is too thick. Add a little warm milk or water to the batter.)

Carefully remove the rings and flip the crumpets over. Cook for about 3 minutes on the other side. The crumpets should be floppy.

Keep the cooked crumpets warm in a tea-towel in the oven while you cook the remaining batter. Serve crumpets hot or toasted, with butter and jam or cheese.

These keep well, stored in a plastic bag. Reheat in a hot oven or toast them before serving.

Pikelets

12 LARGE OR 24 SMALL PIKELETS

A 'pikelet' is a yeasted pancake, still very popular in the north of England. According to more than one authority, they are the Yorkshire–Lancashire version of crumpets. But they differ from crumpets in that they are not baked in rings, so they are larger and thinner, with a nice golden colour. The word is said to be a corruption of the Welsh word *pyglyd*, or *bara pyglyd* – a 'pitchy bread'. Pikelets are filling and have a spongy texture.

1 teaspoon active dried yeast
¼ pint (140ml) lukewarm water
¼ pint (140ml) lukewarm milk
2 eggs

2 teaspoons melted unsalted butter
8oz (225g) unbleached white flour
1 teaspoon salt

Dissolve the yeast in the lukewarm water and add the lukewarm milk. Let it sit for 10 minutes. Beat in the eggs and melted butter.

Combine the salt and flour and beat into the liquids. Beat until you have a smooth, thick batter. Cover it with clingfilm and set it in a warm spot for 1½ hours, or until bubbly.

Heat a griddle or heavy frying pan over medium–low heat and brush it with butter or margarine. Ladle on to the griddle full or half ladlefuls of the batter, depending on how big you want your pikelets to be. Cook them on one side until holes break through and you can turn them easily. Cook them for about a minute on the other side, or until brown. The pikelets take about 3–4 minutes in all to cook.

Wrap the cooked pikelets in a tea-towel and keep them warm in the oven until all the batter is cooked.

These can be wrapped in foil and reheated in a warm oven.

Welsh Oatmeal Pancakes

12–14 LARGE PANCAKES

These tasty, spongy pancakes are based on an Elizabeth David recipe. The batter will keep for several days in the refrigerator, and can be brought back to life by stirring vigorously and leaving at room temperature until bubbly.

4oz (115g) fine oatmeal
1 pint (570ml) water
1 teaspoon active dried yeast
2 tablespoons lukewarm water

2 tablespoons buttermilk
1 teaspoon salt
8oz (225g) unbleached white flour
2 eggs

Soak the oatmeal overnight, or for 12 hours, in the water. Drain, but retain the water.

The next morning, or 12 hours later, dissolve the yeast in the lukewarm water and stir in the buttermilk.

Combine the flour, salt and drained oatmeal in a large bowl, then break in the eggs. Beat into the yeast mixture. Stir together well and add about ½ pint (285ml) of the water in which you soaked the oatmeal to make a thick batter. Cover it with clingfilm and place it in a warm spot for 1½–2 hours, until risen and bubbly.

Heat a lightly greased griddle or a heavy iron frying pan over medium–low heat. Drop on the batter in scant ladlefuls – each equivalent to about 2–3 tablespoons – and let it spread. The pancakes should be about 6–7 inches in diameter and fairly thin. Cook until holes break through and the pancakes are firm enough to turn. Cook them for about 30 seconds on the other side.

Keep the cooked pancakes warm in the oven in a tea-towel as you use up the rest of the batter.

Yeasted Oatmeal Pancakes

ABOUT 24 PANCAKES

These are also based on a recipe from Elizabeth David. They are a bit heavier than the preceding recipe, as they contain no eggs, and they are quite moist on the inside.

1 teaspoon active dried yeast
¾ pint (425ml) lukewarm water
¾ pint (425ml) lukewarm milk
1½ teaspoons salt

8oz (225g) 85 per cent wholemeal
flour
8oz (225g) fine oatmeal

Dissolve the yeast in the lukewarm water and add the milk. Combine the flour, oatmeal and salt and stir into the liquids. Beat until you have a smooth batter. Add more water if it seems very thick. Cover it and let it rise for an hour.

Heat a griddle or heavy frying pan over medium–low heat and brush it with butter or margarine. Drop scant ladlefuls (each equivalent to 2–3 tablespoons) on to the heated griddle and cook until bubbles break through and the pancakes can be turned easily. Cook for another 30 seconds, or until browned, on the other side.

Keep the cooked pancakes warm in a tea-towel in the oven while you use up the rest of the batter.

Barley Pancakes

24 CRÊPE-LIKE PANCAKES

This batter, based on an Elizabeth David recipe, is like crêpe batter, and the pungent pancakes are really more like crêpes. They are cooked in the same manner.

1 teaspoon active dried yeast
2 tablespoons lukewarm water
½ pint (285ml) lukewarm milk
3oz (85g) unbleached white flour
3oz (85g) barley flour

½ teaspoon salt (or more, to taste)
4 eggs
¼ pint (140ml) additional
*   lukewarm milk*

Dissolve the yeast in the water and add the ½ pint (285ml) milk. Let it sit for 10 minutes. Mix together the flours and salt. Whisk into the yeast mixture and mix well. Cover and let it rise in a warm spot for 1–1½ hours, or longer, until spongy and bubbly.

Beat the eggs with the remaining milk, and beat into the batter. Cover and let the batter rise for another hour or two in a warm spot.

Lightly grease a 7-inch crêpe pan or omelette pan and heat it over medium–low heat. Ladle in about 2–3 tablespoons of the batter, tilting the pan to distribute the batter evenly. Cook until small holes appear and you can turn the pancakes with a spatula. Cook for 15–30 seconds on the other side, then turn them on to a plate.

This is a nice crêpe to serve with cheese or eggs, or any of the other suggestions for buckwheat crêpes, p. 256.

Irish and Scottish Oatcakes

Scottish oatcakes were one of my earliest delightful gastronomic discoveries when I came to Britain for the first time in 1980. The crisp, grainy biscuits make such a nutritious, tasty snack, and they go very well with cheese. The only thing I don't like about many of the packaged oatcakes is that they often have a very high fat content, and sometimes they are too salty. When I researched recipes for this book the amount of fat was almost always very low, as you will see below.

However, I must admit that these don't taste or look exactly like the packaged variety: they are more rustic, not quite as neat, and have a grainier texture. They are also fresher tasting and healthier.

The secret of making these is to have a lot of extra oatmeal for rubbing on your work surface and on the surface of the oatcakes.

I am giving two recipes below, as I can't decide which I like better. The Elizabeth David recipe requires more time, but makes more oatcakes.

Elizabeth David's Donegal Oatcakes

12–15 OATCAKES

1lb (450g) fine oatmeal
1½ teaspoons salt
1–2oz (30–55g) unsalted butter

about ¾ pint (425ml) boiling water

Place the oatmeal in a bowl. Dissolve the salt and butter in about ½ pint (285ml) of the boiling water and pour over the oatmeal. Add enough additional boiling water to make a thick, sticky mixture. Cover it with clingfilm and leave it overnight, or for several hours.

Butter a baking sheet and press the dough out on to it, sprinkling the dough with oatmeal all the time so that it doesn't stick to your hands. Press the dough out until it is very thin – about ⅛ inch thick. Leave it to dry for 1–2 hours.

Turn on the oven at its lowest setting and place the baking sheet in it, right at the bottom. Bake for 2–3 hours, until the biscuit is hard. Allow it to cool and break it into pieces. Store the oatcakes in a jar.

Scottish Oatcakes

ABOUT 8 OATCAKES

4oz (115g) fine or medium oatmeal
a pinch of bicarbonate of soda
a pinch of salt

1 teaspoon unsalted butter
enough hot water to make a stiff dough

Mix together the oatmeal, bicarbonate of soda and salt. Melt the butter in about 2fl. oz (60ml) of hot water. Pour it over the oatmeal, and add enough additional water to make a stiff dough.

Place the dough on an oatmeal-strewn work surface and press it flat.

Coat it with oatmeal and roll it out thin, dusting the dough constantly with oatmeal to prevent sticking.

Heat a heavy griddle over a medium heat and brush it with butter or margarine.

Invert a 5–7-inch round plate over the dough and cut a large round. Cut this into quarters. Slide a thin spatula under the oatcakes and transfer them to the hot griddle. Cook until the edges brown and begin to curl. Turn and bake for about a minute on the other side. Place the oatcakes in a warm oven for about 5 minutes, then remove from the heat and allow them to cool. Repeat with the remaining dough.

Oatmeal Pastries

ABOUT 20 PASTRIES

These, based on a Jane Grigson recipe, are more like a flaky pastry than like the pure oatcakes on pp. 150–1. They are made with a combination of oatmeal and flour, and contain more butter. The dough would also make a nice pastry case.

4oz (115g) medium oatmeal
4oz (115g) unbleached white flour
¾–1 teaspoon salt (to taste)
2oz (55g) unsalted butter

enough water to make a soft but not tacky dough (about 4fl. oz/120ml)

Combine the oatmeal, flour and salt, and rub in the butter. Add enough water to make a soft but not sticky dough, and gather it into a ball.

Sprinkle your work surface with oatmeal, then roll out the dough to about ⅛ inch thick, sprinkling the surface with oatmeal as necessary. Cut circles, using either a scone cutter or biscuit cutter, or a glass; or lay a 5–7-inch plate over the dough, cut a large circle and cut this into quarters.

Heat a lightly greased griddle over medium–high heat, and cook the pastries on one side, until brown around the edges. Turn and cook for about 15 seconds on the other side, then remove from the heat. Allow them to cool and store them in a jar.

Singing Hinnies

ABOUT 24 CAKES

These are rich pancakes, which have their origins in the north-east of England. ('Hinny' is a local endearment, from 'honey'.) Jane Grigson reminisces about eating singing hinnies at birthday parties as a child in the 1930s. Coins were always hidden inside their greaseproof wrappers. They are called 'singing hinnies' because of the sound of the batter sizzling when it hits the griddle. I find them a bit bland, but couldn't leave them out of this chapter.

8oz (225g) unbleached white flour
½ teaspoon salt
1–2 tablespoons white sugar (to taste)
1 teaspoon baking powder
2oz (55g) unsalted butter

2oz (55g) lard (margarine may be substituted)
2–3oz (55–85g) currants (to taste)
milk, as necessary (about 4fl. oz/120ml)

Sift together the flour, salt, sugar and baking powder. Rub in the butter and the lard. (This can be done in a food processor, fitted with the steel blade, using the pulse action, or in a mixer.) Mix in the currants. Add enough milk to make a firm dough. Roll out the dough and cut it into 2½-inch rounds.

Heat your griddle over medium–low heat and brush it with butter. Cook the cakes for about 3 minutes on each side, until mottled brown.

Keep the cooked cakes warm in the oven in a tea-towel while you use up the rest of the batter. You can eat these split and buttered.

English Muffins

8 MUFFINS

I grew up on packaged English muffins in the United States, and even long after I had begun making bread I always thought English muffins were one of those mysterious things one couldn't easily make at home. When I was researching this book I learned how easy they are to make, and how satisfying freshly made English muffins can be. The secret of making them successfully is to have a very moist dough – a dough which is really too moist to knead by hand, and which will drive you crazy as it gets all over your hands when you shape the muffins.

1½ teaspoons active dried yeast	8oz (225g) unbleached white flour,
4fl. oz (120ml) lukewarm water	plus extra (or use rice flour) for
½ teaspoon sugar	sprinkling
6fl. oz (180ml) lukewarm milk	8oz (225g) wholemeal flour
2 tablespoons olive oil or melted	2 teaspoons salt
unsalted butter	

Dissolve the yeast in the water and add the sugar. Let it sit for 10 minutes. Add the milk and melted butter.

Mix together the flours and salt, and add to the liquid. Stir together using a wooden spoon or the mixing attachment of an electric mixer. Beat for about 5 minutes, until the dough is uniform and elastic. It will be too wet to knead properly. Cover the bowl with clingfilm and a tea-towel and set it in a warm place for the dough to rise for 1½ hours.

Dust your work surface generously with flour. Divide the dough into eight equal portions and transfer them to the work surface. Sprinkle the portions with flour (or rice flour) and gently shape them into rounds or squares. They will be very sticky, so work quickly. Dust them with more flour. Cover them loosely with a tea-towel and let the dough rest for 35–45 minutes.

Warm a griddle over a very low heat and brush it with butter or margarine. Pre-heat the oven to 325°F/170°C/gas mark 3. Quickly and carefully, slide a wide spatula under one of the pieces of dough and transfer it to the griddle. Cook for 5 minutes on one side, then flip it over and cook for 5 minutes on the other side. Flip back, cook for another 3–5 minutes (or until brown and the edges have a baked film around them), then flip again and cook for 3–5 minutes on the other side. Remove the muffin from the heat and place it in the oven for 5 minutes. Continue cooking one muffin at a time until you have used up all the dough.

The muffins should be brown on the top and bottom, and light in the middle. Cool them on a rack. Split them in half and toast them under the grill or in a toaster. Serve them with butter and jam.

Note

English muffins can be made with other doughs, such as any of the sourdoughs in Chapter 3. But the dough must be quite moist, so add water until you achieve a sticky dough like the one in this recipe.

5: Other Favourites: a Selection of European and American Yeast Breads

This chapter could have been the longest one in the book, because I'm sure that I could find hundreds of breads to love from every country in the world. But what I wanted to include here was a kind of record of my tried and true breads, those I have made often at home, for dinners and for catering. Some of them date from my early catering days in Austin, Texas. Others are more recent and reflect my travels in Europe.

You will find many savoury herb breads in this chapter, crisp breadsticks inspired by Italian sojourns, as well as breads studded with sesame seeds, bagels and black breads from Central Europe. A few of them are sponge-method breads, but most of them are fairly uncomplicated with two risings only.

I often make a selection of these breads for parties, especially the black breads and herb breads, because they go well with other foods that I like to serve – cheeses and savoury dips and spreads – and they slice nicely. A couple of long black *baguettes* and wheatgerm *baguettes* go a very long way and look lovely in a basket.

The techniques involved in making these breads are, for the most part, the basics described in the introduction. Where unusual shapes – braids, bagels, bread rings, ladder-shapes – are required, instructions are given in the recipe.

Potato Bread

2 SMALL–MEDIUM LOAVES

Potatoes enrich bread with an earthy taste and give it a moist, hearty texture. This version, made with half wholemeal and half unbleached white flour, has a distinctive potato flavour and a coarse texture.

½lb (225g) potatoes, peeled and scrubbed

8fl. oz (225ml) warm water from cooking the potatoes

2 teaspoons active dried yeast

4fl. oz (120ml) lukewarm water

1 egg, at room temperature

8fl. oz (225ml) low-fat natural yoghurt or buttermilk

1 tablespoon sunflower, safflower or vegetable oil

1lb (450g) wholemeal flour

2½ teaspoons salt

up to 1lb (450g) unbleached white flour

Mixing the dough and kneading

Quarter the potatoes and boil them until tender. Drain them and retain the water. Mash the potatoes and allow them to cool.

Dissolve the yeast in the lukewarm water in a large bowl and let it sit for about 10 minutes.

Beat the egg and put it in a measuring jug. Add the water from the potatoes and the yoghurt or buttermilk. Add more warm water, as necessary, to make 1 pint.

If kneading the dough by hand. Add the liquids and the oil to the yeast, then beat in the mashed potatoes. Mix together the wholemeal flour and the salt, and stir into the liquid ingredients. Add the unbleached white flour, a cupful at a time, and as soon as you can turn the dough out in one piece, scrape it out on to a lightly floured work surface. Knead for about 15 minutes, using a pastry scraper to help you turn the dough, and adding unbleached flour as necessary. The dough will be slightly dense, but resilient, and at the end of kneading should be soft, elastic and smooth.

If using an electric mixer. Stir the liquid ingredients into the yeast mixture. Using the mixing attachment, beat in the potatoes, then add the wholemeal flour and salt and mix in. Change to the dough hook and add half the unbleached white flour. Knead for 2 minutes at low speed (1 on a Kenwood), then for 8 minutes at medium speed (2 on a Kenwood). Add more unbleached white flour if the mixture seems too sticky. Finish kneading by hand, for about 2–3 minutes, on your lightly floured work surface.

Rising, forming the loaves and baking

Knead the dough into a ball, clean and oil your bowl, and place the dough in it, seam side up first, then seam side down. Cover the bowl with clingfilm and a tea-towel and set it in a warm place for the dough to rise for about 1½ hours, until doubled in bulk.

Punch down the dough, knead it for a couple of minutes, then divide it in two. Form the pieces into round loaves and place them, rounded side up, on one or two baking sheets that have been oiled and dusted with cornmeal (or you can use a *banneton* – see p. 11). Dust the tops with flour, cover with a tea-towel and allow the loaves to rise for about 45 minutes.

Pre-heat the oven to 400°F/200°C/gas mark 6. Spray the loaves with water (see p. 12), dust them with flour and slash the tops with a razor blade or a sharp knife. Bake for an hour, or until the bread is brown and responds to tapping with a hollow thumping sound. Remove it from the heat and cool it on racks.

Potato Bread with Caraway

1 VERY LARGE LOAF OR 2 SMALLER LOAVES

This version of potato bread, made with three-quarters unbleached white flour and one-quarter wholemeal, has a close crumb and slices beautifully. Caraway seeds add a pungent flavour.

½lb (225g) potatoes, scrubbed
2½ teaspoons active dried yeast
1 pint (570ml) lukewarm water
8oz (225g) wholemeal flour

1 tablespoon salt
½ tablespoon caraway seeds
1½lb (680g) unbleached white
flour

Mixing the dough and kneading

Boil the potatoes in their skins until tender, then drain, peel and mash them. Allow them to cool.

Dissolve the yeast in 4fl. oz (120ml) of the warm water in a large bowl, stir in 3 tablespoons of the wholemeal flour, and allow this to sit in a warm place for 30 minutes, loosely covered with clingfilm.

If kneading the dough by hand. Stir the remaining warm water into the yeast mixture. Add the mashed potatoes and mix well. Mix together the remaining wholemeal flour, salt and caraway seeds and stir into the water and yeast mixture. Add the unbleached white flour, a cupful at a time. As soon as the dough can be scraped out of the bowl in one piece, scrape it on to a floured work surface and begin to knead, adding flour as necessary. The dough will soon become resistant and elastic. Knead for about 15 minutes. At the end of the kneading the dough will be firm, smooth and elastic. Shape it into a ball.

If using an electric mixer. Stir the remaining warm water into the yeast mixture. Using the mixing attachment, beat in the potatoes, then add the remaining wholemeal flour, the salt and caraway seeds and mix in. Change to the dough hook and add 1lb (450g) of the unbleached flour. Knead for 2 minutes at low speed (1 on a Kenwood), then for 8 minutes at medium speed (2 on a Kenwood). Add more unbleached flour if the mixture seems too sticky. Turn out the dough on to a lightly floured surface and finish kneading by hand for a minute or two. Shape the dough into a ball.

Rising, forming the loaves and baking

Clean and oil your bowl, and place the dough in it, seam side up first, then seam side down. Cover the bowl with clingfilm and a tea-towel, place it in a warm spot, and allow the dough to rise for 1–2 hours, until doubled in bulk.

Punch down the dough and knead it for about 5 minutes on a lightly floured surface. Shape it into a tight ball, or divide it into two equal pieces and shape into two balls, place it on a baking sheet, oiled and lightly dusted with cornmeal (or use a *banneton* – see p. 11), and let it rise again for 45 minutes.

Meanwhile, pre-heat the oven to 400°F/200°C/gas mark 6. If necessary, reshape the dough and let it rise for another 15 minutes. Slash the dough, spray it with water (see p. 12), and bake for an hour, or until the bread is a nice brown colour and responds to tapping with a hollow thumping sound. Remove it from the heat and cool it on a rack.

Baguettes with Wheatgerm

4 BAGUETTES

The addition of wheatgerm and a little bit of wholemeal flour gives this French bread recipe a sweet, nutty flavour. The bread is light and delicate, the dough sticky and elastic. With a glaze your crust will be shiny but not as hard as without, and certainly unlike a French *baguette*.

2½ teaspoons active dried yeast
1 pint (570ml) lukewarm water
a pinch of sugar
1 tablespoon melted butter or
*   safflower oil*
1 scant tablespoon salt
4oz (115g) wheatgerm

4oz (115g) wholemeal flour
1¾lb (780g) unbleached white
*   flour, plus up to 4oz (115g)*
*   extra for kneading*
1 egg, beaten with 3 tablespoons
*   water, for glaze (optional)*

Mixing the dough and kneading

Dissolve the yeast in the lukewarm water in a large bowl, or in the bowl of your electric mixer, add the pinch of sugar and let it sit 10 minutes.

If kneading the bread by hand. Fold the melted butter or safflower oil into the yeast mixture. Mix together the flours, wheatgerm and salt, and fold into the liquids, a cupful at a time. As soon as you can, scrape the dough out on to a floured kneading surface. Knead, adding extra unbleached flour as necessary, for 10 minutes. The dough will be sticky at first but will become very elastic, though it will remain tacky on the surface. Shape it into a ball.

If using an electric mixer. Combine the flours, wheatgerm and salt, and add all at once to the bowl along with the melted butter or oil. Mix together with the mixing attachment, then change to the dough hook. Mix at low speed (1 on a Kenwood) for 2 minutes, then at medium speed (2 on a Kenwood) for 6–8 minutes. If the dough seems very wet and sticky, sprinkle in up to 2oz (55g) extra unbleached flour. Scrape the dough out on to a lightly floured surface and knead it by hand for a minute or so. Shape it into a ball.

Rising, forming the baguettes and baking

Rinse out your bowl, dry and oil it. Place the dough in it, seam side up first, then seam side down. Cover the bowl with clingfilm and a tea-towel, and set it in a warm place for the dough to rise for 1½ hours, or until it has doubled in size.

Punch down the dough and let it rise again until doubled in bulk – about an hour. Meanwhile, butter or oil a baking sheet or *baguette* tins (see p. 28) and sprinkle with cornmeal. Lightly flour a board and turn out the dough. It will be soft and sticky. Keep your hands and the board lightly floured, and work quickly.

Divide the dough into four equal pieces and shape them into balls, covering them lightly with clingfilm to prevent the dough drying out. Shape into *baguettes* (see p. 27) and place them in the *baguette* tins or on the baking sheets. Brush with the glaze, if using. Cover the loaves with a dry tea-towel and let them rise for 20–30 minutes.

Meanwhile, pre-heat the oven to 400°F/200°C/gas mark 6. Slash each *baguette* three or four times across the top with a sharp knife or a razor blade. Create steam by using the baking-tin method (see p. 12) and spray the loaves and the inside of the oven with water (see p. 12). Bake for 35–45 minutes, until the loaves are golden-brown and respond to tapping with a hollow sound. For extra-shiny bread, brush the loaves several times with glaze during baking. Remove the loaves from the heat, take them out of the *baguette* tins, if using, and cool them on a rack.

French Herb Bread

4 *BAGUETTES* OR SMALL LOAVES, OR 2 OF EACH

This savoury bread with rosemary, thyme, garlic and onion goes very nicely with cheese. The dough – which is basically the same as that for the wheatgerm *baguette* on p. 159, with the herb-and-onion mixture added – is light, sticky and elastic.

For the herb-and-onion mixture

1 tablespoon melted unsalted butter
 or safflower oil
1 medium-sized onion, finely
 chopped
3 cloves garlic, finely chopped or
 crushed
1 tablespoon chopped fresh dill
 (if available)

2 teaspoons chopped fresh
 rosemary, or ¾ teaspoon dried
1½ teaspoons fresh thyme, or ¾
 teaspoon dried
3 tablespoons finely chopped fresh
 parsley

For the dough

2½ teaspoons active dried yeast
1 pint (570ml) lukewarm water
a pinch of sugar
1 tablespoon melted unsalted butter
  or safflower oil
1 scant tablespoon salt

4oz (115g) wheatgerm
4oz (115g) wholemeal flour
1¾lb (580g) unbleached white
  flour, plus up to 4oz (115g)
  extra for kneading

For the topping (optional)

1 egg, beaten with 3 tablespoons
  water

Preparing the onion and the herbs

Sauté the onion in 1 tablespoon of the butter or oil until tender. Remove from the heat. Place the garlic, dill, rosemary, thyme and parsley in a mortar and pestle or a herb-mill and mash together.

Mixing the dough and kneading

Dissolve the yeast in the lukewarm water in a large bowl, or in the bowl of your electric mixer, add the pinch of sugar and let it sit for 10 minutes.

If kneading the dough by hand. Fold in the melted butter or safflower oil, the sautéed onion and the herb mixture. Mix together the flours, wheatgerm and salt, and fold in, a cupful at a time. As soon as you can, scrape the dough out on to a floured work surface. Knead for 10 minutes, adding extra unbleached flour as necessary. The dough will be sticky at first but will become very elastic, though it will remain tacky on the surface. Shape it into a ball.

If using an electric mixer. Combine the flours, wheatgerm and salt, and add all at once to the bowl along with the melted butter or oil, the sautéed onion and the herb mixture. Mix together with the mixing attachment, then change to the dough hook. Mix at low speed (1 on a Kenwood) for 2 minutes, then at medium speed (2 on a Kenwood) for 6–8 minutes. If the dough seems very wet and sticky, sprinkle in up to 2oz (55g) extra unbleached flour. Scrape out the dough on to a lightly floured work surface and knead by hand for a minute or so. Shape the dough into a ball.

Rising, forming the loaves and baking

Rinse out your bowl, dry and oil it. Place the dough in it, seam side up first, then seam side down. Cover the bowl with clingfilm and a tea-towel, and set it in a warm place for the dough to rise for 1½ hours, or until it has doubled in size.

Punch down the dough and let it rise again until doubled in bulk – about an hour. Meanwhile, butter or oil a baking sheet or *baguette* tins (see p. 28) and sprinkle them with cornmeal. Lightly flour a board and turn out the dough. It will be soft and sticky. Keep your hands and the board lightly floured, and work quickly. Divide the dough into four equal pieces and shape them into balls, covering them lightly with clingfilm to prevent the dough drying out. Shape the dough into *baguettes* or round loaves (see p. 27), and place in the *baguette* tins or on the baking sheets. Brush with the glaze, if using. Cover the loaves with a dry tea-towel and let them rise for 20–30 minutes.

Meanwhile, pre-heat the oven to 400°F/200°C/gas mark 6. Slash each loaf three or four times across the top with a sharp knife or a razor blade. Create steam by using the baking-tin method (see p. 12) and spray the loaves and the inside of the oven with water (see p. 12). Bake for 35–45 minutes, until the bread is golden-brown and responds to tapping with a hollow sound. For extra-shiny bread, brush the loaves several times with glaze during baking. Remove the loaves from the heat, take them out of the *baguette* tins, if using, and cool them on a rack.

Herbed Wholemeal Bread

2 LOAVES

This is a savoury, wholesome bread. The dough is soft and sticky, and the loaves have a close crumb and slice very neatly.

¾ pint (425ml) lukewarm water
1 tablespoon active dried yeast
1 tablespoon mild-flavoured honey
5 tablespoons safflower oil
1 small onion, finely chopped
1 clove garlic, finely chopped or
  crushed
8fl. oz (225ml) low-fat natural
  yoghurt, at room temperature
1 scant tablespoon salt
2 teaspoons fresh thyme, or 1
  teaspoon dried (to taste)

2 tablespoons dill
2 teaspoons dried sage
1½lb (680g) finely milled
  100 per cent or 85 per cent
  wholemeal flour
8oz (225g) unbleached white flour,
  plus extra for kneading
1 egg, beaten with 2 tablespoons
  water, for glaze
dill seeds, for decoration (optional)

Mixing the dough and kneading

Dissolve the yeast in the lukewarm water in a large bowl. Add the honey and let it sit for 5 minutes.

Meanwhile, heat 1 tablespoon of the safflower oil in a frying pan and sauté the onion with the garlic, stirring over medium–low heat until the onion is tender. Remove from the heat.

Stir the yoghurt into the yeast mixture, add the remaining 4 tablespoons safflower oil, the salt, thyme, dill and sage. Stir in the sautéed onion and garlic. Whisk in 12oz (340g) of the wholemeal flour, then gradually fold in the rest. Fold in half the unbleached flour and place the remaining half on your kneading surface. Scrape the dough out on to your kneading surface (you can knead in the bowl if the dough is too sticky). Knead for 10 minutes, flouring your hands often and using a pastry scraper to scrape up and fold over the dough if it is sticky and hard to work with. When the dough is stiff and elastic, knead it into a ball.

Rising, forming the loaves and baking

Oil your bowl and place the dough in it, seam side up first, then seam side down. Cover the bowl with a damp tea-towel or with clingfilm and set it in a warm spot for the dough to rise for 1½ hours, or until doubled in bulk.

Punch down the dough and turn it out on to a lightly floured work surface. Oil two loaf tins. Knead the dough for a minute or two, cut it into two equal pieces and form each piece into a ball. Then roll each ball into a loaf shape and place them in the oiled loaf tins, seam side up first, then seam side down. Cover with a damp tea-towel and set the tins in a warm place to rise until the dough has doubled in bulk, or until it rises above the edges of the tins – about an hour.

Meanwhile, pre-heat the oven to 375°F/190°C/gas mark 5. Brush the loaves gently with the glaze, then sprinkle them with the optional dill seeds. Brush again with glaze, slash the loaves and bake for 45–50 minutes, or until the bread is golden-brown and responds to tapping with a hollow thumping sound. Remove it from the tins and cool it on a rack.

Cumin and Cornmeal Bread

1 LOAF

This dough is very much like that for the herbed wholemeal bread on p. 163 – very moist and somewhat dense. The cornmeal gives the bread a marvellous grainy texture. It has a rich, buttery taste, although there's no butter in it. This is a convenient bread to make, because it doesn't require too much rising time.

4fl. oz (120ml) lukewarm water
1 tablespoon active dried yeast
1 tablespoon mild-flavoured honey
8fl. oz (225ml) low-fat natural
   yoghurt
1 egg
2 tablespoons safflower oil
1½ teaspoons salt

2 tablespoons cumin seeds
5oz (140g) stoneground cornmeal
12oz (340g) 100 per cent or 85
   per cent wholemeal flour
unbleached white flour for
   kneading, as necessary
1 additional egg, beaten, for glaze

Mixing the dough and kneading

Dissolve the yeast in the water and stir in the honey. Let it sit for 10 minutes. Add the yoghurt, egg, safflower oil, salt and cumin seeds and mix well. Fold in the cornmeal, then gradually fold in the wholemeal flour. The dough will be sticky, yet solid enough to turn out of the bowl after you have added about two-thirds of the flour. Place the remaining third on your board and turn out the dough. Knead for 10 minutes, adding unbleached flour as necessary. The dough will be sticky. Shape it into a ball.

Rising, forming the loaf and baking

Oil your bowl, return the dough to it and let it rise, covered, in a warm place for 1½ hours, until doubled in bulk.

Punch down the dough, turn it out and form it into a loaf. Place it in an oiled loaf tin and let it rise again, covered, in a warm place for an hour, or until the dough rises above the edges of the tin.

Pre-heat the oven to 375°F/190°C/gas mark 5. Brush the loaf lightly with beaten egg, slash the top with a razor blade or a sharp knife and bake for 50 minutes, or until the bread is golden-brown and responds to tapping with a hollow thumping sound. Remove it from the tin and cool it on a rack.

Pesto Bread

2 SMALL LOAVES

This savoury, garlicky bread is inspired by Carol Field's pesto bread, which I came across in her lovely book, *The Italian Baker*. It makes a delicious addition to an Italian meal, and it's also great with cheese. Naturally, it's a bread to make in spring and summer when fresh basil is readily available.

The dough for this bread is soft, pliable and silky – a pleasure to work with.

For the pesto

2oz (55g) fresh basil leaves,
  washed and dried
2 large cloves garlic
¼ teaspoon salt

4fl. oz (120ml) fruity olive oil
3oz (85g) freshly grated Parmesan
  cheese

For the bread

½ pint (285ml) lukewarm water
2½ teaspoons active dried yeast
2 teaspoons salt
8oz (225g) wholemeal flour

8oz (225g) unbleached white flour,
  plus up to 1oz (30g) extra for
  kneading

Making the pesto

Combine the basil, garlic and salt in a food processor and purée them together, or pound them together in a mortar and pestle. Drizzle in the olive oil (with the processor still going, if using) and continue to blend until smooth. Add the Parmesan cheese and combine well. Set the pesto aside.

Mixing the dough and kneading

Dissolve the yeast in the lukewarm water in a large bowl or in the bowl of your electric mixer, and let it sit for 10 minutes. Stir in the pesto and combine thoroughly.

If kneading the bread by hand. Combine the wholemeal flour and the salt, and fold into the liquid. Fold in the unbleached flour and turn out the dough on to a lightly floured surface. Knead for 10 minutes, or until the dough is smooth and elastic. Shape it into a ball.

If using an electric mixer. Combine the flours and salt, and add all at once to the bowl. Mix together with the mixing attachment, then change to the dough hook. Mix at low speed (1 on a Kenwood) for 2 minutes, then at medium speed (2 on a Kenwood) for 6–8 minutes. If the dough seems very wet and sticky, sprinkle in up to 2oz (55g) extra unbleached flour. Scrape out the dough on to a lightly flavoured surface and knead by hand for a minute or so. Shape the dough into a ball.

Rising, forming the loaves and baking

Clean and oil your bowl, place the dough in it, seam side up first, then seam side down. Cover the bowl with clingfilm and a tea-towel, and set it in a warm place for the dough to rise for 1½ hours, or until it has doubled in size.

Punch down the dough and divide it into two equal pieces. Knead each piece briefly, then shape it into a tight, round loaf (alternatively, you can make one large loaf). Place the loaves on an oiled and cornmeal-dusted baking sheet. Cover them and let them rise in a warm place for 45–60 minutes, until doubled in bulk.

Meanwhile, pre-heat the oven to 450°F/230°C/gas mark 8. Slash the loaves with a sharp knife or razor blade and put them in the oven. Turn down the heat to 400°F/200°C/gas mark 6, then spray the oven with water three times in the first ten minutes (see p. 12). Bake for 40 minutes, until the loaves are deep brown and respond to tapping with a hollow sound. Remove them from the oven and cool them on a rack.

Wholemeal Sesame Breadsticks

20–24 BREADSTICKS

How different these are from commercial breadsticks, which are loaded with fat but have very little character. These are very easy to make, and the dough is easy to handle. They require only one rise and shaping them takes no time at all. They're a great item to have on hand, and they always impress guests.

2 teaspoons active dried yeast
12fl. oz (340ml) lukewarm water
1 tablespoon malt extract, or 1
  teaspoon mild-flavoured honey
2 tablespoons olive oil, plus extra
  for brushing the dough
1½ teaspoons salt
4 tablespoons sesame seeds

4oz (115g) unbleached white flour
12oz (340g) wholemeal flour, plus
  extra for kneading, as necessary
1 egg white, lightly beaten, for
  glaze
4 tablespoons sesame seeds, for
  topping

Mixing the dough and kneading

Dissolve the yeast in the water in a large bowl, stir in the malt extract or honey and allow it to sit for 10 minutes, until the water is cloudy and the yeast beginning to bubble.

Stir in the olive oil, salt and sesame seeds. Stir in the unbleached white flour, then fold in the wholemeal flour, a cupful at a time. After the second cup you should be able to scrape the dough out on to a lightly floured kneading surface. Knead, adding additional wholemeal flour as necessary, for about 10 minutes, until the dough is stiff and elastic.

Rising, forming the loaves and baking

Lightly flour a large cutting board. Using your hands or a rolling pin, press the dough into a rectangle on the board, about 14 inches long by 4 inches wide. Lightly oil the top of the dough and cover it with clingfilm and a tea-towel. Place it in a warm spot to rise for an hour.

Pre-heat the oven to 400°F/200°C/gas mark 6. Oil three baking sheets. Cut the dough crosswise into four equal pieces. Brush each piece with beaten egg white, and sprinkle each with 1 heaped tablespoon of sesame seeds. Now cut these pieces crosswise into six short strips (they'll be like fat fingers).

There are two ways to shape the breadsticks. You can roll them between your hands and the board until they are as long as the width of your baking sheet, then twist them to get a pretty shape. Or you can take each strip and stretch it out, squeezing gently, to the width of your baking sheet. I wrap both hands around the pieces of dough, and squeeze and pull from the centre out. They are shaped very quickly. Lay the breadsticks on the baking sheets, about an inch apart.

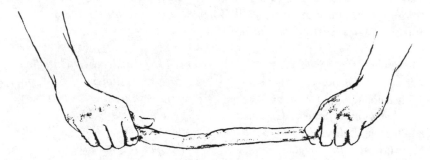

Place two baking sheets in the middle–upper part of the oven and refrigerate the third until the first two are done. Bake for 25 minutes, switching the position of the baking sheets and turning the breadsticks over halfway through baking. When they are golden-brown (they will probably be darker on one side), turn off the oven and leave the breadsticks in for another 15 minutes. Remove them from the oven and cool them on racks. They will keep for several days in a breadbin, and can be frozen.

Parmesan Breadsticks

Follow the recipe for wholemeal sesame breadsticks above, but omit the sesame seeds. Towards the end of the kneading add 2oz (55g) grated Parmesan cheese and work it into the dough. Bake at 450°F/230°C/gas mark 8 for 12–15 minutes.

Thyme Breadsticks

Follow the recipe for wholemeal sesame breadsticks above, but omit the sesame seeds. Add 1 tablespoon fresh thyme (or ½ tablespoon dried) along with the salt and flour.

Spinach and Garlic Breadsticks

Follow the recipe for wholemeal sesame breadsticks above, but omit the sesame seeds. Use 8oz (225g) unbleached white flour and 10oz (285g) wholemeal flour. Add 1 garlic clove, finely chopped or crushed, to the yeast-and-water mixture when you add the salt. At the end of kneading, knead in 2oz (55g) fresh spinach, washed, dried thoroughly and very finely chopped.

Rosemary and Thyme Bread

2 SMALL LOAVES OR 1 LARGE LOAF

I was first inspired to make this savoury bread in Provence, where these herbs grow into big bushes all over the countryside. The smell of the dough rising is enticing, and the baking loaves smell even better.

This bread is best made with fresh herbs, but if that isn't possible use dried herbs and halve the quantities. The dough is soft, elastic and easy to work with, the bread crusty and dense.

1 tablespoon active dried yeast
¼ pint (425ml) lukewarm water
2 tablespoons olive oil
1 tablespoon salt
4 tablespoons finely chopped fresh
  rosemary, or 2 tablespoons
  chopped dried

2 tablespoons fresh thyme leaves, or
  1 tablespoon dried
4oz (115g) wholemeal flour
1¼lb (565g) unbleached white
  flour

Mixing the dough and kneading

Dissolve the yeast in the lukewarm water in a large bowl, or in the bowl of your electric mixer, and let it sit for 10 minutes. Stir in the olive oil.

If kneading the bread by hand. Mix together the herbs, wholemeal flour and salt, and fold into the liquids, a cupful at a time. Begin adding unbleached flour and, as soon as you can, scrape the dough out on to a floured kneading surface. Knead for 10 minutes, adding unbleached flour as necessary. Shape the dough into a ball.

If using an electric mixer. Combine the herbs, flours and salt, and add all at once to the bowl. Mix together with the mixing attachment, then change to the dough hook. Mix at low speed (1 on a Kenwood) for 2 minutes, then at medium speed (2 on a Kenwood) for 6–8 minutes. If the dough seems very wet and sticky, sprinkle in up to 2oz (55g) more unbleached flour. Scrape out the dough on to a lightly floured surface and knead it by hand for a minute or so. Shape the dough into a ball.

Rising and forming the loaves

Clean and oil your bowl and return the dough to it. Cover the bowl with clingfilm and a tea-towel, and set it in a warm place for the dough to rise for 1½ hours, or until it has doubled in size.

Punch down the dough and turn it out on to your work surface. Divide it into two equal pieces and shape these into tight, round loaves.

If using bannetons. Dust the surface of the loaves with flour and place them in *bannetons* (see p. 11), rounded side down. Cover with a tea-towel and let the loaves rise in a wàrm spot for 45–60 minutes, until almost doubled in volume. Just before baking, turn out the dough on to an oiled baking sheet or, preferably, baking stones (see p. 12) which you have warmed as the oven pre-heated and then dusted with cornmeal.

If not using a banneton. Let the dough rise right side up on a lightly oiled and cornmeal-dusted baking sheet for 45–60 minutes. Reshape gently if necessary and let it rise again while you pre-heat the oven.

Baking

Pre-heat the oven to 450°F/230°C/gas mark 8. Slash the tops of the loaves with a razor blade or sharp knife and place in the hot oven. Spray the inside of the oven with water three times during the first ten minutes (see p. 12). Reduce the heat to 400°F/200°C/gas mark 6 and bake for 30–35 minutes longer, until the loaves are brown and respond to tapping with a hollow sound. Remove them from the heat and cool them on racks.

Black Bread

2 LOAVES

This is a lovely, slightly sweet, dark loaf with a close crumb. I often make it for parties and catering, because it slices very nicely and you can get a lot of thin slices out of a long loaf. It goes very well with savoury dips and smoked salmon.

The dough is wet and soft, but stiffens up as you knead. The surface will remain tacky.

For the sponge

12fl. oz (340ml) lukewarm water
1 tablespoon active dried yeast
¼ pint (140ml) strong black coffee
  (can be instant), cooled to
  lukewarm

3 tablespoons black treacle
½ teaspoon ground ginger
4oz (115g) fresh wholemeal
  breadcrumbs
8oz (225g) unbleached white flour

For the dough

2 teaspoons salt
12oz (340g) rye flour
4 tablespoons safflower or
  sunflower oil

4oz (115g) wholemeal flour
up to 4oz (115g) unbleached white
  flour for kneading

For the topping

½ teaspoon instant coffee
4 tablespoons hot water
1 egg

sesame seeds or poppy seeds
  (optional)

Mixing the sponge

Dissolve the yeast in the water and let it sit for 5 minutes. Stir in the coffee and the treacle. Add the ground ginger and the wholemeal breadcrumbs and mix well. Stir in the unbleached flour, a cupful at a time, and mix well. Stir about 100 times, changing direction every now and then, and cover with clingfilm and a tea-towel. Set the bowl in a warm place for the dough to rise for 50–60 minutes.

Mixing the dough and kneading

If kneading the dough by hand. Mix together the rye flour and the salt. Fold the oil into the sponge, then the wholemeal flour. Flour your work surface and scrape out the dough. Knead for 10–15 minutes, using a pastry scraper to help you turn the dough and adding flour as necessary. At the beginning the moistness of the dough will be discouraging, but it will stiffen up quickly. At the end of kneading it will be stiff and elastic, but may still be tacky on the surface. Shape it into a ball.

If using an electric mixer. Mix together the rye flour, the salt and the wholemeal flour. Add the oil and the flour mixture to the sponge. Mix together using the mixing attachment, then change to the dough hook. Mix at low speed (1 on a Kenwood) for 2 minutes, then at medium speed (2 on a Kenwood) for 6 minutes, adding extra unbleached flour if the mixture seems too liquid. Turn out the dough on to a floured work surface and knead for a minute. Shape the dough into a ball.

Rising, forming the loaves and baking

Rinse out the bowl, dry and oil it. Place the dough in the bowl, seam side up first, then seam side down. Cover the bowl and let the dough rise for about 1½ hours, until doubled in bulk.

Punch down the dough and turn it out on to a lightly floured work surface. Divide it into two equal pieces and shape the pieces into long or round loaves. Make them high, as the dough will spread out. You can place them directly in *baguette* tins if you are using these.

Prepare a glaze by dissolving the instant coffee in the 4 tablespoons hot water, then beating in the egg. Brush the loaves with the glaze and sprinkle them with poppy seeds or sesame seeds if you wish. Let them rise for 40–45 minutes.

Meanwhile, pre-heat the oven to 400°F/200°C/gas mark 6. Slash the loaves and bake for 40–45 minutes, until the bread is a dark blackish-brown and responds to tapping with a hollow sound. For extra-shiny bread, brush the loaves again with the glaze halfway through baking. Remove them from the heat and cool them on racks.

Strong Black Pumpernickel

3 SMALL OR 2 LARGE LOAVES

This is another black bread, heavier and with a stronger, spicier flavour than the one on p. 171, because of the addition of vinegar, chocolate and caraway seeds. Like all rye breads, the dough is sticky, dense, heavy and unwieldy. Bear with it: the bread is delicious. Slice it thin and eat it with cheese, ham, salads – or anything.

1 pint (570ml) lukewarm water
1oz (30g) unsweetened chocolate
4 tablespoons cider vinegar
4 tablespoons black treacle
2 tablespoons caraway seeds
2 teaspoons instant coffee powder
2 tablespoons active dried yeast
1 teaspoon sugar
1 lb (450g) rye flour
1 tablespoon salt

2oz (55g) bran
1lb (450g) unbleached white flour,
  or a combination of 85 per cent
  wholemeal and unbleached white
  flour
1 egg, beaten with 2 tablespoons
  water, for glaze
1 tablespoon poppy seeds for
  topping (optional)

Mixing the dough and kneading

Combine ¾ pint (425ml) of the water, the chocolate, vinegar, treacle, caraway seeds and coffee powder in a heavy-bottomed saucepan, or in the top of a double boiler, and heat through, stirring, until the chocolate and coffee are thoroughly dissolved. Remove from the heat and allow to cool to lukewarm.

Dissolve the yeast in the remaining lukewarm water in a large bowl, or in the bowl of your electric mixer, add the sugar and let it sit for 10 minutes. When the chocolate-and-coffee mixture is lukewarm, stir it in.

If kneading the dough by hand. Mix together the rye flour, salt and bran, and fold in, a cupful at a time. Let the mixture sit for 10 minutes. Begin adding the unbleached flour (or combination of wholemeal and unbleached flours) and, as soon as you can, scrape the dough out on to a floured kneading surface. Knead, adding extra unbleached flour as necessary, for 10 minutes. Shape the dough into a ball.

If using an electric mixer. Combine the rye flour, salt and bran, and add all at once to the bowl. Mix together with the mixing attachment, then let the mixture sit for 10 minutes. Add three-quarters of the unbleached flour (or combination of unbleached and wholemeal flours). Change to the dough hook and mix at low speed (1 on a Kenwood) for 2 minutes, then at medium speed (2 on a Kenwood) for 6–8 minutes. Add extra unbleached flour as necessary until the dough comes away from the sides of the bowl. Scrape out the dough on to a lightly floured surface and knead by hand for a minute or so. Shape the dough into a ball.

Rising, forming the loaves and baking

Clean and oil your bowl and put the dough in it. Cover the bowl with clingfilm and a tea-towel, and set it in a warm place for the dough to rise for 1½ hours, or until it has doubled in size.

Oil two baking sheets and sprinkle them with cornmeal. Punch down the dough, turn it out on to your work surface and shape it into a ball. Cut it into two or three pieces, depending on the size of loaf you want, and shape the pieces into round or oval loaves. Cover them with a tea-towel and let the dough rise until it has doubled – about an hour. The dough will spread out considerably; reshape it gently before pre-heating the oven.

Pre-heat the oven to 375°F/190°C/gas mark 5. Brush the loaves lightly with glaze, sprinkle with poppy seeds if desired, then brush again with glaze. Bake for 45 minutes, brushing again halfway through baking. The loaves are done when they are dark brown – almost black – and shiny and respond to tapping with a hollow thumping sound. Remove them from the oven and cool them on a rack.

Bagels

1 DOZEN

I was weaned on bagels, but I never made one until I moved to Paris. Then I got homesick for them and found that making them was extremely easy. The dough is easy to work with and has only one long rise, and shaping the bagels is no problem – as you will see.

Bagels can be varied with a number of toppings, such as sesame seeds, poppy seeds, caraway or chopped onion. The dough can be made with white flour, wholemeal, or rye for pumpernickel bagels. My standard bagel recipe combines wholemeal and white, and I like the balance. Other variations follow the standard recipe.

For the dough

12fl. oz (340ml) lukewarm water
2 tablespoons active dried yeast
1 tablespoon mild-flavoured honey
  or malt extract
1 scant tablespoon salt

12oz (340g) wholemeal flour or
  wholemeal pastry flour
4–6oz (115–170g) unbleached
  white flour, as necessary

For the boiling

4 pints (2½ litres) water

1 tablespoon sugar or malt extract

For the topping

1 egg white
1 tablespoon water

2 tablespoons sesame seeds, or
  poppy seeds, or coarse salt, or
  chopped onion, or caraway seeds
  (these are all optional)

Mixing the dough and kneading

Dissolve the yeast in the lukewarm water in a large bowl, or in the bowl of your electric mixer, stir in the honey or malt extract and let it sit for 10 minutes. Stir in half the wholemeal flour and the salt, and beat vigorously with a whisk or at medium speed (2 on a Kenwood) in a mixer fitted with the mixing attachment for about 5 minutes.

If kneading the dough by hand. Fold in the remaining wholemeal flour. Place 4oz (115g) of the unbleached flour on a floured work surface and scrape out the dough. Knead, adding more unbleached flour as necessary, for 10 minutes, until the dough is stiff and elastic. Shape it into a ball.

If using an electric mixer. Add the remaining wholemeal flour and 4oz (115g) of the unbleached flour. Mix together with the mixing attachment, then change to the dough hook. Mix at low speed (1 on a Kenwood) for 2 minutes, then at medium speed (2 on a Kenwood) for 6–8 minutes. If the dough seems very wet and sticky, sprinkle in up to 2oz (55g) more unbleached flour. Scrape out the dough on to a lightly floured surface and knead it by hand for a minute or so, until it is stiff and elastic. Shape it into a ball.

Rising, forming the bagels and baking

Clean and oil your bowl and place the dough in it, seam side up first, then seam side down. Cover the bowl with clingfilm and a tea-towel, and set it in a warm place for the dough to rise for 1½ hours, or until it has doubled in size.

Punch down the dough and turn it out on to your work surface. Divide it into twelve equal pieces, shape these into balls and let the dough rest for 5 minutes, covered lightly with clingfilm.

Meanwhile, combine the 4 pints (2½ litres) water and the sugar or malt extract and bring it to a boil in a large pan over a high heat.

Now shape the bagels. Gently flatten each ball *slightly* and make a hole in the centre by sticking your thumb through the dough and

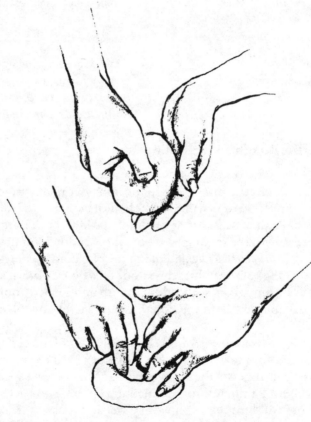

spreading the dough apart with your fingers. Stretch the hole out so that it is a little larger than you want it to look when the bagels are done – as they prove and bake the holes will shrink.

Place the bagels on a lightly floured surface and cover them lightly with clingfilm or a tea-towel. Let them rise for 10 minutes. Pre-heat the oven to 450°F/230°C/gas mark 8.

Now you will boil the bagels to form the beginning of their sleek, chewy crust. Have the water gently boiling. Using a wide spatula or a skimmer, gently lift the bagels, in batches of two or three, and lower them into the simmering water. After 30 seconds flip the bagels over so that they boil on both sides. Simmer for 30 seconds more, then carefully lift them from the water with a skimmer or slotted spatula and drain them on a tea-towel. Repeat with the remaining bagels.

Oil two baking sheets and sprinkle them with cornmeal. Beat together the egg white and water and gently brush the bagels. Sprinkle them with the topping of your choice and transfer them to the baking sheets. Bake them in the middle–upper part of the hot oven for 30 minutes, switching the position of the baking sheets halfway through. Ten minutes before the bagels are done, flip them over so that the bottom side won't brown too much. Bagels are done when they are dark brown and shiny. Remove them from the heat and cool them on a rack.

Plain Bagels

Follow the basic recipe above but use all unbleached white flour in place of the wholemeal flour.

Pumpernickel Bagels

Follow the basic recipe above but dissolve 2 teaspoons instant coffee and 2 tablespoons black treacle in the water along with the yeast. Omit the wholemeal flour, and use 8oz (225g) rye flour and 8–10oz (225–285g) unbleached white flour, as needed.

Herbed Cottage Cheese Bread

1 LOAF

This is a high-protein, very easy-to-make bread. It requires only one rising, and the finished bread has a firm texture and savoury flavour. It slices very well and works well for sandwiches. The dough is firm and elastic.

2fl. oz (60ml) lukewarm water
1 tablespoon active dried yeast
1 teaspoon sugar or mild-flavoured
  honey
8oz (225g) cottage cheese, at room
  temperature
1 egg, at room temperature
1 tablespoon grated onion
2 tablespoons sunflower or
  safflower oil

¼ teaspoon bicarbonate of soda
4 tablespoons chopped fresh dill or
  parsley
1½ teaspoons salt
8oz (225g) 85 per cent wholemeal
  flour
4–6oz (115–170g) unbleached
  white flour, as necessary

Mixing the dough and kneading

Dissolve the yeast in the lukewarm water in a large bowl, or in the bowl of your electric mixer, and stir in the sugar or honey. Let it sit for 10 minutes.

Press the cottage cheese through a sieve, or purée it in a food processor fitted with the steel blade, then stir it into the yeast mixture. Beat in the egg and add the onion, oil, bicarbonate of soda and the herbs. Mix together well.

If kneading the dough by hand. Mix together the wholemeal flour and salt, and fold in, a cupful at a time. As soon as you can, scrape the dough out on to a floured kneading surface. Knead, adding unbleached flour as necessary, for 10 minutes. The dough should be fairly smooth and elastic, and should spring back when indented with the fingers. Shape it into a ball.

If using an electric mixer. Combine the wholemeal flour and salt, and add all at once to the bowl along with 4oz (115g) of the unbleached flour. Mix together with the mixing attachment, then change to the dough hook. Mix at low speed (1 on a Kenwood) for 2 minutes, then at medium speed (2 on a Kenwood) for 6–8 minutes. If the dough seems very wet and sticky, sprinkle in up to 2oz (55g) more unbleached flour. Scrape out the dough on to a lightly floured surface and knead by hand for a minute or so. Shape the dough into a ball.

Rising, forming the loaf and baking

Butter a loaf tin generously. Shape the dough into a loaf and place it in the tin, seam side up first, then seam side down. Brush the top of the loaf with melted butter or oil. Cover it with a lightly dusted tea-towel and let it rise in a warm spot until it has doubled in bulk, or until the dough rises above the sides of the tin – about 2 hours.

Pre-heat the oven to 375°F/190°C/gas mark 5. Bake the bread for 35–40 minutes, until it is golden and sounds hollow when you tap it. Remove it from the tin and cool it on a rack.

Broa – Portuguese Yeast-raised Cornbread

2 SMALL LOAVES

This is a Portuguese country bread. The cornmeal gives it a heavenly sweet flavour and crunchy texture. It's a lovely, moist bread with a thick, hard crust. The dough is slightly sticky, but resilient and not very difficult to handle.

1 tablespoon active dried yeast
12fl. oz (340ml) lukewarm water
1 tablespoon sugar or
   mild-flavoured honey
12oz (340g) stoneground yellow
   cornmeal

1½lb (680g) unbleached white
   flour
8fl. oz lukewarm milk
2 tablespoons sunflower oil
2½ teaspoons salt

Mixing the dough and kneading

Dissolve the yeast in the lukewarm water with the sugar or honey and let it sit for 5 minutes. Add half the cornmeal and 4oz (115g) of the unbleached flour, and stir together 100 times, or until there are no lumps. Cover with clingfilm and a tea-towel and set it in a warm spot for 45 minutes, until bubbling.

Fold the milk into the sponge, then fold in the sunflower oil and the salt. Fold in the remaining cornmeal, and begin folding in the remaining unbleached flour. As soon as you can, scrape the dough out on to a well-floured board, and begin to knead, using a pastry scraper to facilitate folding the dough. Knead for 10 minutes, until the dough is smooth and elastic, frequently flouring your hands and the kneading surface. Shape the dough into a ball.

Rising, forming the loaves and baking

Clean and oil your bowl and place the dough in it, seam side up first, then seam side down. Cover the bowl with clingfilm and a tea-towel, and set it in a warm place for the dough to rise for 1½ hours, or until doubled in bulk.

Punch down the dough, turn it out on to a board and knead for 5 minutes. Shape it into a ball again, place it in the oiled bowl, cover it and let it rise for another hour, or until doubled in bulk.

Turn out the dough on to a floured surface, knead for a few minutes and divide it in two. Shape into two tight, round loaves and place them in oiled, cornmeal-dusted cake tins, or on a baking sheet. Sprinkle the tops with cornmeal or flour. Cover them loosely with a tea-towel and let them rise for 30–45 minutes.

Meanwhile, pre-heat the oven to 500°F/250°C/gas mark 10. Create steam by using the baking-tin method (see p. 12) and spray the loaves and the oven (see p. 12). Place in the hot oven for 15 minutes, spraying every 5 minutes, then turn down the heat to 400°F/200°C/gas mark 6 and bake for another 15 minutes, again spraying every 5 minutes. When the loaves are dark brown and respond to tapping with a hollow sound, remove them from the heat. Cool them on a rack.

Sicilian Bread

1 LARGE OR 2 SMALL LOAVES

This is one of the many gastronomic pleasures of Sicily – a pale yellowish-white loaf with a hard crust covered with sesame seeds. Sicilian bakers shape the bread in a number of ways: rolled into a long cylinder and curled back and forth over itself, or shaped like a small ladder; shaped like a coiled S or as a crown; or simply left as a *baguette* or round loaf – which is the easiest, and to which I have stuck here.

The dough is smooth, stiff and easy to handle. The finished bread has a dense, grainy texture and a satisfying, nutty taste. It's especially nice toasted.

2½ teaspoons active dried yeast
½ pint (285ml) warm water
1 teaspoon malt extract or
   mild-flavoured honey
1 tablespoon olive oil

2 teaspoons salt
1lb (450g) finely ground semolina
   flour
4oz (115g) unbleached white flour
4 tablespoons sesame seeds

Mixing the dough and kneading

Dissolve the yeast in the water in a large bowl, or in the bowl of your electric mixer, and let it sit for 10 minutes. Stir in the malt extract or honey and the olive oil. Mix together the salt and semolina flour.

If kneading the dough by hand. Stir in the semolina flour, a cupful at a time. Place the unbleached flour on your kneading surface, turn out the dough and knead until smooth and firm – about 10 minutes. Shape the dough into a ball.

If using an electric mixer. Add the dry ingredients to the liquid. Mix together with the mixing attachment, then change to the dough hook. Beat at low speed (1 on a Kenwood) for 2 minutes. Beat at medium speed (2 on a Kenwood) for 8 minutes. Scrape the dough out of the bowl and knead for a minute by hand on a lightly floured surface. Shape the dough into a ball.

Rising, forming the loaf and baking

Place the dough in a lightly oiled bowl, seam side up first, then seam side down. Cover the bowl with clingfilm and allow the dough to rise in a warm place until doubled in bulk – about 1¼ hours.

Punch down the dough, knead it a few times on a floured surface, then either shape it into a large round loaf, or into two *baguettes* (see p. 27) or round loaves. Place the loaves on a lightly oiled baking sheet and brush them thoroughly with water. Sprinkle them with the sesame seeds and gently pat the seeds into the dough. Brush again with water. Cover the loaves lightly with a tea-towel and let them rise for an hour, or until doubled in bulk.

Meanwhile, pre-heat the oven to 425°F/220°C/gas mark 7. Place the bread in the oven and spray the loaves with water three times during the first 10 minutes. Turn the heat down to 400°F/200°C/gas mark 6 and bake for 25–30 minutes longer, until the bread is golden-brown and responds to tapping with a hollow sound. Remove it from the heat and cool it on a rack.

Bran Bread

1 LOAF

This is my version of a delicious bran bread made by an excellent baker in Apt, a Provençal town in the valley of the Luberon mountains. It is a very wet dough, best kneaded in an electric mixer; if you don't have a mixer, knead it in the bowl, use a pastry scraper to turn it and keep flouring your hands generously. It resembles the sourdough bran bread on p. 84.

2 teaspoons active dried yeast
¾ pint (425ml) lukewarm water
1 teaspoon mild-flavoured honey
1 tablespoon olive oil
1oz (30g) bran
4oz (115g) coarsely ground
  wholemeal flour

8oz (225g) 85 per cent or 100
  per cent wholemeal flour
2 teaspoons salt
10oz (285g) unbleached white
  flour

Mixing the dough and kneading

Dissolve the yeast in the lukewarm water in a large bowl, or in the bowl of your electric mixer, stir in the honey and let it sit for 10 minutes.

If kneading the dough by hand. Fold the oil and bran into the yeast mixture. Mix together the wholemeal flours and salt, and fold in, a cupful at a time. Begin adding the unbleached flour and, as soon as you can, scrape the dough out on to a well-floured kneading surface, or knead the dough in the bowl (it is very sticky, and this might facilitate kneading). Knead, adding more unbleached flour as necessary, for 10 minutes. The dough will remain sticky.

If using an electric mixer. Combine the bran, flours and salt, and add all at once to the bowl along with the oil. Mix together with the mixing attachment, then change to the dough hook. Mix at low speed (1 on a Kenwood) for 2 minutes, then at medium speed (2 on a Kenwood) for 6–8 minutes. If the dough seems very wet and sticky, sprinkle in up to 2oz (55g) more unbleached flour. Scrape out the dough on to a lightly floured surface and shape it into a ball.

Rising and forming the loaf

Clean and oil your bowl and place the dough in it. Cover the bowl with clingfilm and a tea-towel, and set it in a warm place to rise for 2 hours, or until the dough has doubled in size.

Flour your work surface and your hands well, and scrape out the dough. Knead for a minute or so, flouring your hands and work surface as necessary, and shape the dough into a ball.

If you are using a banneton. Dust the surface of the dough with flour and place it in the *banneton* (see p. 11), rounded side down. Cover it with a tea-towel and let the dough rise in a warm spot for 1–1½ hours, until almost doubled in bulk. You can also let the dough rise in the refrigerator for several hours or overnight.

If you are not using a banneton. Let the dough rise in an oiled bowl for 1–1½ hours, until doubled in bulk. Flour your hands, reshape the dough gently and place it on a baking sheet which has been oiled and sprinkled with cornmeal. Let it rise for about 20 minutes while you pre-heat the oven.

Baking

Pre-heat the oven to 425°F/220°C/gas mark 7, with a baking stone in it if you have one (see p. 12). Turn the dough on to the baking stone, or place the baking sheet on top of the stone, slash the loaf and bake for 40–45 minutes, until the crust is hard and brown, and the bread responds to tapping with a hollow sound. Remove it from the oven and cool it on a rack.

Fougasse

1 LOAF

A *fougasse* is a lattice-shaped bread that is usually made with *baguette* dough in southern France, where it is a speciality. French bakers often add anchovies, olives, nuts or herbs to their *fougasse* dough. My version incorporates a small amount of wholemeal flour, giving the loaf a nutty flavour. The dough is light, pliable and slightly sticky.

2½ teaspoons active dried yeast
12fl. oz (340ml) lukewarm water
1 tablespoon olive oil
2½ teaspoons salt

12oz (340g) unbleached white
flour, plus up to 2oz (55g) extra
for kneading
6oz (170g) wholemeal flour

Optional

4oz (115g) black olives, pitted and
chopped, or 2oz (55g) anchovy
fillets, chopped, or 2oz (55g)

chopped walnuts, or a handful of
chopped fresh herbs (such as
rosemary or thyme)

Mixing the dough and kneading

Dissolve the yeast in the lukewarm water in a large bowl, or in the bowl of your electric mixer, and let it sit for 10 minutes. Stir in the olive oil.

If kneading the dough by hand. Mix together the flours and salt, and fold in, a cupful at a time. As soon as you can, scrape the dough out on to a floured work surface. Knead, adding unbleached white flour as necessary, for 10 minutes. Shape the dough into a ball.

If using an electric mixer. Combine the flours and salt, and add all at once to the bowl. Mix together with the mixing attachment, then change to the dough hook. Mix at low speed (1 on a Kenwood) for 2 minutes, then at medium speed (2 on a Kenwood) for 6–8 minutes. If the dough seems very wet and sticky, sprinkle in up to 2oz (55g) extra unbleached flour. Scrape out the dough on to a lightly floured surface and knead by hand for a minute or so. Shape the dough into a ball.

Rising, forming the loaf and baking

Clean and oil your bowl, and place the dough in it. Cover the bowl with clingfilm and a tea-towel, and set it in a warm place for the dough to rise for 1½ hours, or until it has doubled in size.

Scrape the dough out on to a floured work surface. If adding any of the optional ingredients, sprinkle them over the dough. Knead for a couple of minutes, then press or roll out the dough into a rectangle about 12 inches long by 6–8 inches wide. Place the rectangle length-wise on your work surface. Starting 2 inches from the top, make three incisions across the dough, at equal intervals along its length, to within 2 inches of the sides of the rectangle. Pull the dough apart at these incisions, so that it looks like a ladder with a rung across the top, one across the bottom and two in the middle. Place it on an oiled baking sheet dusted with cornmeal, and cover it with a damp tea-towel. Let it rise for 1½ hours.

Pre-heat the oven to 400°F/200°C/gas mark 6. Bake the bread for 45 minutes, until it is golden and crusty, and responds to tapping with a hollow sound. Remove it from the oven and cool it on a rack.

Sesame Bread Rings

8–12 RINGS

This is my version of a bread sold by street vendors in Cairo and Athens. They string these hard, nutty bracelets of sesame-encrusted bread on thin ropes and sell them throughout the day. I have enriched the recipe by using part wholemeal flour.

This dough is a sticky one, but there is a small amount of it so it isn't too difficult to handle.

1 teaspoon active dried yeast
2fl. oz (60ml) lukewarm water
a pinch of sugar
3fl. oz (90ml) lukewarm milk
1 tablespoon olive or safflower oil
½ teaspoon salt
2oz (55g) 85 per cent wholemeal
  flour

1oz (30g) finely ground semolina
  or semolina flour
3–4oz (85–115g) unbleached
  white flour,
plus extra for kneading
1 egg, beaten
3oz (85g) sesame seeds

Mixing the dough and kneading

Dissolve the yeast in the water and add the pinch of sugar. Let it sit for 10 minutes. Stir in the milk and oil. Combine the wholemeal flour, semolina and salt, and stir into the liquids. Add 3oz (85g) of the unbleached flour and knead for a few minutes in the bowl, adding a little water if the dough is too stiff. Let it rest for 15 minutes.

Now turn the dough out on to a lightly floured board and knead vigorously for 10 minutes, adding more unbleached flour if necessary. Shape the dough into a ball.

Rising, forming the rings and baking

Clean and oil your bowl, and place the dough in it, seam side up first, then seam side down. Cover the bowl with clingfilm and set it in a warm place for the dough to rise for about 2 hours, until doubled in size.

Punch down the dough and turn it out on to your kneading surface. Cut it into 8–12 pieces, and roll out each piece into a thin sausage shape.

Place the sesame seeds on a baking sheet. Brush each sausage-like piece of dough with beaten egg and roll it in the sesame seeds. Then join the ends, so that each piece of dough forms a bracelet-like circle. Brush them again with egg. Place the rings on oiled baking sheets, leaving space for rising, and cover them lightly with greaseproof paper or a tea-towel. Set them in a warm spot to rise for 30 minutes.

Meanwhile, pre-heat the oven to 425°F/230°C/gas mark 8. Bake the rings for 10 minutes, then turn the heat down to 325°F/170°C/gas mark 3 and bake for another 10–20 minutes, until the bread is golden-brown and responds when tapped with a hollow sound. Remove the rings from the heat and cool them on racks.

Cheese and Mustard Bread

1 LOAF

This unique bread smells and tastes like a cheese sandwich, with the cheese and mustard baked right into the loaf. When you toast it, the fragrance of the mustard and cheese emerge. Vary the amount of mustard (see below), depending on how strong you want it to taste. I've made the bread both with Dijon mustard and with a grainy English type, and have liked both equally. The bread freezes well.

2½ teaspoons active dried yeast
4fl. oz (120ml) lukewarm water
4fl. oz (120ml) lukewarm milk
1 tablespoon mild-flavoured honey
1 tablespoon safflower, sunflower or olive oil
1 egg, lightly beaten
2–4oz (55–115g) prepared mustard (such as Dijon, or a grainier mustard)
1 tablespoon grated onion (optional)

4oz (115g) sharp Cheddar cheese, grated
4oz (115g) 85 per cent wholemeal flour
8oz (225g) unbleached white flour, plus up to 4oz (115g) extra for kneading
1¼ teaspoons salt
1 egg, beaten with 2 tablespoons water, for glaze (optional)

Mixing the dough and kneading

Dissolve the yeast in the lukewarm water in a large bowl, or in the bowl of your electric mixer, and let it sit for 10 minutes. Stir in the milk, honey, oil, egg, mustard, onion and cheese.

If kneading the dough by hand. Mix together the flours and salt, and fold into the yeast mixture, a cupful at a time. As soon as you can, scrape out the dough on to a floured work surface. Knead, adding unbleached white flour as necessary, for 10 minutes. Shape the dough into a ball.

If using an electric mixer. Combine the flours and salt, and add all at once to the bowl with the yeast mixture. Mix together with the mixing attachment, then change to the dough hook. Mix at low speed (1 on a Kenwood) for 2 minutes, then at medium speed (2 on a Kenwood) for 6–8 minutes. If the dough seems very wet and sticky, sprinkle in up to 2oz (55g) more unbleached flour. Scrape out the dough on to a lightly floured surface and knead by hand for a minute or so. Shape the dough into a ball.

Rising, forming the loaf and baking

Clean and oil your bowl and place the dough in it, seam side up first, then seam side down. Cover the bowl with clingfilm and a tea-towel, and set it in a warm place to rise for 1½ hours, or until the dough has doubled in size.

Punch down the dough and turn it out on to your work surface. Knead for a minute, then shape it into a loaf. Oil a loaf tin and place the dough in it, seam side up first, then seam side down. Cover it with a towel and let the dough rise in a warm spot for an hour, or until it rises above the edges of the tin.

Towards the end of the rising time, pre-heat the oven to 350°F/ 180°C/gas mark 4. Slash the top of the loaf, brush it with glaze if desired, and bake for 50 minutes, until the loaf is golden-brown and responds to tapping with a hollow sound. Remove it from the tin and cool it on a rack.

Alternative method

The flavours in the dough develop overnight using this method. After the first kneading, let the dough rise in an oiled bowl for 30 minutes. Shape it into a loaf and place it in the oiled loaf tin. Cover it loosely with clingfilm and refrigerate overnight. In the morning, remove it from the refrigerator and let it stand in a warm place for 45 minutes, while you pre-heat the oven. Bake as above.

Challah

2 VERY LARGE OR 3 MEDIUM-SIZED LOAVES

Challah is a rich, eggy bread. The loaves are braided and shiny with glaze, beautiful to look at and heavenly to eat. Traditional *challah* is made with white flour only, but I like adding a little wholemeal for its nutty flavour and nutritional value. This dough is smooth and easy to work with.

4fl. oz (120ml) lukewarm water
1 tablespoon active dried yeast
8fl. oz (225ml) lukewarm milk
3 eggs
3 tablespoons mild-flavoured honey
1lb (450g) unbleached white flour,
    plus up to 2oz (55g) extra for
    kneading

4 tablespoons melted unsalted butter
    or sunflower oil
2½ teaspoons salt
8oz (225g) 85 per cent wholemeal
    flour or wholemeal pastry flour
1 egg, beaten with 2 tablespoons
    water, for glaze
2–3 tablespoons poppy seeds or
    sesame seeds (optional)

Mixing the dough and kneading

Dissolve the yeast in the lukewarm water in a large bowl, or in the bowl of your electric mixer, and let it sit for 10 minutes. Beat in the warm milk, the eggs and the honey. Whisk in 12oz (340g) of the unbleached white flour, a cupful at a time, to make a sponge. Stir 100 times, changing direction every now and then, cover with clingfilm and set it in a warm spot for an hour.

If kneading the dough by hand. Fold the melted butter or oil into the sponge. Mix together the remaining unbleached flour and salt, and fold in. Begin adding the wholemeal flour, and as soon as you can, scrape the dough out on to your kneading surface. Knead, adding more flour as necessary, for 10 minutes. The dough should be stiff, very elastic and somewhat silky. Shape it into a ball.

If using an electric mixer. Combine the remaining flours and salt, and add all at once to the bowl along with the melted butter or oil. Mix together with the mixing attachment, then change to the dough hook. Mix at low speed (1 on a Kenwood) for 2 minutes, then at medium speed (2 on a Kenwood) for 6–8 minutes. If the dough seems very wet and sticky, sprinkle in up to 2oz (55g) more unbleached flour. Scrape out the dough on to a lightly floured surface and knead by hand for a minute or so. The dough should be stiff, very elastic and somewhat silky. Shape it into a ball.

Rising, forming the loaves and baking

Clean and oil your bowl and place the dough in it, seam side up first, then seam side down. Cover the bowl with clingfilm and a tea-towel, and set it in a warm place for the dough to rise for 1½ hours, or until it has doubled in size.

Punch down the dough and turn it out on to your lightly floured work surface. Divide the dough into six equal pieces for very large loaves, nine pieces for medium-sized loaves. Shape each piece into a ball and cover lightly with clingfilm.

Take three balls, shape each one into a rectangle, as if you were making a thin *baguette* (see p. 27), then shape it into a thin, tight cylinder about 12–14 inches long. Attach three cylinders by pinching the ends together at one end, and fold the pinched part under. Make a braid with the three long dough cylinders. Fold the other end under, place the braid on an oiled baking sheet and brush it with oil. Repeat the braiding process with the remaining dough, using two baking sheets if necessary.

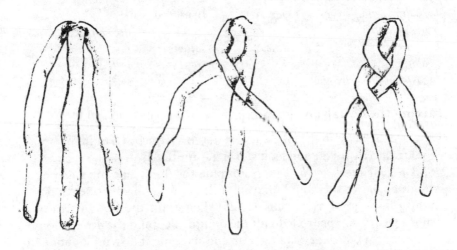

Brush the loaves with glaze, then sprinkle with poppy seeds or sesame seeds if desired. Brush again with glaze to stick the seeds on. Cover with a clean, dry tea-towel and set in a warm spot to rise for 30 minutes.

Meanwhile, pre-heat the oven to 375°F/190°C/gas mark 5. Bake for 40 minutes, brushing the loaves again with glaze halfway through baking. Remove them from the oven and cool them on a rack.

Brioche

2 LOAVES OR 8 OR 9 SMALL *BRIOCHES*

The first time I saw a recipe for *brioche* I couldn't believe the amount of butter in it. I made the rich, eggy bread and realised why it always tastes so luxurious. When I took a pastry course at the Ecole de Gastronomie Française Ritz-Escoffier in Paris I made *brioche* again, and their recipe had even more butter in it than the first one I had used (James Beard's version, I think that was). There was half as much butter as flour, which adds up to almost a tablespoon per serving. It's just too much for my taste, so I have reduced the amount by a third in my recipe. This version is based on the Ritz recipe, but I will never be able to make the dough as smooth as the baker who taught that class. Nevertheless, it makes a delicious *brioche*. *Brioche* is one of my *péchés mignons* – sinful foods I can't resist!

2 teaspoons active dried yeast	3 tablespoons white sugar (use
4 tablespoons lukewarm water	2 tablespoons for a less sweet
4 medium or large eggs, at room	brioche)
temperature	4oz (115g) unsalted butter,
12–14oz (340–395g) unbleached	softened
white flour	1 egg, beaten, for glaze
1 teaspoon salt	

Mixing the dough and kneading

Dissolve the yeast in the lukewarm water in a large bowl or in the bowl of your electric mixer and let it sit for 5 minutes. Beat in the eggs.

If kneading the dough by hand. Combine the flour, salt and sugar and add gradually to the liquid mixture, folding in with a wooden spoon. Lightly flour your work surface and scrape out the dough. Knead, using a pastry scraper to help lift the dough, slapping the dough down on to the work surface, pulling it up and slapping it down for about 15 minutes, flouring your hands often. The dough will be sticky. When it begins to come away from your fingers easily, knead in the butter by placing the butter on the dough, pushing it in and squeezing the buttery dough between your fingers. Lift and slap the dough down, then squeeze it through your fingers again. Continue until the butter has been amalgamated into the dough.

If using an electric mixer. Add the flour, sugar and salt to the liquids. Beat them together using the mixing attachment, then change to the dough hook. Beat at low speed (1 on a Kenwood) for a minute, and at medium speed (2 on a Kenwood) for 8 minutes. Add the softened butter and beat for 2 minutes longer, or until the butter is amalgamated.

Rising, forming the brioches and baking

Cover the bowl with clingfilm and a tea-towel and place it in a warm spot for the dough to rise for an hour. Punch down the dough, cover again and let it rise for another hour.

Punch down the dough again, then scrape it out on to your work surface. Weigh the dough and divide it into two equal pieces, or eight or nine pieces for small *brioches*.

Shaping large brioches. These can take on several shapes. They can have a top-knot and be baked in a fluted mould – the traditional *brioche* shape; they can be made in tall cylindrical moulds (these are called *mousseline brioches*); or they can be baked in loaf tins, either like a split loaf made by placing two equal-sized round balls side by side in the tin, or like a normal loaf.

To make the traditional large top-knotted *brioches*, weigh each piece of dough and divide it into two, one piece weighing one-third of the total weight, the other weighing two-thirds. Shape tight balls with each of these pieces. Butter *brioche* tins generously. Place the larger ball in a tin and make a depression in the centre with your thumb. Place the smaller ball on top of this depression and press it down lightly.

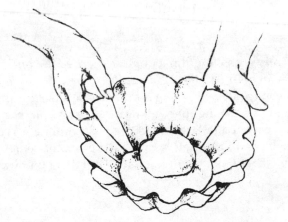

For split *brioches*, divide each piece into two balls and place these side by side in small buttered loaf tins.

Shaping small brioches. Shape the dough into tight balls. Make a circle with your thumb and forefinger, and grab the dough about one-third of the way down. Squeeze the dough so that you form a 'neck' and a small top-knot. Then press this top-knot down into the centre of the remaining ball so that it sits squarely on top. Place it in a buttered *brioche* mould. Repeat with the remaining pieces.

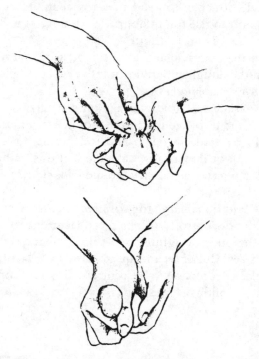

Cover the *brioches* with clingfilm and place them in the refrigerator for the final rise – an hour or a little longer.

Pre-heat the oven to 400°F/200°C/gas mark 6. Heat baking sheets in the oven. Brush the *brioches* lightly with beaten egg and place them on the hot baking sheets. Bake large *brioches* for 30 minutes, brushing again with glaze halfway through baking. Bake small *brioches* for 15 minutes. Remove them from the moulds and cool them on racks.

Croissants

12 CROISSANTS

The rich flaky layers in a *croissant* are thin layers of dough spread with lots of butter. I learned to make them at the Ecole de Gastronomie Française Ritz-Escoffier in Paris; this recipe is based on theirs but, as always, I've reduced the amount of butter.

1 teaspoon active dried yeast
6fl. oz (180ml) water, at room
  temperature
2 tablespoons white sugar
2 tablespoons double cream

1 teaspoon salt
11oz (300g) unbleached white
  flour
4oz (115g) cold unsalted butter
1 egg, beaten, for glaze

Mixing the dough and kneading

Dissolve the yeast in the water in a large bowl, or in the bowl of your electric mixer, and let it sit for 10 minutes.

If kneading the dough by hand. Add the sugar and cream to the water. Mix together the flour and salt, and fold into the liquid. As soon as you can, scrape the dough out on to a lightly floured board and knead for 10–15 minutes. The dough will be sticky. Shape it into a ball.

If using an electric mixer. Add the sugar and cream to the liquid. Mix together the flour and salt and add to the bowl. Mix together using the mixing attachment, then scrape the dough off the mixing attachment and change to the dough hook. Knead at low speed (1 on a Kenwood) for 2 minutes, then at medium speed (2 on a Kenwood) for 6–8 minutes, adding more unbleached flour if the dough is very sticky. Scrape it out of the bowl and shape it into a ball.

Rising, forming the croissants and baking

Clean the bowl and place the dough in it. Cover it with clingfilm and a tea-towel, and set it in a warm spot for the dough to rise for 2 hours.

Punch down the dough, cover it and let it rise in the refrigerator for an hour.

Turning the dough. Roll out the dough into a square about ⅜ inch thick, slightly thicker in the centre. Place the butter on the table and slap it with a rolling pin to soften it. Place it in the centre of the dough, then fold in the sides of the dough over the butter all the way around to enclose it completely. Now roll out this piece of dough into a rect-angle, three times longer than it is wide.

First turn: fold the dough like a business letter, so that you have three layers. Give the dough a quarter-turn, so that the edge of the top layer is now facing right. Place the dough in a plastic bag and put it in the refrigerator for 10 minutes.

Turns two and three: with the top edge of the dough still facing right, roll out the dough again so that it is three times longer than it is wide. Fold it again like a business letter, then give it another quarter-turn. Place it in the plastic bag and refrigerate it again for 10 minutes. Repeat once more, refrigerating for 10 minutes after the third turn.

Cutting and shaping the croissants. Roll out the dough to a thickness of about ⅛ inch. Cut the dough into bands about 8 inches wide, then cut each band crosswise into triangles, about 4–5 inches wide at the wide end. Roll up the triangles, beginning at the wide end, and curl the ends in slightly once the crescents are rolled up.

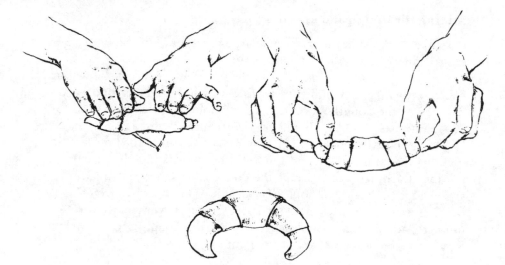

Line baking sheets with greaseproof paper, or butter non-stick baking sheets. Place the *croissants* on the baking sheets, leaving space between each one. Cover them loosely with a tea-towel and let them rise in a warm spot for 1½ hours.

Pre-heat the oven to 400°F/200°C/gas mark 6. Brush the *croissants* with beaten egg and bake them for 18 minutes, until brown. Cool them on a rack.

6: Sweet and Spicy Yeasted Breads and Quick Breads

I've lumped together my recipes for sweet yeasted breads and for quick breads in one chapter. Sweet usually means spicy too; many of the loaves you will find in this chapter are fragrant with spices like cinnamon, anise, nutmeg, allspice and cloves. They are speciality breads – breads to give as gifts, to have on hand for treats for the children, to slice thin and eat with tea, or to serve for a special breakfast or brunch. As Christmas nears my kitchen becomes strewn with these recipes and my cupboards filled with dried fruit, honey and spices. A nice braided bread with currants and spices, a hefty bread bursting with fruit, or a *pain d'épices* which gets better as the days go by make perfect presents for friends and neighbours.

Unlike many sweet breads sold in wholefood shops and bakeries, mine are not cloying or heavy. They are as healthful as can be, without sacrificing flavour and lightness. The fruit and spices in many of these recipes reduces the need for vast quantities of sugar or honey.

There are many more sweet yeasted and chemically raised breads in Chapter 4, on English breads. The ones given here are inspired by American and Scandinavian recipes.

Spicy Challah with Currants

2 VERY LARGE OR 3 MEDIUM-SIZED LOAVES

This is a special, slightly sweet *challah* which I usually make for Christmas gifts during the holiday season. The method is exactly the same as for the basic *challah* (p. 188) and the dough is similar. There are just a few more flavourful ingredients in it.

4fl. oz (120ml) lukewarm water
1 tablespoon active dried yeast
8fl. oz (225ml) lukewarm milk
3 eggs
4 tablespoons mild-flavoured honey
1 teaspoon vanilla essence
½ teaspoon ground allspice
½ teaspoon ground cardamom
2 tablespoons freshly grated orange rind
1lb (450g) unbleached white flour, plus up to 2oz (55g) extra for kneading

4 tablespoons melted unsalted butter or sunflower oil
2½ teaspoons salt
8oz (225g) 85 per cent wholemeal flour or wholemeal pastry flour
4oz (115g) currants
1 egg, beaten with 2 tablespoons water, for glaze
2–3 tablespoons poppy seeds or sesame seeds (optional)

Mixing the dough and kneading

Dissolve the yeast in the lukewarm water in a large bowl, or in the bowl of your electric mixer, and let it sit for 10 minutes. Beat in the warm milk, eggs, honey, vanilla, allspice, cardamom and orange rind. Whisk in 12oz (340g) of the unbleached flour, a cupful at a time, to make a sponge. Stir 100 times, changing direction every now and then, cover with clingfilm and set in a warm spot for an hour.

If kneading the dough by hand. Fold the melted butter or oil into the sponge. Mix together the remaining unbleached flour and salt, and fold in. Begin adding the wholemeal flour, and as soon as you can, scrape the dough out on to a floured work surface. Knead, adding flour as necessary, for 10 minutes. The dough should be stiff, very elastic and somewhat silky. Shape it into a ball.

If using an electric mixer. Combine the remaining flours and salt, and add all at once to the bowl along with the melted butter or oil. Mix together with the mixing attachment, then change to the dough hook. Mix at low speed (1 on a Kenwood) for 2 minutes, then at medium speed (2 on a Kenwood) for 6–8 minutes. If the dough seems very wet and sticky, sprinkle in up to 2oz (55g) more unbleached flour. Scrape out the dough on to a lightly floured surface and knead by hand for a minute or so. The dough should be stiff, very elastic and somewhat silky. Shape it into a ball.

Rising, forming the loaves and baking

Clean and oil your bowl and place the dough in it, seam side up first, then seam side down. Cover the bowl with clingfilm and a tea-towel, and set it in a warm place for the dough to rise for 1½ hours, or until it has doubled in size.

Punch down the dough and turn it out on to your lightly floured work surface. Press out the dough and sprinkle the currants over the top. Fold the dough over and knead until the currants are evenly distributed. Divide the dough into six equal pieces for very large loaves, nine pieces for medium-sized loaves. Shape each piece into a ball and cover them lightly with clingfilm.

Take three balls, shape each one into a rectangle, as if you were making a thin *baguette* (see p. 27), then shape it into a thin, tight cylinder, about 12–14 inches long. Attach three cylinders by pinching the ends together at one end, and fold the pinched part under. Make a braid with the three long dough cylinders. Fold the other end under, then place the braid on an oiled baking sheet and brush it with oil. Repeat the braiding process with the remaining dough, using two baking sheets if necessary.

Brush the loaves with glaze, then sprinkle them with poppy seeds or sesame seeds if desired. Brush them again with glaze to attach the seeds on. Cover the loaves with a clean, dry tea-towel, and set them in a warm spot to rise for 30 minutes.

Meanwhile, pre-heat the oven to 375°F/190°C/gas mark 5. Bake for 40 minutes, brushing the loaves again with glaze halfway through baking. Remove them from the oven and cool them on a rack.

Traditional Anadama Bread

2 SMALL LOAVES

Anadama bread is a traditional American bread containing black treacle and cornmeal. Some versions are made with wholemeal flour, others with unbleached white. The dough is dense because of the cornmeal, and extremely wet and sticky. In fact, it's so sticky that it's hard to believe that it will really become bread. It is more like a batter than a dough, but I still manage to knead it by using a pastry scraper to fold the dough, and resigning myself to very sticky hands. The bread has a grainy texture and a sweet, earthy flavour.

Legend has it that the bread originated in Massachusetts when a lazy woman named Anna abandoned her husband in the midst of preparing the evening meal, which consisted of nothing more than cornmeal mush and molasses (treacle). Her husband came home, found the cornmeal mush and molasses, and angrily mixed them together, adding yeast, flour and water and muttering all the while, 'Anna, damn her'.

2 tablespoon unsalted butter
3fl. oz (90ml) black treacle (about 6 tablespoons)
1 pint (570ml) water
8oz (225g) stoneground yellow cornmeal
2 teaspoons salt

1 tablespoon active dried yeast
4 fl. oz (120ml) additional lukewarm water
8oz (225g) wholemeal flour
1lb (450g) unbleached white flour, plus 4oz (115g) extra for kneading

Mixing the dough and kneading

Heat together the butter, treacle and 1 pint (570ml) of water, stirring until the butter has melted. Stir in the cornmeal and the salt. Set it aside and allow it to cool to lukewarm.

Dissolve the yeast in the 4fl. oz (120ml) lukewarm water in a large bowl or in the bowl of your electric mixer and let it sit for 10 minutes.

When the cornmeal mixture has cooled to lukewarm, stir it into the yeast mixture and mix well.

If kneading the dough by hand. Fold in the wholemeal flour, then begin to fold in the unbleached flour. As soon as you can, flour your work surface and scrape out the dough. Begin to knead, flouring your hands often and adding flour to the work surface as necessary. The dough is so sticky that kneading will be more like pulling and pressing than neatly folding and leaning. Knead for 10–15 minutes, until the dough is elastic. It won't stop being sticky. Shape the dough into a ball.

If using an electric mixer. Add the wholemeal flour and 1lb (450g) unbleached flour to the yeast-and-cornmeal mixture in the bowl of your mixer. Mix together with the mixing attachment, then scrape the dough off the mixing attachment and change to the dough hook. Knead at low speed (1 on a Kenwood) for 2 minutes, then at medium speed (2 on a Kenwood) for 6 minutes. Add extra unbleached flour if the dough seems too liquid. Scrape out the dough on to a floured surface and knead by hand for a minute, then shape it into a ball.

Rising, forming the loaves and baking

Clean and oil or butter your bowl and place the dough in it. Cover the bowl with clingfilm and a tea-towel and set it in a warm spot for the dough to rise for about 1½ hours, until it has doubled in bulk.

Sprinkle some flour on top of the dough, punch it down and scrape it out on to your work surface. Knead again for a couple of minutes, then divide the dough in half. It will still be sticky and formless, like thick, stretchy batter. Shape each piece into balls and let them sit for 5 minutes. Shape them into loaves and put them in two buttered 8-inch loaf tins, upside down first, then right side up. Cover them with a dry tea-towel and set them in a warm spot until the loaves rise about ½ inch higher than the edges of the tins – about 45 minutes.

Meanwhile, pre-heat the oven to 400°F/200°C/gas mark 6. Slash the loaves and bake for 15 minutes, then turn the heat down to 350°F/180°C/gas mark 4 and bake for another 35–40 minutes, until the bread is golden and responds to tapping with a hollow sound. Remove the loaves from the oven and cool them on racks.

Cranberry Orange Anadama Bread

2 SMALL LOAVES

This is a more festive version of anadama bread (p. 198), sweet with orange juice, honey and treacle, and tart with cranberries. It has the same close crumb as the basic anadama bread and the dough is dense and extremely sticky, like a batter bread.

¾ pint (425ml) orange juice
4oz (115g) stoneground yellow
  cornmeal
3fl. oz (90ml) black treacle
1 scant tablespoon active dried yeast
4fl. oz (120ml) lukewarm water
8oz (225g) wholemeal flour
6oz (170g) whole raw cranberries
1 tablespoon grated orange rind

1 tablespoon mild-flavoured honey
2 tablespoons melted unsalted butter
  or safflower oil
2 teaspoons salt
up to 12oz (370g) unbleached
  white flour
1 egg, beaten with 3 tablespoons
  water, for glaze

Mixing the dough and kneading

Warm the orange juice in a heavy-bottomed saucepan until bubbles form around the rim of the pan. Gradually add the cornmeal in a slow stream, stirring constantly with a wooden spoon. Reduce the heat to low and stir constantly, scraping the cornmeal up from the sides and bottom of the pan, until the mixture is thick. This will take a few minutes. Remove the pan from the heat, stir in the treacle, and allow to cool to lukewarm.

Dissolve the yeast in the warm water in a large bowl, or in the bowl of your electric mixer. When the cornmeal mixture has cooled, add it to the yeast and water. Stir in half the wholemeal flour, stir about 100 times (the mixture will be stiff and difficult to stir), and cover with clingfilm and a tea-towel. Set it in a warm spot for 30 minutes.

Meanwhile, put the cranberries, orange rind and honey in a blender or food processor and blend until the cranberries are coarsely chopped.

If kneading the dough by hand. Fold the melted butter or oil into the cornmeal-and-yeast mixture. Fold in the cranberry mixture, the salt and the remaining wholemeal flour. Add sufficient unbleached flour to make a dough stiff enough to scrape out on to your kneading surface. Flour your board and begin to knead, flouring your hands and the board often. The dough will be thick and sticky. Knead for 10–15 minutes, adding flour as necessary. By the end of the kneading your dough will be stiff and elastic, but it may still be a bit tacky. Shape it into a ball.

If using an electric mixer. Add the melted butter or oil, the cranberry mixture, the salt, remaining wholemeal flour and 8oz (225g) unbleached flour to the cornmeal-and-yeast mixture. Beat together with the mixing attachment, then scrape the dough off the mixing attachment and change to the dough hook. Beat at low speed (1 on a Kenwood) for 2 minutes, then at medium speed (2 on a Kenwood) for 6 minutes. Add extra unbleached flour if the dough seems too liquid. Scrape out the dough on to a floured surface and knead by hand for a minute, then shape it into a ball.

Rising, forming the loaves and baking

Clean your bowl, oil it and place the dough in it, seam side up first, then seam side down. Cover the bowl and set it in a warm place for the dough to rise for 1–1½ hours, until it has doubled in bulk.

Meanwhile, oil or butter two 8-inch loaf tins, or oil a baking sheet and sprinkle it with cornmeal. Turn out the dough and divide it in half. Form each piece into a ball and allow the dough to rest for 5 minutes before forming loaves, if baking in tins. (The dough will be so sticky that you may just have to pat it into the tins rather than forming loaves, which is fine.) Place the loaves in the prepared tins or on the baking sheet. Set them in a warm place and allow them to rise until the tops are higher than the tops of the tins – about 1½ hours.

Towards the end of the rising time, pre-heat the oven to 350°F/180°C/gas mark 4. Slash the loaves and brush them with glaze. Bake for 50 minutes, brushing them once again with glaze halfway through baking. When the loaves are dark brown and respond to tapping with a hollow sound, remove them from the heat and cool them on racks.

Swedish Limpa

1 LARGE LOAF OR 2 SMALLER LOAVES

This sweet, subtly spiced bread is adapted from a James Beard recipe. Like all rye-based doughs, it is sticky and unwieldy – you'll have to be patient. The finished bread is dense, with a fine texture. It toasts beautifully.

1 tablespoon active dried yeast
4 tablespoons lukewarm water
¾ pint (425ml) bitter, heated to
  lukewarm
6 tablespoons mild-flavoured honey
1 teaspoon ground cardamom
1 teaspoon crushed anise seeds
2 tablespoons grated orange rind

10oz (285g) rye flour
up to 1lb (450g) unbleached white
  flour, as necessary
2 tablespoons melted unsalted butter
  or safflower oil
2 teaspoons salt
1 egg, beaten with 2 tablespoons
  water, for glaze (optional)

Mixing the dough and kneading

Dissolve the yeast in the water in a large bowl, or in the bowl of your electric mixer, and let it sit for 10 minutes. Add the bitter, honey, cardamom, anise seeds and orange rind and mix together well.

Mix together the flours and fold 12oz (340g) into the yeast mixture. Stir 100 times, cover with clingfilm or a damp tea-towel, and set this sponge in a warm place for an hour.

Stir the sponge and fold in the melted butter or oil and the salt.

If kneading the dough by hand. Fold in additional flour until you can turn out the dough, which will be sticky, on to a floured kneading surface. Knead for 10–15 minutes, adding only enough flour to make the dough workable. When the dough is stiff, form it into a ball.

If using an electric mixer. Add the remaining flour all at once to the bowl. Mix together with the mixing attachment, then change to the dough hook. Mix at low speed (1 on a Kenwood) for 2 minutes, then at medium speed (2 on a Kenwood) for 6–8 minutes. If the dough seems very wet and sticky, sprinkle in up to 2oz (55g) more unbleached white flour. Scrape the dough out on to a lightly floured surface and knead by hand for a minute or so. Shape it into a ball.

Rising, forming the loaf and baking

Clean and oil your bowl and place the dough in it, seam side up first, then seam side down. Cover the bowl with clingfilm and a tea-towel, and set it in a warm place for the dough to rise for 1½ hours, or until it has doubled in size.

Punch down the dough and shape it into one large ball or two smaller balls. Place them on an oiled baking sheet, brush with oil or melted butter, cover loosely with greaseproof paper or clingfilm, and refrigerate for 2–3 hours.

Remove the loaves from the refrigerator and let them sit for 15 minutes while you pre-heat the oven to 375°F/190°C/gas mark 5. Bake for an hour for a large loaf, 40–45 minutes for smaller loaves, or until the bread is golden-brown and sounds hollow when tapped on the bottom. Cool it on a rack.

Fruit-filled Bread

1 VERY LARGE LOAF

This is a big, rich bread, bursting with a sweet, spicy dried-fruit filling. The finished bread is quite heavy, but that's because of all the fruit; the dough is fairly light. Make it for a Sunday breakfast. It also makes a nice gift.

For the filling

8oz (250g) dried figs, or prunes, or
  apricots, or dates, or raisins, or a
  combination of any of these
8fl. oz (225ml) orange juice
2fl. oz (60ml) water, as necessary
1 teaspoon ground cinnamon
¼ teaspoon freshly grated nutmeg

1 tablespoon grated orange rind
  (optional)
3 tablespoons mild-flavoured honey
1 teaspoon vanilla essence
2 tablespoons melted unsalted butter
2oz (55g) chopped walnuts
  (optional)

For the dough

2½ teaspoons active dried yeast
2fl. oz (60ml) lukewarm water
4fl. oz (120ml) freshly squeezed
  orange juice
4fl. oz (120ml) lukewarm milk
2–3 tablespoons mild-flavoured
  honey (to taste)
2 eggs, beaten
3 tablespoons melted unsalted butter
  or sunflower oil

8oz (225g) 85 per cent wholemeal
  flour
12oz (340g) unbleached white
  flour
1½ teaspoons salt
1 egg, mixed with 2 tablespoons
  water and 1 teaspoon sugar, for
  glaze

Making the filling

The night before. Pour the orange juice over the fruit and let it soak overnight.

On the day you wish to bake. Drain the orange juice over a saucepan. Remove 4fl. oz (120ml) and add the fruit to the saucepan. Add 2fl. oz (60ml) water if most of the remaining orange juice has been absorbed by the fruit. Add the other ingredients, except the walnuts and melted butter. Bring to a simmer and simmer over a medium heat until the mixture is thick. Remove the pan from the heat and stir in the walnuts and butter. Set aside while you make the dough.

Mixing the dough and kneading

Dissolve the yeast in the lukewarm water in a large bowl, or in the bowl of your electric mixer, and let it sit for 10 minutes. Stir in the orange juice, honey, milk, butter or oil and eggs.

If kneading the dough by hand. Mix together the flours and salt, and fold in, a cupful at a time. As soon as you can, scrape out the dough on to a floured kneading surface. Knead, adding more unbleached flour as necessary, for 10 minutes. Shape the dough into a ball.

If using an electric mixer. Combine the flours and salt, and add all at once to the bowl. Mix together with the mixing attachment, then change to the dough hook. Mix at low speed (1 on a Kenwood) for 2 minutes, then at medium speed (2 on a Kenwood) for 6–8 minutes. If the dough seems very wet and sticky, sprinkle in up to 2oz (55g) more unbleached flour. Scrape the dough out on to a lightly floured surface and knead by hand for a minute or so. Shape the dough into a ball.

Rising, forming the loaf and baking

Clean and oil your bowl and place the dough in it, seam side up first, then seam side down. Cover the bowl with clingfilm and a tea-towel, and set it in a warm place for the dough to rise for 1½ hours, or until it has doubled in size.

Punch down the dough and turn it out on to your work surface. Shape it into a ball, then roll it out into a long, wide rectangle – about 12 × 14 inches. Spread the fruit lengthwise down the centre of the rectangle. Fold in both short ends over the fruit. There are two ways to construct the loaf (see illustrations, pp. 205–6):

1. Fold one side of the dough all the way over the fruit, and the other side over this, then pinch together the top layer with the side of the

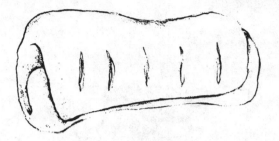

dough. Take a sharp knife and cut slits across the top of the dough at 1½-inch intervals, all down the length of the dough. *Or:*

2. Cut the sides of the dough on either side of the filling into 1½-inch strips, and fold the strips over the fruit, overlapping the strips and pulling and twisting the dough to cover the fruit entirely.

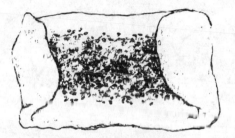

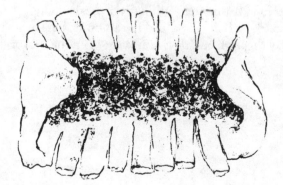

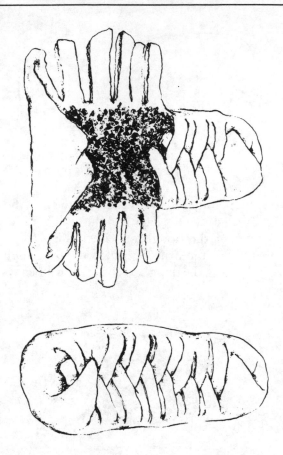

Carefully transfer the dough to a buttered baking sheet and brush it with the glaze. It will be quite heavy with all the fruit in it. Let it rise in a warm place for 20 minutes, while you pre-heat the oven to 350°F/180°C/gas mark 4. Bake the bread for an hour, brushing it again with glaze halfway through baking. Remove it from the heat and cool it on a rack.

Pecan Rolls

2 DOZEN ROLLS

These pecan rolls resemble French *pains aux raisins* in shape and flavour, but they have much less butter and are made in part with wholemeal pastry flour. The dough is very sticky, but once it has risen it is not difficult to roll out and finish the rolls. These make a real breakfast treat.

6oz (170g) raisins or sultanas
boiling water to cover the raisins
6fl. oz (180ml) lukewarm milk
4fl. oz (120ml) lukewarm orange
  juice
1 tablespoon active dried yeast
6 tablespoons mild-flavoured honey
6 tablespoons safflower oil or
  melted unsalted butter
2 eggs, beaten
1 teaspoon salt

½ teaspoon ground mace or nutmeg
8oz (225g) wholemeal flour
1¼lb (565g) unbleached white
  flour, or as necessary
4 tablespoons additional unsalted
  butter, melted
2 tablespoons additional
  mild-flavoured honey
ground cinnamon
6oz (170g) chopped pecans

For the topping

6 tablespoons unsalted butter,
  melted
4 tablespoons mild-flavoured
  honey, warmed with the butter

½ teaspoon ground cinnamon
1 egg, beaten with 2 tablespoons
  water, for glaze

Mixing the dough and kneading

Soak the raisins or sultanas in enough boiling water to cover them for 15 minutes, then drain them over a bowl. Retain 4fl. oz (120ml) of the water and allow it to cool to lukewarm.

Dissolve the yeast in the cooled water from the raisins, and add the milk, orange juice and honey. Let it sit for about 10 minutes.

If kneading the dough by hand. Stir the safflower oil or melted butter into the yeast mixture, then add the eggs and raisins or sultanas. Mix together the wholemeal flour, salt and spices and fold in, a cupful at a time. Begin folding in the unbleached flour and when the dough comes away from the sides of the bowl, turn it out on to a floured surface. The dough will be very sticky. Knead for 10–15 minutes, using a pastry scraper to help turn the dough and adding flour to the kneading surface as necessary. Shape the dough into a ball.

If using an electric mixer. Add the safflower oil or melted butter to the yeast mixture, then add the eggs and raisins or sultanas. Mix together the flours, spices and salt and add to the mixture all at once. Mix together with the mixing attachment, then change to the dough hook. Knead at low speed (1 on a Kenwood) for 2 minutes, then at medium speed (2 on a Kenwood) for 8 minutes. Turn out the dough on to your floured work surface, knead it by hand a few times and shape it into a ball.

Rising, forming the rolls and baking

Clean the bowl and oil it. Place the dough in it, seam side down, then seam side up. Cover with clingfilm and a damp tea-towel and let the dough rise in a warm place for 1½–2 hours, until doubled in bulk.

Punch down the dough, knead it a few times and cut it in two. Roll out each half into a large rectangle (about 12 × 14 inches) about ¼ inch thick.

Melt the additional 4 tablespoons butter and the 2 tablespoons honey together over a low heat. Brush the rectangles with this mixture and sprinkle them generously with cinnamon. Divide the pecans in half and spread them evenly over each rectangle. Roll up the dough lengthwise, tightly, like a Swiss roll.

Cut each cylinder into twelve rolls, about 1½–2 inches thick. Place them on buttered baking sheets and cover them lightly with a floured tea-towel or greaseproof paper. Set them in a warm place to rise for an hour.

Melt together the butter and honey for the topping, and add the cinnamon. Brush the rolls gently with this mixture, then brush them with the glaze.

Pre-heat the oven to 400°F/200°C/gas mark 6. Bake for 15–20 minutes, until golden-brown. Five minutes before the end of baking, brush the rolls again with the glaze. Remove them from the heat, carefully lift them from the baking sheets with a spatula and cool them on a rack.

Pain d'Epices

1 LOAF

This French spice bread is rich and sweet with honey and spices, and very easy to make. The garam masala, which is my own addition to a traditional recipe, gives the bread a peppery flavour. The spices ripen over time and the bread tastes best a few days after it is made. It goes wonderfully with tea. This is another bread I often make to give away at Christmas.

4oz (115g) unsalted butter
4fl. oz (120ml) strong-flavoured honey
6fl. oz (180ml) milk
1 egg
8oz (225g) 85 per cent wholemeal flour
2oz (55g) unbleached white flour

1 teaspoon bicarbonate of soda
1½ tablespoons ground anise
¼ teaspoon ground allspice
½ teaspoon garam masala
½ teaspoon freshly grated nutmeg
¼ teaspoon ground ginger
¼ teaspoon ground cloves
¼ teaspoon salt

Pre-heat the oven to 375°F/190°C/gas mark 5. Butter a loaf tin or a special tin for *pain d'épices*, and line it with buttered greaseproof paper.

Cream together the butter and honey. Beat in the milk and egg. Sift together the flours, bicarbonate of soda, spices and salt. Stir into the liquid ingredients and mix together well.

Turn the batter into the prepared loaf tin and bake for 50–60 minutes, or until a knife inserted into the centre comes out clean. Remove the loaf from the heat and let it cool for 10–15 minutes in the tin, then turn it out on to a rack. Carefully peel off the greaseproof paper and let the bread cool completely. Wrap it tightly in foil and let it sit for several days before eating. This will keep for two weeks.

Boston Brown Bread

2 LARGE OR SEVERAL SMALL LOAVES

This is one of my favourite American breads. It is practically black in colour, with a moist, chewy, wholesome texture. The bread is steamed like a Christmas pudding and has great staying power if kept in the refrigerator in a well-sealed plastic bag. I love it at breakfast or tea time, spread with a little ricotta cheese or *fromage blanc*.

You can steam this bread in coffee tins or juice or vegetable tins, or in pudding basins. It steams for hours, so plan to do this while you're at home.

This particular version is made from my own mixture of flours and is high in protein.

4oz (115g) rye flour	*1 teaspoon salt*
3½oz (100g) stoneground yellow	*¼ pint (140ml) black treacle*
cornmeal	*¾ pint (425ml) buttermilk, or a*
3oz (85g) wholemeal flour	*combination of low-fat natural*
1oz (30g) soya flour	*yoghurt and milk*
2 teaspoons bicarbonate of soda	*6oz (170g) raisins*

Sift together the rye flour, cornmeal, wholemeal flour, soya flour, bicarbonate of soda and salt. Stir in the treacle and buttermilk or yoghurt-and-milk mixture, and blend well. Stir in the raisins.

Generously butter two 1lb (450g) coffee or juice tins, or several small tins or pudding basins. Fill each three-quarters full of the batter. Butter pieces of foil and cover the tins or basins, sealing well with tape if necessary.

Place the tins or basins in a large pan (deep enough to enable you to cover it with the tins or basins in it) and pour in water to the depth of 2 inches. Bring the water to a boil on top of the stove. Cover the pan, then reduce the heat and simmer for 3 hours, checking every so often to make sure that the water hasn't boiled away.

Remove the tins or basins from the pan, turn out the loaves and cool them on a rack. If your bread seems too moist, place it in a 375°F/190°C/gas mark 5 oven for 10 minutes.

Banana Bread

1 LOAF

Banana bread is usually very sweet. Here most of the sweetness comes from the spices and the bananas themselves. This bread freezes well and is delicious for breakfast or tea.

4oz (115g) 85 per cent wholemeal flour
4oz (115g) unbleached white flour
1 teaspoon bicarbonate of soda
1 teaspoon ground cinnamon
½ teaspoon freshly grated nutmeg
½ teaspoon salt
4 tablespoons Demerara sugar
4 tablespoons melted unsalted butter or sunflower oil

2fl. oz (60ml) mild-flavoured honey
1 teaspoon vanilla essence
2 eggs
4 tablespoons low-fat natural yoghurt
1lb (450g) ripe bananas, mashed
5oz (140g) chopped walnuts

Pre-heat the oven to 375°F/190°C/gas mark 5. Butter an 8 × 5 × 3-inch loaf tin.

Sift together the flours, bicarbonate of soda, spices, salt and sugar. Beat together the honey, eggs, butter or oil, vanilla essence, yoghurt and mashed banana. Quickly stir in the mixed dry ingredients and mix together well, but don't over-beat. Fold in the walnuts.

Turn the batter into the prepared loaf tin. Bake for 50–60 minutes, until the loaf is firm and a knife inserted into the centre comes out clean. Remove the bread from the oven. Let it cool in the tin for 10–15 minutes, then turn it out on to a rack to cool completely.

Courgette and Apricot Bread

1 LOAF

This is a moist, spicy bread. It is only moderately sweet, so if you want it sweeter add an ounce or two more sugar. The courgettes are hardly discernible, but they give the bread its moist texture.

4 eggs
4fl. oz (120ml) safflower or vegetable oil
4oz (115g) Demerara sugar
2 teaspoons vanilla essence
2fl. oz (60ml) milk
1 tablespoon grated orange rind
8oz (225g) grated courgettes
4oz (115g) wholemeal pastry flour
4oz (115g) unbleached white flour

2 teaspoons baking powder
1 teaspoon bicarbonate of soda
½ teaspoon salt
2 teaspoons ground cinnamon
1 teaspoon ground cloves
1 teaspoon ground nutmeg
½ teaspoon ground allspice
3oz (85g) shelled walnuts or pecans, chopped
3oz (85g) dried apricots, chopped

Pre-heat the oven to 350°F/180°C/gas mark 4. Butter an 8 or 9 × 5-inch loaf tin.

Beat together the eggs, oil, sugar, milk and vanilla essence. Stir in the grated courgettes and orange rind. Sift together the flours, baking powder, bicarbonate of soda, salt and spices. Stir into the liquid mixture and mix just until well blended. Fold in the nuts and apricots.

Pour the batter into the prepared loaf tin and bake on the middle shelf for 1¼ hours, or until a knife inserted into the centre comes out clean. Cool the bread for 10 minutes in the tin, then turn it out on to a rack and cool it completely. Wrap it in foil and let it sit overnight so that the flavours will develop. This makes a very nice tea or dessert bread.

Carrot Cake

1 LOAF

This is very much like the courgette bread opposite, with grated carrots instead of courgettes, no nuts, and sultanas instead of apricots. It is less cloying than most carrot cakes.

4oz (115g) sultanas
boiling water to cover the sultanas
4 eggs
4fl. oz (120ml) safflower or
    vegetable oil
4oz (115g) unrefined brown sugar
2 teaspoons vanilla essence
1 tablespoon grated lemon rind
8oz (225g) grated carrots

4oz (115g) wholemeal pastry flour
4oz (115g) unbleached white flour
2 teaspoons baking powder
1 teaspoon bicarbonate of soda
½ teaspoon salt
2 teaspoons ground cinnamon
1 teaspoon ground cloves
1 teaspoon ground nutmeg
½ teaspoon ground allspice

Pre-heat the oven to 350°F/180°C/gas mark 4. Butter an 8 or 9 × 5-inch loaf tin.

Place the sultanas in a bowl and cover them with boiling water. Let them sit for 3–5 minutes, then drain and pat them dry. Set them aside.

Beat together the eggs, oil, sugar and vanilla essence. Stir in the grated carrots and lemon rind. Sift together the flours, baking powder, bicarbonate of soda, salt and spices. Stir into the liquid mixture and mix just until well blended. Fold in the sultanas.

Pour the batter into the prepared loaf tin and bake on the middle shelf for 1¼ hours, or until a knife inserted into the centre comes out clean. Cool the cake for 10 minutes in the pan, then turn it out on to a rack and cool it completely. Wrap it in foil and let it sit overnight so that the flavours will develop. This makes a very nice tea or dessert bread.

7: American-style Biscuits, Cornbread, Panbread and Muffins

In this chapter my true American origins surface, along with the legacy of the twelve years I lived in Texas. Since moving to Europe in 1981, I've baked more cornbread, biscuits (which are really savoury scones) and muffins than I ever did when I lived in Texas. I guess these foods were so easy to come by then that I took them for granted. When you went out to breakfast at a Texas café, the waitress put a basket of hot, fresh-baked biscuits on the table and poured you a big cup of (lousy) coffee before you'd even looked at the menu. Walking down the street in New York, every deli on every block sells huge muffins, and I suppose that's what most New Yorkers eat for breakfast, on their way to work or when they get there. These are not the griddle-baked yeasted English muffins, but batter breads baked in small moulds, like cupcakes.

When I moved to Paris I began to crave these American specialities, so I would make cornbread for a dinner party, muffins for a brunch. And the French loved them. They had nothing resembling these cake-like breads, some crunchy with grains, others sweet with fruit; they were a big hit, and my cravings for them have not diminished over the years.

One of the things I like best about the breads in this chapter is that they are so quick to throw together. None are yeast breads, yet many have the same satisfying, sustaining character. The savoury breads go marvellously with soups, stews and salads, and the muffins are great for breakfast and with tea.

Texas Cornbread

8–12 SERVINGS

This is my favourite cornbread recipe. I brought it with me to Europe from Texas and make it often. It is moist and rich, with a grainy texture and a sweet corn flavour. It goes very well with soups and stews. It is very quick to throw together.

6oz (170g) stoneground cornmeal
2oz (55g) wholemeal flour
¾ teaspoon salt
1 tablespoon baking powder
½ teaspoon bicarbonate of soda

8fl. oz (225ml) low-fat natural
  yoghurt or buttermilk
4fl. oz (120ml) milk
1 tablespoon mild-flavoured honey
2 eggs
3 tablespoons unsalted butter

Pre-heat the oven to 450°F/230°C/gas mark 8.

Sift together the cornmeal, flour, salt, baking powder and bicarbonate of soda in a large bowl. Beat together the yoghurt, milk, honey and eggs in another bowl.

Put the butter in a 9 × 9-inch baking tin or a 9-inch cast-iron frying pan and place it in the oven for about 3–4 minutes, until the butter melts. Remove from the heat, brush the butter over the sides and bottom of the tin and pour the remaining melted butter into the yoghurt-and-egg mixture. Stir this together well, then fold the liquid mixture into the dry mixture. Do this quickly, with just a few strokes of a wooden spoon or plastic spatula. Don't worry about lumps. You don't want to over-work the batter.

Pour the batter into the warm, greased tin, place it in the oven and bake for 30–35 minutes, until the top is golden-brown and a toothpick inserted comes out clean. Let the loaf cool in the tin, or serve it hot.

Savoury Oatmeal Panbread

8 SERVINGS

This easy, quick bread, based on a recipe by Jacques Pepin, tastes rather like a stuffing. It is savoury and filling, and makes a nice accompaniment to soups and salads. It's the kind of bread you can whip up at a moment's notice.

4oz (115g) porridge oats
2 teaspoons baking powder
2oz (55g) unbleached white flour
   or 85 per cent wholemeal flour
½oz (15g) chopped parsley
   (a teacupful)
½ small onion, grated

1 large egg
½ teaspoon salt
¼ teaspoon freshly ground black
   pepper
4fl. oz (120ml) milk
2½ tablespoons olive, safflower or
   sunflower oil

Pre-heat the oven to 400°F/200°C/gas mark 6.

Mix together all the ingredients except the oil in a bowl, or in a food processor fitted with the steel blade. Place an 8-inch pie dish or a heavy 7- or 8-inch ovenproof frying pan in the hot oven with 2 tablespoons of oil in it. Heat for about 5 minutes. Spread the batter in the hot dish and brush the remaining oil over the top.

Return the dish to the oven and bake for 20 minutes. Flip the bread over – either like a crêpe, using a wide spatula, or by sliding it on to a plate and reversing it back into the dish. Bake for another 5–8 minutes, until the loaf is brown and a toothpick inserted comes out clean. Remove it from the heat, let it cool for a couple of minutes, then cut it into wedges. Serve this bread warm (reheat in a warm oven if it has cooled).

Southern Spoonbread

6–8 SERVINGS

Spoonbread isn't really a bread – it's more like a pudding or a soufflé, but because this chapter is full of nostalgia for Texas, I thought I'd include it. A traditional dish of the American South, it is said to have originated when a cook put too much water into a cornbread batter, and the baked bread had to be spooned out of the tin.

8fl. oz (225ml) water
½ teaspoon salt
6oz (170g) stoneground cornmeal
12fl. oz (340ml) milk
½ teaspoon mild-flavoured honey
2 tablespoons unsalted butter

3 eggs, separated
kernels from 1 ear of corn
  (optional)
1 fresh green chilli, finely chopped,
  or 1 small sweet green pepper,
  finely chopped (optional)

Pre-heat the oven to 350°F/180°C/gas mark 4. Butter a 3-pint (1.75-litre) soufflé dish, baking dish or a 10-inch cast-iron frying pan.

Bring the water to a boil in a 2-pint (1.25-litre) heavy-bottomed saucepan or in the top of a double boiler. Add the salt and very slowly pour in the cornmeal, stirring continually with a wooden spoon. Stir in the milk and cook over a low heat or over boiling water, stirring all the time, for 10–15 minutes, until you have a thick, smooth mixture. Remove from the heat and stir in the honey and butter. Stir in the egg yolks, one at a time.

Beat the egg whites until they form stiff peaks. Stir one-quarter of the egg whites into the cornmeal mixture until just mixed. Gently fold in the rest of the egg whites, then the optional corn and/or chilli or pepper. Spoon the mixture into the prepared baking dish and bake for 30 minutes, until puffed and beginning to brown. Serve at once.

Thyme Scones

12 SCONES

In the United States we would call these 'biscuits', the American version of a scone. They are savoury and light, go well with cheese and with soups, and are also terrific with herb-flavoured jellies.

4oz (115g) unbleached white flour
4oz (115g) wholemeal flour or
  wholemeal pastry flour
¾ teaspoon salt
1 teaspoon sugar
2 teaspoons baking powder
½ teaspoon bicarbonate of soda

1 tablespoon finely chopped fresh
  thyme, or 1½ teaspoons dried
  thyme
2½oz (70g) unsalted butter
6fl. oz (180ml) sour milk,
  buttermilk or low-fat natural
  yoghurt

Pre-heat the oven to 450°F/230°C/gas mark 8. Butter a baking sheet.

Sift together the flours, salt, sugar, baking powder and bicarbonate of soda. Stir in the thyme. Rub in the butter until the mixture has the consistency of coarse cornmeal. (This can also be done in a food processor fitted with the steel blade, using the pulse action, or in an electric mixer.)

Stir the milk and buttermilk or yoghurt into the mixture. Gather up the dough and gently knead it, not working it as you would bread dough, but just pressing it together so that it comes together in a cohesive lump. It will be slightly sticky, so lightly flour your hands. The less you work the dough, the lighter your scones (or biscuits) will be. Roll out the dough to a thickness of about ¾ inch and cut it into squares, triangles or rounds.

Place the scones on the prepared baking sheet and bake for 12–15 minutes, until they begin to brown. Serve them warm.

Wheatgerm Sourdough Biscuits

12–15 BISCUITS

These are excellent American-style 'biscuits'. They are flaky and melt in your mouth, with a rich, earthy, slightly sour taste.

6oz (170g) wholemeal pastry flour
8fl. oz (225ml) sourdough starter
  (see p. 96)
2fl. oz (60ml) milk
2 teaspoons baking powder
½ teaspoon bicarbonate of soda

¾ teaspoon salt
2oz (55g) wheatgerm
4oz (115g) unsalted butter
up to 2oz (55g) unbleached white
  flour for kneading

The day before

In a bowl, combine 2oz (55g) of the wholemeal flour, the starter and the milk, and mix well. Cover and let it stand in a draught-free place for 18–24 hours. (Replenish the starter – see p. 96.)

The next day

Butter two baking sheets.

Sift together the remaining flour, the baking powder, bicarbonate of soda and salt. Stir in the wheatgerm and quickly rub in the butter, until the mixture resembles coarse cornmeal. (This can be done in a food processor fitted with the steel blade, using the pulse action, or in an electric mixer.) Stir in the sourdough mixture. Add more flour until you get a light dough that comes away easily from the sides of the bowl or food processor.

Turn out the dough on to a lightly floured board and knead gently 10–15 times, until the ingredients are just amalgamated. Roll or press out the dough into a rectangle about ¾ inch thick, and cut it into squares, circles or triangles. Place the biscuits on the baking sheets and allow them to rest for 30 minutes.

Meanwhile, pre-heat the oven to 425°F/220°C/gas mark 7. Bake for 10–15 minutes, until the biscuits are lightly browned. Serve them warm.

Cornmeal Drop Biscuits

12 BISCUITS

These biscuits have a grainy texture and a rich, earthy flavour. They go well with soups and stews as well as with tea.

4oz (115g) unbleached white flour
2oz (55g) wholemeal flour
4oz (115g) stoneground yellow
 cornmeal
2 teaspoons baking powder
½ teaspoon bicarbonate of soda

½ teaspoon salt
4oz (115g) cold unsalted butter, cut
 into pieces
1 large egg
4–5fl. oz (120–140ml) buttermilk
1 tablespoon mild-flavoured honey

Pre-heat the oven to 425°F/220°C/gas mark 7. Butter two baking sheets.

Sift together the flours, cornmeal, baking powder, bicarbonate of soda and salt. Rub in the butter until the mixture resembles coarse cornmeal. (This can also be done in a food processor fitted with the steel blade, using the pulse action, or in an electric mixer.) Beat together the egg, honey and 4fl. oz (120ml) buttermilk. Stir into the flour mixture and mix to form a dough. If the mixture is dry, add a little more buttermilk.

Drop heaped tablespoons of the batter (2–3 tablespoons of dough per biscuit) on to the prepared baking sheets. Bake for 12–15 minutes, until the biscuits are golden. Serve them warm.

Overnight Bran Muffins

16–20 MUFFINS

You don't *have* to let this batter sit overnight, but it does make breakfast very easy. It will last for a week in the refrigerator, so you could make up a large quantity on Sunday night and have the makings for fresh muffins for every day of the week. The muffins are moist and sweet. If you don't like the taste of treacle, reduce the amount to 1 tablespoon, or omit it altogether and substitute honey.

6oz (170g) raisins, or sultanas, or chopped figs, or chopped apricots
12fl. oz (340ml) boiling water
4oz (170g) bran
2 eggs
4fl. oz (120ml) sunflower oil or melted butter
4fl. oz (120ml) mild-flavoured honey

2fl. oz (60ml) black treacle
12fl. oz (340ml) buttermilk, or milk soured with 1 tablespoon lemon juice
6oz (170g) wholemeal flour
4oz (115g) unbleached white flour
2½ teaspoons bicarbonate of soda
½ teaspoon salt
2oz (55g) wheatgerm

Place the raisins or chopped dried fruit in a bowl and pour on the boiling water. Let it sit for 5 minutes, then stir in the bran and let the mixture sit for another 10 minutes.

Beat together the eggs, oil or melted butter and the honey and treacle. Stir in the buttermilk or sour milk. Stir the raisins and bran, with their liquid, into the milk-and-egg mixture. Combine well.

Sift together the flours, bicarbonate of soda and salt in a separate bowl. Stir in the wheatgerm. Fold this into the liquid mixture. Cover the bowl with clingfilm or foil and refrigerate overnight, or bake right away.

In the morning, pre-heat the oven to 400°F/200°C/gas mark 6 and oil muffin tins. Give the batter a stir, and spoon it into the tins. Bake for 20–30 minutes, until the muffins are puffed, brown and cooked through. Remove them from the oven, allow them to cool for 15 minutes (or more) in the tins, then remove them and cool further on racks.

Savoury Rye Muffins

10–12 MUFFINS

These have a firm, grainy texture and a rich savoury flavour. They go well with soups, salads and cheese.

1 tablespoon safflower or vegetable
  oil
4 tablespoons finely chopped onion
2oz (55g) stoneground cornmeal
3oz (85g) unbleached white flour
3oz (85g) rye flour
2 teaspoons baking powder
½ teaspoon salt
½ teaspoon dried thyme

½ teaspoon dried sage
2 eggs
2 teaspoons mild-flavoured honey
3 additional tablespoons safflower
  oil or melted unsalted butter
8fl. oz (225ml) milk, low fat
  natural yoghurt, or a
  combination

Pre-heat the oven to 400°F/200°C/gas mark 6. Oil or butter muffin tins.

Heat the first tablespoon of oil in a frying pan and sauté the finely chopped onion until it is translucent – about 3–5 minutes. Remove from the heat.

Sift together the cornmeal, flours, baking powder and salt. Stir in the thyme and sage. Beat together the eggs, honey, safflower oil or butter, and the milk or yoghurt. Quickly stir into the flour mixture, then fold in the sautéed onion. Spoon the batter into the prepared muffin tins. Bake for 20 minutes, until the muffins are golden. Allow the muffins to cool for 10 minutes in the tins, then remove them and cool further on a rack.

Sweet or Savoury Cornmeal Muffins

12 MUFFINS

These can be rich and slightly sweet, like the Texas cornbread on p. 216, either plain or with added sweetcorn. Or you can make them savoury by adding sage and/or hot green chillis. This is a versatile muffin.

6oz (170g) stoneground cornmeal
4oz (115g) wholemeal flour
½ teaspoon salt
1 tablespoon baking powder
½ teaspoon bicarbonate of soda

8fl. oz (225ml) low-fat natural
*   yoghurt or buttermilk*
4fl. oz (120ml) milk
2 tablespoons mild-flavoured honey
2 eggs
3 tablespoons melted unsalted butter

Optional

1–2 teaspoons rubbed sage
*   (to taste)*
1 small tin sweetcorn, drained

1–2 hot green chillis, seeded and
*   chopped*

Pre-heat the oven to 425°F/220°C/gas mark 7. Oil muffin tins.

Sift together the cornmeal, flour, salt, baking powder and bicarbonate of soda in a large bowl. Stir in the sage, if using. In another bowl beat together the yoghurt or buttermilk, the milk, honey, eggs and melted butter. Fold the dry ingredients into the liquid mixture. Fold in the optional sweetcorn and/or chillis.

Heat the oiled muffin tins for 5 minutes in the pre-heated oven. Spoon the batter into the tins and bake for 20 minutes. Allow the muffins to cool in the tins for 10 minutes, then remove them and cool them further on a rack.

Lemon Muffins

10–12 MUFFINS

These are cakey and sweet. They go nicely with puréed berries or soft fruits.

8oz (225g) unbleached white flour
1 tablespoon baking powder
¼ teaspoon salt
2oz (55g) white sugar
grated rind of 1 lemon

2 eggs
2fl. oz (60 ml) sunflower oil or
*   melted unsalted butter*
2fl. oz (60ml) lemon juice
6fl. oz (180ml) milk

Pre-heat the oven to 400°F/200°C/gas mark 6. Oil or butter muffin tins.

Sift together the flour, baking powder, sugar and salt. Stir in the lemon rind. Beat together the eggs, oil or melted butter, lemon juice and milk. Quickly stir into the flour mixture. Spoon the batter into the muffin tins.

Bake for 20 minutes, until the muffins are lightly browned. Allow them to cool in the tins for 10 minutes, then remove them and cool further on a rack.

Cheese Muffins with Sweet Red Pepper

10 MUFFINS

These savoury muffins have lots of protein and flavour baked into them.

4oz (115g) 85 per cent wholemeal flour	4 tablespoons safflower or vegetable oil
4oz (115g) unbleached white flour	8fl. oz (225ml) milk
½ teaspoon salt	4oz (115g) grated Cheddar cheese
2½ teaspoons baking powder	1 sweet red pepper, diced
2 eggs	

Pre-heat the oven to 375°F/190°C/gas mark 5. Oil or butter muffin tins.

Sift together the flours, salt and baking powder. Beat together the eggs, oil and milk. Stir in the cheese. Quickly stir the wet ingredients into the dry, and fold in the diced red pepper.

Spoon the batter into the muffin tins and bake for 20 minutes. Allow the muffins to cool for a few minutes in the tins, then remove them and cool further on a rack.

Oat and Apple Muffins

10 MUFFINS

These are sweet, moist, spicy and delicious.

6fl. oz (170ml) milk
4oz (115g) rolled or flaked oats
4oz (115g) wholemeal flour
2½ teaspoons baking powder
¼ teaspoon salt
1 teaspoon ground cinnamon
½ teaspoon ground nutmeg

3oz (85g) unrefined brown sugar
2 eggs
4 tablespoons melted unsalted butter
*   or safflower oil*
1 medium-sized cooking apple,
*   peeled, cored and diced*

Pre-heat the oven to 400°F/200°C/gas mark 6. Oil or butter muffin tins.

Combine the milk and the oats and let them sit for 10 minutes.

Sift together the flour, baking powder, salt, cinnamon, nutmeg and sugar. Beat together the eggs and melted butter or oil. Stir in the milk and oats, then the dry ingredients. Fold in the chopped apple.

Spoon the batter into the muffin tins and bake for 25–30 minutes. Remove the muffins from the heat, cool in the tins for 10 minutes, then remove them and cool further on a rack.

Maple Pecan Muffins

12 MUFFINS

4oz (115g) unbleached white flour
4oz (115g) wholemeal flour
1½ teaspoons baking powder
¼ teaspoon salt
2 eggs
5fl. oz (140ml) milk

3fl. oz (90ml) maple syrup
4 tablespoons melted unsalted butter
*   or safflower oil*
2oz (55g) chopped pecans
12 unbroken pecan halves

Pre-heat the oven to 375°F/190°C/gas mark 5. Oil or butter muffin tins. Sift together the flours, baking powder and salt. Beat together the eggs, milk, maple syrup and melted butter or oil. Quickly stir into the dry ingredients. Fold in the chopped pecans.

Spoon the batter into muffin tins. Top each muffin with an un-broken pecan half. Bake for 20 minutes. Allow the muffins to cool for a few minutes in the tins, then remove them and cool further on a rack.

Orange Date Muffins

12 MUFFINS

6oz (170g) unbleached white flour
2oz (55g) wholemeal pastry flour
2½ teaspoons baking powder
½ teaspoon ground cinnamon
¼ teaspoon salt
2 oranges
2fl. oz (60ml) milk

2fl. oz (60ml) mild-flavoured
  honey
2 eggs
4 tablespoons melted unsalted butter
  or sunflower oil
3oz (85g) chopped dates

Pre-heat the oven to 400°F/200°C/gas mark 6.

Sift together the flours, cinnamon, baking powder and salt. Squeeze the oranges and measure out 4fl. oz (120ml) of the juice. Take the rind of one of the squeezed oranges and chop it coarsely. Place it in a blender with the milk, orange juice, honey, eggs and melted butter or oil. Blend until the orange rind is finely chopped. Pour the mixture into a bowl.

Stir the dry ingredients into the wet ingredients, mix together briefly and fold in the chopped dates.

Spoon the batter into muffin tins and bake for 15–20 minutes. Cool the muffins in the tins for 10 minutes, then remove them and cool further on a rack.

Popovers

10–12 POPOVERS

Popovers are almost like *choux* pastries, but softer and more fragile. A mixture of flour, water and eggs is baked in muffin tins or pudding basins and puffs up like a cream puff. You have to be sure to butter the tins generously so that you can get the popovers out right away, because they fall as quickly as they rise. These are wonderful with savoury dishes, and even better spread with butter and jam.

8fl. oz (225ml) milk
3 eggs
1 teaspoon sugar (optional)

2 tablespoons melted unsalted butter
4oz (115g) unbleached white flour
¼ teaspoon salt

In a blender or food processor, combine all the ingredients. Blend until smooth, stopping the machine every now and then to stir down flour from the sides of the bowl.

Pre-heat the oven to 400°F/200°C/gas mark 6. *Generously* butter muffin tins, Yorkshire pudding tins or custard cups. Pour in the batter, filling the tins about half full. Bake for 35–40 minutes, until the popovers are puffed, browned and firm to the touch. Avoid opening the oven until the end of the baking time. Serve the popovers hot.

8: Pizza, Calzoni, Focaccia and Quiche

This chapter has a decidedly Mediterranean flavour. Unfortunately I don't have a wood-fire pizza oven like the best Italian and French bakers do (but then, I imagine most of my readers don't either), but even so, when I bake these breads in my small apartment, the fragrance of Italy and southern France pervades my kitchen and I'm transported to the sun.

If you've never made pizza before, get ready to be spoiled for ever; it will be difficult to find such crisp, tangy crusts in pizza houses. *Calzoni* are like pizzas, with the crust folded over the fillings, and *focacce* are the flat, dimpled Italian breads you often find in Italian delis. All of these breads are versatile; you can top them or fill them with any number of foods, including leftovers.

When it comes to pizza, *focacce*, *calzoni* and quiche, it's the bread or pastry itself that makes the difference between the ordinary and the extravagant. No matter how good the tomato sauce or cheese filling that goes on top, it's the crust that people remember.

For those of you with little time, one of the pizza doughs in this chapter (p. 231) is a quick one which can be put together in minutes. With the yeast doughs, though, the recipe makes a large enough quantity for you to be able to freeze portions of the dough to use up whenever you get a craving for an extraordinary pizza.

Partly Wholemeal Pizza Crust

12–14-INCH CRUST

This is a delicious, crunchy crust with a slightly sour, earthy flavour, which develops during the dough's long rising time. If you don't have this much time, double the quantity of yeast and allow the dough to rise for 2 hours.

The pizza can be topped with any number of combinations (see recipes below). Make sure you bake it at the highest possible heat to get the best texture.

If you want more than one pizza, simply double or triple the quantities in this recipe. You could do this anyway, to give yourself a head start for future pizza dinners, and freeze the extra dough. Frozen dough will thaw in about 2 hours – and how convenient it is to have it to hand. It can be frozen for up to six months.

For the dough

1 scant teaspoon active dried yeast
5fl. oz (140ml) lukewarm water
1 tablespoon olive oil
½ teaspoon salt

4oz (115g) wholemeal pastry flour
4–5oz (115–140g) unbleached
  white flour

For the garlic olive oil

3 tablespoons olive oil

2 large cloves garlic, finely chopped
  or crushed

Mixing the dough and kneading

Dissolve the yeast in the water in a large bowl, or in the bowl of your electric mixer, and let it stand for 10 minutes.

If kneading the dough by hand. Add the olive oil and mix well. Combine the wholemeal flour and the salt and stir into the mixture. Begin adding the unbleached flour and, as soon as you can, scrape the dough out of the bowl and knead it on a lightly floured surface for 10–15 minutes. The dough will be sticky, but keep flouring your hands and add only enough flour to prevent the dough sticking to the kneading surface.

If using an electric mixer. Add the olive oil and mix well. Combine the salt, the wholemeal flour and 4oz (115g) of the unbleached white flour, and add to the liquid all at once. Mix together using the mixing attachment, then change to the dough hook. Knead at low speed (1 on a Kenwood) for 2 minutes, then at medium speed (2 on a Kenwood) for 8 minutes. Add no more than 1oz (30g) of flour if the dough seems very sticky.

Rising, shaping and baking

Shape the dough into a ball on a floured work surface and place it in an oiled bowl, seam side up, then seam side down. Cover the bowl and let the dough rise for 4–8 hours. If the dough doubles in size before this, punch it down: it needs this amount of time to develop its full flavour.

To shape, oil your hands and the top of the dough. Punch it down and turn it out on to a floured work surface. Shape it into a ball and let it rest under a tea-towel for 30 minutes.

Oil a 12–15-inch pizza tin or baking sheet. Place the pieces of dough on the tin, and press and stretch them with your hands, keeping your hands oiled so that the dough doesn't stick. Press out the dough into a circle ⅛ inch thick, with a thick edge. Pinch the edges all the way round to make an attractive border. The dough can stand, covered with a tea-towel, for up to an hour before being topped and baked.

Pre-heat the oven to 500–550°F/250–270°C/gas mark 10–12. If possible, heat baking tiles or a baking stone in the oven for 30 minutes before baking the pizza. (If you are using a baking stone (see p. 12), place the rolled-out pizza dough on a floured board and slide it on to the stone in the pre-heated oven when ready to bake.)

Combine the olive oil and garlic and brush the pizza crust before you add the topping. This creates a very fragrant protective seal so that the pizza does not become soggy when you add the topping and bake. Cover the dough with the topping of your choice (see suggestions on pp. 232–5) and place the pizza tins in the oven, on top of the baking tiles if you are using them. Bake until the edges of the dough are browned – about 15–20 minutes. If you are using cheese in the topping, don't add it until halfway through the baking or it will burn.

Quick Wholemeal Pizza Crust (Unyeasted)

This is an easy pizza crust which I learned to make in Provence. You can assemble it very quickly and top it with any of the combinations on pp. 232–5.

8oz (225g) wholemeal pastry flour
½ teaspoon salt
1 teaspoon baking powder
½ teaspoon bicarbonate of soda

5fl. oz (140ml) water, or more as
  necessary
2 tablespoons olive oil

Mix together the flour, salt, baking powder and bicarbonate of soda. Add the water and work it in with your hands, then add the oil and work it in. (This can also be done in an electric mixer or a food processor.) The dough will be stiff and dry.

Oil a 10-inch pie dish, pizza tin or quiche dish. Roll out the dough to about ¼ inch thick and line the tin. As the dough is stiff, this will take some elbow grease. Just keep pounding down with the rolling pin and rolling out until you get a nice flat, round dough. Don't worry if it tears: you can always patch it together. Pinch a nice border round the top edge and refrigerate the dough until you are ready to use it. (The pizza crust can also be frozen at this point. Defrost before continuing.)

Pre-heat the oven to 450°F/230°C/gas mark 8. Spread the desired topping over the pizza crust and bake for 15–20 minutes, or until the crust is brown and crisp.

Sweet Pepper Topping

This is a very pretty, easy topping. The peppers can be sautéed hours in advance and reheated gently just before baking.

1 tablespoon olive oil
1lb (450g) sweet red peppers,
    seeded and thinly sliced
1lb (450g) sweet yellow peppers,
    seeded and thinly sliced
2 cloves garlic, finely chopped

1 tablespoon fresh thyme, or
    1 teaspoon dried
salt and freshly ground pepper (to
    taste)
garlic olive oil (see pp. 230–1;
    optional)

Heat the oil in a heavy-bottomed or non-stick frying pan and sauté the peppers and garlic together, stirring, for about 10 minutes, until they are softened but still have some texture. Stir in the thyme and add salt and freshly ground pepper.

Pre-heat the oven to 500–550°F/250–270°C/gas mark 10–12. Brush the prepared pizza dough with the optional garlic olive oil and spread with the sautéed peppers. Bake for 15–20 minutes, until the crust is browned. Remove the pizza from the heat and serve.

Wild Mushroom Topping

1oz (30g) dried porcini
   mushrooms
boiling water to cover the
   mushrooms
2 tablespoons olive oil
4 large cloves of garlic, finely
   chopped
1–2 teaspoons soya sauce (to taste)
3 tablespoons dry white wine

2 tablespoons chopped fresh parsley
1 tablespoon chopped fresh sage
   leaves
salt and freshly ground pepper (to
   taste)
garlic olive oil (see pp. 230–1)
1–2oz (15–30g) freshly grated
   Parmesan cheese (to taste)

Cover the mushrooms with boiling water and soak for 30 minutes. Squeeze the liquid out of the mushrooms over a bowl, and strain off the soaking liquid through a strainer lined with paper towels or cheese-cloth. Retain the liquid and rinse the mushrooms thoroughly. Squeeze them dry.

Heat the oil in a small saucepan and add the mushrooms and garlic. Sauté over medium heat for about 5 minutes, stirring, until the garlic is beginning to colour. Add the soya sauce and the white wine and continue to sauté for another 5 minutes. Add the soaking liquid from the mushrooms, then the parsley, and turn the heat to medium–high. Cook until the liquid has been reduced to a glaze, stirring often. Stir in the sage and add salt and freshly ground pepper to taste. Remove the pan from the heat.

Pre heat the oven to 500–550°F/250–270°C/gas mark 10–12. Brush the pizza dough with the garlic olive oil and bake it for 7 minutes. Remove it from the oven, spread the mushroom mixture over the crust in an even layer and sprinkle with Parmesan cheese. Return the pizza to the oven and bake for 8–10 minutes, until it is golden-brown and fragrant. Remove it from the heat and serve.

Tomato, Goat's Cheese, Red Pepper and Caper Topping

2 ripe tomatoes, tinned or fresh,
   peeled, seeded and chopped
1 sweet red pepper, seeded and
   sliced

3oz (85g) goat's cheese, thinly
   sliced
2 tablespoons capers, rinsed
garlic olive oil (see pp. 230–1)
freshly ground pepper

Brush the prepared pizza crust with the garlic olive oil. Sprinkle on the tomatoes, red pepper, goat's cheese and capers. Bake for 15 minutes at 500°F/250°C/gas mark 10, or until the pizza is brown and crisp.

Tomato–Onion Topping

The tomato sauce for this gutsy pizza can be used with other combinations besides onions, such as green peppers, cheese, anchovies or mushrooms (see p. 235).

For the tomato sauce

1 tablespoon olive oil
2–3 cloves garlic, finely chopped or
    crushed
2lb (900g) tomatoes, fresh or
    tinned, seeded and chopped
1 tablespoon tomato purée

salt and freshly ground pepper (to
    taste)
1 teaspoon dried oregano
½ teaspoon dried thyme, or
    1 teaspoon fresh
a pinch of ground cinnamon

For the onion topping

1 tablespoon olive oil
2–3 onions (to taste), sliced in rings
salt and freshly ground pepper (to
    taste)

1oz (30g) freshly grated Parmesan
    cheese
garlic olive oil (see pp. 230–1;
    optional)

For the tomato sauce, heat the oil in a heavy-bottomed frying pan or casserole and sauté the garlic for about a minute. Add the tomatoes and tomato purée and bring to a simmer. Add salt to taste and cook, uncovered, for about 30 minutes over medium–low heat, stirring from time to time. Add the oregano and thyme and cook another 10 minutes. Add a pinch of cinnamon and freshly ground pepper to taste. Taste and adjust seasonings, adding more salt, garlic or herbs if you wish. Set aside.

Heat the oil in a frying pan and sauté the onions over a medium heat for 10 minutes, stirring often. They should just be beginning to brown. Remove from the heat.

Brush the prepared pizza crust with garlic olive oil (see p. 231) if desired. Spread the crust with the tomato sauce, then top with the onions. Sprinkle with Parmesan cheese.

Pre-heat the oven to 500°F/250°C/gas mark 10 and bake for 15–20 minutes, until the crust is nicely browned.

Other toppings to accompany the tomato sauce

2 green peppers, sliced
8oz (225g) Mozzarella cheese,
  thinly sliced
4oz (115g) olives, pitted and
  halved
16 anchovy fillets

1–2 jars artichoke hearts, drained
  and sliced
up to 2oz (55g) freshly grated
  Parmesan cheese
2 tablespoons capers, rinsed
garlic olive oil (see pp. 230–1;

Spread the tomato sauce over the prepared pizza crust (brush before-hand with the optional garlic olive oil – see p. 231). Top the tomato sauce with any of the above ingredients, alone or in combination, and bake as directed above. Note that cheese should be added halfway through to prevent burning.

Pissaladière

SERVES 8

Pissaladière is a Provençal onion pizza, and most of my books contain recipes for it. Each recipe is a little different, because I've found so many versions. Some people make it in a pastry case, others use a pizza crust, which I prefer. Sometimes *pissaladière* is thick with onions, at other times the layer is thin. The important thing is to cook the onions until they become sweet and slightly caramelised.

You can use this crust, or either of the pizza crusts on pp. 229–31.

For the crust

2 teaspoons active dried yeast
6fl. oz (180ml) lukewarm water
¾ teaspoon salt
2 tablespoons olive oil

8oz (225g) wholemeal or
  wholemeal pastry flour, or use
  half wholemeal, half unbleached
  white flour
unbleached white flour for
  kneading, as necessary

For the filling

4lb (2kg) onions, very thinly sliced
3 tablespoons olive oil (or more, as
  necessary)
1 tablespoon unsalted butter
salt and freshly ground pepper (to
  taste)

¼ teaspoon dried thyme (or more,
  to taste)
2 teaspoons mild-flavoured honey
  or sugar
2fl. oz (60ml) red wine
1 small tin anchovy fillets
2oz (55g) black Niçoise olives

Mixing the dough and kneading

Dissolve the yeast in the lukewarm water in a large bowl or in the bowl of your electric mixer. Let it sit for 10 minutes, or until the mixture begins to bubble. Stir in the salt and oil.

If you are kneading by hand. Add the flour, a cupful at a time, and mix thoroughly, first with a whisk and then, when it becomes too thick for a whisk, with a large wooden spoon. Turn out the dough on to a lightly floured board and knead for 10 minutes, adding only enough flour to keep the dough from sticking. If you work briskly and use a pastry scraper to manipulate the dough, it won't stick too much.

If using an electric mixer. Add the flour to the liquid all at once in the bowl of your mixer. Mix together using the mixing attachment, then change to the dough hook. Knead at low speed (1 on a Kenwood) for 2 minutes, then at medium speed (2 on a Kenwood) for 8 minutes. Add up to 1oz (30g) more flour if the dough seems very sticky. Shape the dough into a ball.

Rising, shaping and baking

Shape the dough into a ball, then place it in a lightly oiled bowl, rounded side down first, then rounded side up. Cover with a damp tea-towel or clingfilm and set the bowl in a warm place for the dough to rise until it has doubled in bulk – 1–1½ hours.

Meanwhile, prepare the onions. Heat the olive oil and butter in a large frying pan over a low heat. Add the onions and cook over a low heat, stirring from time to time, until they are translucent. Add the honey, wine and thyme and cook gently, stirring occasionally, for 1–1½ hours, until the onions are golden-brown and beginning to caramelise. Add salt and freshly ground pepper to taste. The onions should not brown or stick to the pan. Add extra oil or butter as needed.

When the dough has doubled in size, punch it down, then let it rise for another 40 minutes (while the onions are still cooking).

Pre-heat the oven to 450°F/230°C/gas mark 8. Turn out the dough on to a lightly floured work surface and roll it out to about ¼ inch thick, or a little thinner. Oil a 12–14-inch pizza tin or *tarte* tin and line it with the dough. Pinch a lip around the edge. Bake for 7–10 minutes, until the surface is crisp and the edges are beginning to brown.

Spread the crust with the onions. Top with anchovies and olives and bake again for 15 minutes, or until the crust is browned and crisp. Remove the *pissaladière* from the heat and serve it hot, or let it cool and serve it at room temperature.

Calzoni

6 CALZONI

Calzoni are Italian stuffed turnovers. A pizza dough is rolled out into an oval shape, topped with a filling, folded over and sealed at the edges. You can fill them with any number of combinations.

double the quantity of pizza dough given on p. 229	*1 egg, beaten with 2 tablespoons water*
the filling of your choice (see pp. 239–40)	*2fl. oz (60ml) olive oil*
	2 cloves garlic, finely chopped or crushed

Follow the recipe for pizza dough on p. 229, doubling the quantities for the ingredients. After the dough has risen, punch it down, divide it into six equal pieces and shape these into balls. Place them on a lightly floured surface, cover with a tea-towel and let them sit for 30 minutes. Roll or press out each ball into an oval, about ⅛–¼ inch thick. If the dough is very sticky, flour it lightly or oil your fingertips.

Spread the filling over half the oval. Brush the edges of the oval with beaten egg, and fold the dough in half. Pinch the edges together. Mix together the 2oz (60ml) olive oil and the garlic, and brush the *calzoni* with this mixture.

Pre-heat the oven to 450°F/230°C/gas mark 8. Place the *calzoni* on a hot baking stone (see p. 12) or on oiled baking sheets. Brush the *calzoni* with the garlic-scented olive oil and bake for 20–25 minutes, until brown. Brush again with the garlic olive oil and serve hot.

An Alternative Calzoni Dough

This is a breadier crust than the one above, and I like it a little less for that reason. However, it's very easy to work with and is high in protein, so I thought it worth giving.

2½ teaspoons active dried yeast
1 teaspoon sugar
4 tablespoons lukewarm water
8fl. oz (225ml) lukewarm milk
2 tablespoons olive oil

1½ teaspoons salt
4oz (115g) wholemeal flour
up to 12oz (340g) unbleached
    white flour, as necessary

Mixing the dough and kneading

Dissolve the yeast in the lukewarm water in a large bowl, or in the bowl of your electric mixer, stir in the sugar and let it sit for 10 minutes.

If kneading the bread by hand. Stir the milk and olive oil into the yeast mixture. Mix together the flours and salt, and fold in, a cupful at a time. As soon as you can, scrape the dough out on to a floured kneading surface. Knead, adding extra unbleached flour as necessary, for 10 minutes. Shape the dough into a ball.

If using an electric mixer. Add the milk and olive oil to the yeast mixture. Combine the wholemeal flour, 10oz (285g) of the unbleached white flour and salt, and add all at once to the bowl. Mix together with the mixing attachment, then change to the dough hook. Mix at low speed (1 on a Kenwood) for 2 minutes, then at medium speed (2 on a Kenwood) for 6–8 minutes. If the dough seems very wet and sticky, sprinkle in up to 2oz (55g) more unbleached flour. Scrape out the dough on to a lightly floured surface and knead by hand for a minute or so. Shape the dough into a ball.

Rising, shaping and baking

Put the dough into your bowl. Cover the bowl with clingfilm and a tea-towel and set it in a warm place for the dough to rise for 2 hours, or until it has doubled in size.

Punch down the dough and turn it out on to your work surface. Shape it into a ball. Divide it into six equal pieces, shape these into balls, and proceed with shaping, filling and baking the *calzoni* as in the above recipe.

Tomato–Mozzarella Filling

1 tablespoon olive oil
2 large cloves garlic, finely chopped
  or crushed
2lb (900g) tomatoes, peeled, seeded
  and chopped, or a 28oz (800g)
  tin
salt and freshly ground pepper (to
  taste)

a pinch of sugar
2 tablespoons chopped fresh basil,
  or ½ teaspoon dried thyme or
  oregano
8oz (225g) Mozzarella cheese,
  shredded
2oz (55g) freshly grated Parmesan
  cheese

Heat the olive oil in a heavy-bottomed frying pan and add the garlic. Sauté over medium–low heat until the garlic begins to colour, then add the tomatoes and turn up the heat. Add salt and pepper and the pinch of sugar, and sauté, stirring often, over medium–high heat for 15 minutes. Add the herbs, adjust the seasonings and set aside.

Spread the tomato sauce over the rolled out *calzoni*. Top with Mozzarella and Parmesan cheese. Seal and bake as p. 237.

Goat's Cheese and Olive Filling

8oz (225g) mild goat's cheese
4oz (115g) black olives, pitted and
  coarsely chopped
2 cloves garlic, finely chopped or
  crushed

½–1 teaspoon dried thyme (to
  taste)
½ teaspoon crumbled dried
  rosemary, or 1 teaspoon chopped
  fresh
freshly ground pepper (to taste)

Mash the goat's cheese with a wooden spoon and combine it in a bowl with all the above ingredients. Spread the mixture over the *calzoni*. Seal and bake as p. 237.

Goat's Cheese and Herb Filling

8oz (225g) mild goat's cheese
2 tablespoons low-fat natural
  yoghurt
4oz (115g) Mozzarella cheese
2 tablespoons chopped fresh chives
1 teaspoon dried thyme

1 teaspoon crushed dried or fresh
  rosemary
2 cloves garlic, finely chopped or
  crushed
freshly ground pepper

Mash the goat's cheese with the yoghurt and stir in the herbs, Mozzarella cheese, garlic and pepper. Spread the mixture over the *calzoni*. Seal and bake as p. 237.

White Bean and Sage Filling

½lb (225g) white haricot beans, cooked, or two 14oz (400g) tins white beans, drained
2 tablespoons chopped fresh sage
½ teaspoon dried thyme
4 tablespoons chopped fresh parsley
1–2 cloves garlic, finely chopped or crushed

salt and freshly ground pepper (to taste)
2oz (55g) freshly grated Parmesan cheese
2 tomatoes, peeled, seeded and chopped (optional)

Mix together all the ingredients in a bowl. Spread the mixture over the *calzoni*. Seal and bake as p. 237.

Note

Although tinned beans are more convenient here, they are not as good as dried beans which you have cooked yourself; tinned beans tend to have a viscous texture.

Potato and Pesto Filling

½lb (680g) waxy potatoes, scrubbed and diced
4 tablespoons pesto (see p. 168)
½oz (15g) dried porcini mushrooms
boiling water to cover the mushrooms

2 cloves garlic, finely chopped or crushed
2oz (55g) freshly grated Parmesan cheese
2 tablespoons olive oil
salt and freshly ground pepper (to taste)

Steam the potatoes until tender, then drain them. Cover the mushrooms with boiling water and soak them for 15–30 minutes. Drain and rinse them thoroughly (save the soaking liquid for another purpose). Toss together the potatoes, pesto, mushrooms, garlic, Parmesan cheese, olive oil, and add salt and freshly ground pepper to taste.

Spread this mixture over the *calzoni*. Seal and bake as p. 237.

Focaccia

THREE 9–10-INCH ROUND *FOCACCE*, OR TWO 10½ × 15½-INCH RECTANGULAR *FOCACCE*

Focacce are found all over Italy, under one name or another (*sardinaira* or *sardenara* in western Liguria, *schiacciata* in Florence, *pinze* in southern Italy). They are rustic, round or rectangular, leavened breads, about ¾–1 inch thick, with dimpled tops and a variety of seasonings. Sometimes they are merely sprinkled with coarse salt and olive oil, or they can be flavoured with herbs such as sage or rosemary, or studded with olives, anchovies or garlic. They are fragrant with olive oil (even though there really isn't too much in the doughs) and they are very easy to make. I often serve them, cut into small squares, with cocktails.

The dough is light and easy to work with. It requires a long rising time.

2½ teaspoons active dried yeast
1 pint (570ml) lukewarm water
4 tablespoons olive oil
1 scant tablespoon salt

1½lb (680g) unbleached white flour, or more as necessary for kneading
olive oil

Mixing the dough and kneading

Dissolve the yeast in the water in a large bowl, or in the bowl of your electric mixer, and let it sit for 10 minutes. Stir in the olive oil.

If kneading the dough by hand. Combine the flour and salt. Fold into the yeast mixture, a cupful at a time. As soon as the dough holds together, turn it out on to a lightly floured surface and knead, adding more flour as necessary, for 10 minutes, until the dough is smooth and elastic.

If using an electric mixer. Combine the flour and salt and add all at once to the liquids. Mix together using the mixing attachment, then change to the dough hook. Knead for 2 minutes at low speed (1 on a Kenwood), then knead for 6–8 minutes at medium speed (2 on a Kenwood). Add more flour as necessary if the dough seems very sticky.

Rising, forming the focacce and baking

Oil your bowl, shape the dough into a ball and place it in the bowl, rounded side down first, then rounded side up. Cover with clingfilm or a damp tea-towel and let the dough rise in a draught-free spot for 1½ hours, until it has doubled in volume.

Turn the dough out on to a lightly floured surface, knead for a minute, then cut it into three pieces for round *focacce*, two pieces for rectangular *focacce*. Oil pie plates or Swiss-roll tins and roll or press out the dough to fit the tins. Place the dough in the tins, cover with damp tea-towels and let the dough rise for 30 minutes.

Using your fingertips, dimple the surface of the dough all over. Cover it again and let it rise for 1½–2 hours.

Pre-heat the oven to 400°F/200°C/gas mark 6. Brush the dough lightly with olive oil and bake for 20–25 minutes, until the tops of the *focacce* are golden-brown. Spray the oven with water three times during the first 10 minutes' baking (see p. 12). Remove the *focacce* from the heat and turn them out on a rack so that the bottoms don't get soggy.

Eat *focacce* warm or at room temperature, preferably the day that you bake them. Do not refrigerate.

Note

Focacce will be improved if you bake them on baking tiles (see p. 12). Pre-heat the tiles for 30 minutes and place the tins directly on the tiles.

Wholemeal Focaccia with Herbs

THREE 10-INCH ROUND *FOCACCE*, OR TWO 10½ × 15½-INCH RECTANGULAR *FOCACCE*

I think this version, made with a combination of wholemeal and unbleached white flours, has more flavour than the traditional all-white *focaccia*. It is the recipe I usually use. It calls for more flour than the white version, but you don't necessarily use it; wholemeal doughs can be stickier than all-white flour doughs.

2½ teaspoons active dried yeast
1 pint (570ml) lukewarm water
3 tablespoons olive oil
3 tablespoons chopped fresh sage or
   rosemary

1 scant tablespoon salt
12oz (340g) wholemeal flour
up to 1lb (450g) unbleached white
   flour, or more as necessary for
   kneading

Mixing the dough and kneading

Dissolve the yeast in the water in a large bowl and let it sit for 10 minutes. Stir in the olive oil and sage or rosemary.

If kneading the dough by hand. Combine the wholemeal flour and salt, and whisk into the yeast mixture, a cupful at a time. Fold in the remaining flour, a cupful at a time. As soon as the dough holds together, turn it out on to a lightly floured surface and knead, adding more flour as necessary, for 10 minutes, until the dough is smooth and elastic.

If using an electric mixer. Combine the wholemeal flour, salt and 12oz (340g) of the unbleached white flour and add all at once to the liquids. Mix together using the mixing attachment, then change to the dough hook Knead for 2 minutes at low speed (1 on a Kenwood), then for 6–8 minutes at medium speed (2 on a Kenwood). Add the remaining unbleached flour as necessary.

Rising, forming the focacce and baking

Oil your bowl, shape the dough into a ball and place it in the bowl, rounded side down first, then rounded side up. Cover with clingfilm or a damp tea-towel and let the dough rise in a draught-free spot for 1½ hours, until it has doubled in volume.

Turn the dough out on to a lightly floured surface, knead for a minute and cut it into three pieces for round *focacce*, two pieces for rectangular *focacce*. Oil pie plates or Swiss-roll tins and roll out the dough to fit the tins. Place the dough in the tins, cover with damp tea-towels and let it rise for 30 minutes.

Using your fingertips, dimple the surface of the dough all over. Cover it again and let it rise for 1½–2 hours.

Pre-heat the oven to 400°F/200°C/gas mark 6. Brush the dough lightly with olive oil and bake for 20–25 minutes, until the tops of the *focacce* are golden-brown. Spray the oven with water three times during the first 10 minutes' baking (see p. 12). Remove the *focacce* from the heat and turn them out on a rack so that the bottoms don't get soggy.

Eat *focacce* warm or at room temperature, preferably the day you bake them. Do not refrigerate.

Note

Focacce will be improved if you bake them on baking tiles (see p. 12). Pre-heat the tiles for 30 minutes and place the tins directly on the tiles.

Focaccia with Coarse Salt

Sprinkle 2–3 teaspoons (to taste) coarse salt over each *focaccia* before brushing with olive oil and baking.

Focaccia with Sun-dried Tomatoes

Add 6oz (170g) chopped sun-dried tomatoes to the dough after you
have added the flour and kneaded for a few minutes. Knead the
tomatoes into the dough (the dough will take on an orangey colour).
It's best to use sun-dried tomatoes that have been marinated in olive
oil, because they are less salty. The olive oil can be used in the dough
instead of regular olive oil. These *focacce* have a marvellous savoury
flavour.

Focaccia with Gorgonzola and Parmesan

8oz (225g) Gorgonzola cheese
2oz (55g) freshly grated Parmesan
  cheese

1–2 cloves garlic, finely chopped or
  crushed
2fl. oz (60ml) milk

Mix together all the ingredients in a bowl, or use a food processor, to
form a smooth mixture. After you have shaped the *focacce*, dimple
them and spread this mixture over the top. Let the dough rise for about
1½ hours. Bake as p. 243), until the cheese is bubbly and beginning
to brown.

Focaccia with Sweet Red Peppers

Omit the herbs if desired. Roast 2 large sweet red peppers over a gas
burner or under the grill until blackened on all sides. Remove them
from the heat and place them in a plastic or paper bag until they are cool
enough to handle. Remove the charred skins, cut the flesh in half and
remove the seeds and membranes. Rinse and pat dry. Chop the
peppers into small dice and set aside.

Mix up the *focaccia* dough, and when you are ready to knead, add the
chopped roasted peppers and knead them into the dough. Proceed with
the recipe.

Focaccia with Olives

Omit the herbs if desired. Just before baking, stud the *focaccia* dimples
with 8oz (225g) pitted imported black olives.

Focaccia with Anchovies

Omit the herbs if desired. Chop 8–10 anchovy fillets and mix them with 4 tablespoons olive oil. Brush the mixture over each *focaccia* before baking.

Yeasted Pastry for Quiches and Tarts

A 10–12-INCH CRUST

This brilliant, tender pastry is adapted from Elizabeth David's recipe in *English Bread and Yeast Cookery*. It is rather like a cross between a pizza crust and shortcrust pastry – not as flaky and buttery as shortcrust pastry, nor as crisp or as labour-intensive as a pizza crust. It's quick to mix together, and requires half the butter that a shortcrust quiche pastry requires.

This dough can be mixed up, allowed to rise once, reshaped and left to rise again overnight, or it can be used immediately after the first rising.

2 tablespoons lukewarm water	2oz (55g) 85 per cent wholemeal
½ teaspoon active dried yeast	flour or 100 per cent wholemeal
1 egg, at room temperature	pastry flour
3oz (85g) unbleached white flour	3 tablespoons softened unsalted
½–¾ teaspoon salt (to taste)	butter

Dissolve the yeast in the lukewarm water in a bowl. Let it sit for 10 minutes, then beat in the egg. Combine the flours and salt and stir in. Combine as well as you can, then stir or beat in the butter. (This can all be done in a mixer, using the mixing attachment, or in a food processor.) Dust the mixture lightly with flour if it is very sticky, and knead it gently, only until you can shape it into a ball. Place it in a bowl, cover with clingfilm and set the bowl in a warm place for the dough to rise for 2 hours. The dough will expand and soften.

Flour the top of the dough again, then shape it again into a ball. If you will not be using it right away, place it in the bowl, cover it and set it in a cool place, but not the refrigerator, until the next day.

When you are ready to use it, butter your quiche tin generously, shape the dough into a ball and place it in the centre of the tin. Gently press the dough out, using the palm of your hand and your fingertips, until it reaches the sides of the tin. Now cover it again with clingfilm or a tea-towel and set it in a warm spot to rest for 25 minutes, or until the dough relaxes, becomes very pliable and has risen slightly. Press it out to line the sides of the tin and pinch an attractive lip around the edge.

Pre-heat the oven to 425°F/220°C/gas mark 7. Fill the pastry (see below) and bake it for 15 minutes. Turn the heat down to 375°F/190°C/gas mark 5, cover the quiche lightly with foil if the edges are very browned, and bake for another 10 minutes. Remove the quiche from the heat and serve it at once.

Savoury Fillings

There are any number of combinations for quiches. I sometimes mix up leftovers with eggs and a little Parmesan cheese and spread a thin layer over the pastry for an hors d'oeuvre. For instance, I have taken 4oz (115g) of the leftover salt cod acorda on p. 264, mixed it with 2 eggs, 2oz (55g) freshly grated Parmesan cheese and 2 tablespoons milk, and spread it on this pastry. The resulting quiche was marvellous.

Elizabeth David has a Roquefort filling made with 4oz (115g) Roquefort, 2 eggs, 3 tablespoons thick cream, 4 tablespoons milk, a pinch of nutmeg and freshly ground pepper, all blended together.

My fillings are generally less rich. I tend not to use cream. You could take 4oz (115g) steamed or sautéed chopped vegetables or thick tomato sauce (or leftover acorda, as above), mix it with 2–3 eggs (to taste), 3 tablespoons milk, thick cream or *crème fraîche*, and 2–4oz (55–115g) grated cheese, season with salt and freshly ground pepper to taste, and spread it on the pastry.

Sweet Fillings

This also makes a fabulous pastry case for a fruit tart. First brush the pastry with egg, then fill it with 2lb (900g) sliced, stoned plums, peaches or nectarines, sprinkled with sugar if desired; or with peeled, cored, sliced apples or pears, tossed in the juice of a lemon and sugar to taste. Bake as above.

9: Other Yeasted Flat Breads, Crackers, Crêpes and Pancakes

One could fill an entire book with recipes that fall under these headings. I've gathered together my favourites here, the ones I've often made and love to eat. They conjure up different places for me – Egypt, France, Russia, India; some I've visited, others not.

With the exception of the delicious wholemeal pitta breads and naans, with their various fillings, these recipes are quick to make. The crunchy *carta musica* and the crackers can become addictive; they keep for quite a while and are great to have around the house (much healthier, too, than crisps) to serve up with drinks, alone or with toppings.

There are many more cracker-like breads and pancakes, mostly yeasted, in Chapter 4, on English breads. The ones here – the *blinis* and crêpes – can make terrific meals with the toppings or fillings of your choice, both sweet and savoury. You can make them up in batches and freeze some of them (they thaw quickly), or keep batter on hand in the refrigerator.

Wholemeal Pitta Bread

8–12 PITTAS

These are nothing like the cardboard-like pittas we often find in restaurants and supermarkets. They are moist, pliable and very tasty.

There are two tricks to making pitta. First, the oven must be very hot so that the bread puffs up. Second, the bread should not be left in the oven too long, or it will begin to get crisp and won't be flexible. There is another Middle Eastern bread called *lavash*, which *is* crisp, and it's delicious. If you want to make *lavash*, just leave the pitta in the oven until it crisps, and once it's cool, break it into pieces.

This dough is soft and easy to work with.

2 tablespoons (2 envelopes plus 1
   teaspoon) active dried yeast
¼ teaspoon mild-flavoured honey
¾ pint (425ml) lukewarm water
2 tablespoons safflower oil

1 scant tablespoon salt
12oz (340g) wholemeal flour
8–10oz (225–285g) unbleached
   white flour

Mixing the dough and kneading

Dissolve the yeast and honey in 4fl. oz (120ml) of the lukewarm water in a large bowl, or in the bowl of your mixer, and let it sit for 10 minutes, until the mixture begins to bubble. Add the remaining water and mix well, then whisk in the oil.

If kneading the dough by ha; :. Mix together the wholemeal flour and salt and stir in, a cupful at a time. Fold in 4oz (115g) of the unbleached flour. Place the remaining flour on your board and scrape the dough out of the bowl. Knead for 10–15 minutes, until the dough is smooth and elastic, then shape it into a ball.

If using an electric mixer. Combine the flours and salt, and add all at once to the bowl. Mix together with the mixing attachment, then change to the dough hook. Mix at low speed (1 on a Kenwood) for 2 minutes, then at medium speed (2 on a Kenwood) for 6–8 minutes. If the dough seems very wet and sticky, sprinkle in up to 2oz (55g) more unbleached flour. Scrape out the dough on to a lightly floured surface and knead by hand for a minute or so. Shape the dough into a ball.

Rising, forming the loaves and baking

Oil your bowl and place the dough in it, seam side up first, then seam side down. Cover the bowl with a damp tea-towel or clingfilm and allow the dough to rise in a warm place for 1½–2 hours, or until it has doubled in bulk.

Punch down the dough and turn it out on to your board. Knead for a couple of minutes, then allow it to rest for 10 minutes. Divide it into eight to twelve equal pieces, and shape each piece into a ball. Place the balls on a floured surface, cover them with a tea-towel and let them rise for 30 minutes.

Using a well-floured rolling pin, flatten each ball and roll it out into a circle approximately ⅛ inch thick and 8 inches in diameter. Dust two oiled baking sheets with cornmeal and place two circles on each sheet. (Leave the remaining ones on your lightly floured board.) Cover all the breads with a tea-towel and let them rise again for 30 minutes.

Meanwhile pre-heat the oven to 500°F/250°C/gas mark 10. Place one of the baking sheets on the middle shelf of your oven and bake for 5 minutes without opening the oven door. Check your loaves: if they are beginning to brown remove them from the oven. If they still smell yeasty and not like baking bread, leave them for another 2–5 minutes. Bake the remaining pittas this way, then cool them on racks.

Wholemeal Naans

8 LARGE NAANS

Naans are flat, yeasted breads which are traditionally baked in a Tandoori oven but still yield delicious results when baked under a grill. This version is made with part wholemeal flour, part unbleached white. The dough is fairly easy to work with and becomes resilient and smooth by the end of kneading.

Naans can be plain, or topped with a sweet or savoury mixture. Two different versions follow this recipe.

2fl. oz (60ml) lukewarm water
2 teaspoons active dried yeast
6fl. oz (180ml) lukewarm milk
1 teaspoon mild-flavoured honey
2fl. oz (60ml) low-fat natural
  yoghurt or buttermilk

2 tablespoons safflower oil
1 teaspoon salt
1 teaspoon baking powder
  (optional)
4oz (115g) unbleached white flour
12oz (340g) wholemeal flour

Mixing the dough and kneading

Dissolve the yeast in the water in a large bowl or in the bowl of your electric mixer. Add the milk, honey, yoghurt and oil.

If kneading the dough by hand. Combine the optional baking powder, the unbleached flour and the salt, and fold into the liquid mixture. Fold in the wholemeal flour, a cupful at a time. As soon as the dough has begun to come together into one piece, turn it out on to a generously floured board and begin to knead, adding flour as necessary. Knead for 10 minutes, until the dough is elastic, then form it into a ball.

If using an electric mixer. Add the optional baking powder, the unbleached flour, the salt and 8oz (225g) of the wholemeal flour to the yeast mixture. Mix together with the mixing attachment, then change to the dough hook. Mix at low speed (1 on a Kenwood) for 2 minutes, then at medium speed (2 on a Kenwood) for 8 minutes. Add up to 4oz (115g) more flour, as necessary. Scrape the dough out on to your work surface and shape it into a ball.

Rising, forming the naans and baking

Clean and oil your bowl, then place the dough in it, rounded side down first, then rounded side up. Cover with a damp tea-towel and let the dough rise for 1½–2 hours in a warm place, until it has doubled in bulk.

When the dough has risen, pre-heat the grill. Brush baking sheets with oil. Punch down the dough and turn it out on to a lightly floured work surface. Knead a few times, then divide it into eight equal pieces. Shape these into balls, then roll each one out to a round or oval shape about ¼ inch thick. Place two on each baking sheet, cover them with a damp tea-towel and let them rise for 20 minutes.

These naans cook very quickly under the grill, so you have to watch them carefully. Place them about 3 inches from the grill and let them cook for 2 minutes, after which they should be golden-brown (if they are not, leave them for up to another minute, watching them carefully). Turn them over and repeat this process on the other side. Remove the naans from the heat and serve them hot.

These can be reheated in the oven, wrapped in foil, and will keep for several days in the refrigerator. You can also roll out the naans and keep the dough refrigerated, covered with clingfilm, for up to a day.

Note

For a higher-protein, more earthy-tasting naan, substitute 2oz (55g) chick-pea flour for 2oz (55g) of the unbleached white or wholemeal flour.

Naans with Sweet Pinenut–Sultana Topping

8 LARGE NAANS

These naans are topped with a sweet, anisy paste made with sultanas and pinenuts. They are great for breakfast and tea as well as lunch or dinner.

wholemeal naan dough (see p. 249)
8oz (225g) sultanas
2oz (55g) pinenuts

1¼ teaspoons crushed anise seeds
2fl. oz (60ml) low-fat natural
    yoghurt

Make the naan dough according to the recipe on pp. 249–50 and set it in a warm spot to rise.

Meanwhile, make the filling. Place the sultanas in a bowl and pour on boiling water to cover. Let them plump for 15 minutes, then drain and pat them dry with paper towels. Mash the sultanas to a paste in a mortar and pestle. Add the pinenuts and anise and continue to mash together, but make sure the pinenuts retain some texture (some can remain whole). Work in the yoghurt.

Roll out the naans and grill them on one side, as directed. Turn them over and spread the other side with the sultana–pinenut paste. Return them to the heat and grill them for another minute, as directed, making sure the naans are not too close to the grill, or the topping will burn. Serve them warm.

Naans with Spicy Chick-pea Topping

8 LARGE NAANS

These naans have a hearty, spicy topping. They are filling and high in protein.

wholemeal naan dough (see p. 249)
a 14oz (400g) tin chick peas,
  drained, or 6oz (170g) chick
  peas, cooked and drained
4fl. oz (120ml) low-fat natural
  yoghurt

1 teaspoon crushed cumin seeds
⅛ teaspoon cayenne pepper
  (or to taste)
salt and freshly ground pepper
  (to taste)

Mix up the naan dough as directed on pp. 249–50. While the dough is rising, make the filling. Mash the chick peas coarsely in a mortar and pestle and mix with the yoghurt and spices, which you have crushed in a mortar and pestle or a spice mill. Season to taste with salt, cayenne and freshly ground pepper. The mixture should be a little piquant, and should have a coarse, paste-like consistency.

Roll out the naans and grill on one side, as directed. Turn them over and spread the other side with the chick-pea paste. Return them to the heat and grill them for another minute, as directed, making sure the naans are not too close to the grill, or the chick peas will burn. Serve them warm.

Socca

SERVES 4

Socca is a Niçoise speciality, and I have a great weakness for it. It is a thick chick-pea-flour pancake, almost like polenta in texture, but finer. Whenever I go to Nice or Monte Carlo I make a point of going to the market expressly to eat *socca*, which is made on huge griddles over a wood fire or in a wood-burning oven; greasy portions are scraped off the griddle and served in pieces of greaseproof paper. *Socca* is very easy to make and you can make a quick meal of it. My version is less greasy than authentic *socca*. I make it in a Le Creuset *gratin* dish.

Chick-pea flour can be obtained in wholefood shops and Indian supermarkets.

2 tablespoons olive oil	*8fl. oz (225ml) cold water*
3oz (85g) chick-pea flour	*freshly ground pepper*
¼–½ teaspoon salt (to taste)	

About 30 minutes before you wish to bake the *socca*, pre-heat the oven, lined with baking tiles if possible (see p. 12), to 475°F/240°C/gas mark 9. Brush a 14-inch non-stick cake tin, a pizza tin, tart tin or heavy baking dish (such as a Le Creuset *gratin* dish) all over with 1 tablespoon of the olive oil.

Beat together the flour, salt and water until there are no lumps. (This can be done in a blender at high speed.) Add freshly ground pepper to taste and let it sit for 30 minutes.

Heat the oiled baking tin in the pre-heated oven for about 10–15 minutes until it is very hot, then pour in the batter (it should be about ¼ inch deep in the tin). Drizzle the remaining oil over the top of the batter. Set the tin in the upper third of the oven and bake for about 5 minutes, until the batter has set. Then place the tin under the grill and brown the pancake for 3–4 minutes, turning the tin several times. Remove it from the heat and scrape out servings with a spatula. Don't worry if it sticks to the tin – it does in Nice too.

Socca with Garlic or Herbs

Add 1–2 cloves garlic, finely chopped or crushed, to the batter. You can also add 1–2 teaspoons chopped fresh thyme, sage or rosemary to the batter, with or without the garlic.

Carta Musica

10 LARGE BREADS

Carta musica is paper-thin, crisp Sardinian flat bread. It was a rare treat for me until I learned how easy it is to make at home. The bread lasts for weeks and is great to have on hand for snacks and cocktails. This version is derived from the America-based cook Carlo Middione's recipe, given in his book *The Food of Southern Italy*.

8oz (225g) unbleached white flour
4oz (115g) fine semolina flour
¾ teaspoon salt

8–12fl. oz (225–340ml)
lukewarm water

Mix together the flour, semolina flour and salt in a bowl. Gradually add 8fl. oz (225ml) of the water and stir it into the flour with a wooden spoon. Add more water if necessary to form a smooth, easy-to-handle dough that isn't sticky or elastic. Gather the dough into a ball (dust it with flour if it is sticky) and divide it into ten equal pieces. Form small balls and set them aside on a lightly floured board or baking sheet, covered with clingfilm and a tea-towel, for 20 minutes.

Meanwhile, 20 minutes before baking, pre-heat the oven to 400°F/ 200°C/gas mark 6, with baking sheets or baking stones (see p. 12) in the oven.

On a lightly floured work surface, roll out each piece of dough, adding more flour to the top of the dough and the work surface as necessary to avoid sticking. Roll out each piece into a very thin disc – less than ¹⁄₁₆ inch thick. Transfer them to the hot baking sheets and bake on the bottom shelf of the oven for 2½–3 minutes, until the dough is beginning to blister. Turn the bread over and bake for another 2½ minutes, approximately. Watch carefully, as once the dough begins to burn it will burn very quickly. The flat breads should be paper thin and crisp, with brown bubbles. Cool them on a rack. Proceed in this way with all the breads.

Store in sealed plastic bags in a cool dry place (but *not* in the refrigerator). They will keep for a couple of weeks.

Crêpes

20–30 CRÊPES

Whether you make these with wholemeal or unbleached white flour, or a combination, crêpes are as tasty as can be. You can wrap them around any number of fillings – a great way to transform leftovers into a new dish. Crêpes are very easy to make and store easily. You can keep them in the refrigerator for a couple of days, or freeze them. Stack them between pieces of greaseproof paper and seal them in a plastic bag or foil.

To make crêpes you should have a well seasoned 6–7-inch crêpe pan which you never wash and use only for crêpes. If you don't have one, a non-stick omelette pan will work, though not quite as well.

3 large eggs	4oz (115g) flour (either sifted
5fl. oz (140ml) milk	wholemeal pastry flour; half
5fl. oz (140ml) water	wholemeal pastry flour and half
3 tablespoons melted unsalted butter	unbleached white; all sifted 85
¼ teaspoon salt	per cent wholemeal; or all
	unbleached white)
	butter for cooking the crêpes

Put the eggs, milk, water, melted butter and salt in a blender or a food processor fitted with the steel blade. Turn it on and slowly add the flour. Blend at high speed for a minute. (If you don't have a blender or food processor, sift together the flour and salt. Beat the eggs and stir in the flour. Gradually add the milk and water and the butter, beating vigorously with a whisk. Strain through a sieve.) Refrigerate the batter for 1–2 hours. This allows the flour particles to swell and soften, so that the crêpes will be light.

Have the batter ready in a bowl, with a whisk to hand for stirring, as the flour tends to settle and the batter will need to be stirred every now and then, especially if you are using wholemeal flour. Also have a ladle and a plate on which to put the finished crêpes.

Place the pan over a moderately high heat and brush the bottom with butter. When the pan just begins to smoke, remove it from the heat and ladle in about 3 tablespoons of batter. Immediately tilt the pan from side to side or swirl it to distribute the batter evenly. Return the pan to the heat and cook for about a minute. Loosen the edges of the crêpe gently with a spatula or a palette knife and if the crêpe comes up from the pan easily, turn it over and cook it for about 30 seconds on the other side. If the crêpe sticks, wait another 30 seconds, then turn it. (Don't panic if the first few stick: the pan will eventually become well seasoned and they will come away easily.) Turn the crêpe from the pan on to a plate, with the first side down (the darker, prettier side). When you fill the crêpes, place the filling on the less-cooked side.

Brush the pan again with butter and continue to cook the remainder of the batter. After the first three or four crêpes you won't have to brush the pan each time, but only after every three or four crêpes.

Dessert Crêpes

Using the recipe above, replace 2fl. oz (60ml) of the water with 2fl. oz Grand Marnier or orange juice. Proceed as above.

Buckwheat Crêpes

ABOUT 20 CRÊPES

Buckwheat crêpes are my favourite French 'fast food'. They are made in little stands and in small restaurants called *crêperies* in Paris and all over Brittany, where they originate, topped with a number of nutritious items – cheese, egg, spinach, smoked salmon, tomatoes, ham and others. The French call them *galettes au sarrasin* or *galettes au blé noir*. These crêpes rank among the world's greatest street food, made right in front of you on large round griddles. The vendor pours some of the batter, which he has mixed up in a huge bowl, on to the middle of the griddle, then with a flat spatula he spreads it over the surface. It is so thin that it needs to be cooked on one side only. If you have ordered an *œuf/fromage*, the crêpe-maker will fry the egg right on top of the crêpe, sprinkle on the cheese, fold the crêpe in half, then in half again and wrap it like a cone in a piece of greaseproof paper. He hands it to you, hot and buttery, and *voilà!* – a nutritious and mouthwatering quick lunch.

I make my own buckwheat crêpes like normal crêpes, in a well-seasoned crêpe pan. They are good to have to hand and freeze well.

8fl. oz (225ml) milk
2½fl. oz (90ml) water (or 6
  tablespoons)
3 eggs

½ teaspoon salt
3oz (85g) buckwheat flour
1oz (30g) unbleached white flour
3 tablespoons melted unsalted butter

Place the milk, water, salt and eggs in a blender and turn it on. With the blender still going, add the flours then the melted butter, and blend at high speed for a minute. Refrigerate for 1–2 hours before making the crêpes.

To make the crêpes, use a 6–7-inch crêpe pan (or a larger pan for a more authentic crêpe), or a cast-iron or non-stick skillet. Place the pan over a moderate heat and brush the bottom with butter. When the pan just begins to smoke, remove it from the heat and pour or ladle in the batter – about 3 tablespoons per crêpe. Immediately tilt or twist the pan to distribute the batter evenly, and return it to the heat. Cook the crêpe for about a minute, then gently loosen the edges by running a palette knife or thin spatula around the edge. If the crêpe comes up from the pan easily and is nicely browned, turn it and cook for 30 seconds on the other side. If it sticks, wait another 30 seconds, then turn. Turn the crêpe out on to a plate. Continue cooking crêpes in this way until all the batter is used up.

Buckwheat Crêpes with Egg and Cheese

For each serving, fry one egg and place it on top of a warm crêpe. Sprinkle with 2–3 tablespoons grated Gruyère cheese, fold over if desired, and serve immediately.

Light Blinis

ABOUT 30 *BLINIS*

Blinis can be thick, rich and moist, like the ones opposite, or lighter, thinner and moist, like these. This type is best cooked in a crêpe pan or omelette pan, because the batter spreads when you ladle it in. There are also special *blini* pans with indentations for uniform shapes (but I don't use them).

I often make these *blinis* for parties: they keep very well, so I can make them in advance. I cut them in half or into quarters for finger food.

2 tablespoons active dried yeast
32fl. oz (1 litre) warm milk
4 eggs, separated
2 teaspoons sugar
1 teaspoon salt

4oz (115g) wholemeal flour
4oz (115g) unbleached white flour
2oz (55g) buckwheat flour
2 teaspoons melted unsalted butter

Dissolve the yeast in half the milk. Beat in the egg yolks and sugar. Sift together the flours and salt. Stir half into the liquid mixture and whisk together until completely smooth. Cover and set it in a warm place to rise for an hour.

Beat the remaining milk into the sponge and add the remaining flour mixture and the melted butter. Combine well. Strain through a medium-fine sieve or a *chinois*, cover and let the batter rise for another hour in a warm place. At this point it can be refrigerated for several hours, or overnight.

Just before cooking, beat the egg whites to stiff peaks and fold them into the batter.

Heat a crêpe pan or non-stick skillet over medium–high heat. Brush the pan with butter (it should sizzle). Cook the *blinis*, using about 4–6 tablespoons batter for a large *blini*, and 2 tablespoons for finger-food size. Cook for 30–60 seconds on the first side, until bubbles break through, then turn the *blini* and cook it for 30 seconds on the other side. Stack the finished *blinis* and keep them warm wrapped in a tea-towel in a low oven. If not using them right away, wrap them tightly in foil. Reheat them for 30 minutes in an oven pre-heated to 325°F/170°C/gas mark 3, still wrapped in their foil.

Note

These freeze well. Wrap them in foil and place them in plastic bags. They can be transferred immediately from the freezer, wrapped in the foil, to a 350°F/180°C/gas mark 4 oven and will take about 40 minutes to thaw.

Thick Blinis

15 LARGE OR 24 SMALLER *BLINIS*

These *blinis*, based on an Elizabeth David recipe, are heftier than the ones opposite. The batter is thicker and the *blinis* are too. They are easier to make, however, because the batter doesn't run on the griddle. They have a moist texture and a rich, earthy buckwheat flavour. They are marvellous with smoked salmon and *fromage blanc* or sour cream.

1 teaspoon active dried yeast
2 tablespoons lukewarm water
4oz (115g) buckwheat flour
4oz (115g) unbleached white flour
a scant half pint (about 9fl. oz/
  285ml) lukewarm milk

¼ pint (140ml) buttermilk or
  low-fat natural yoghurt
2 large or 3 medium eggs, separated
¾–1 teaspoon salt, to taste

Dissolve the yeast in the lukewarm water in a large bowl, add the milk and let it sit for 5 minutes. Combine the flours and salt and stir into the milk. Stir in the buttermilk or yoghurt. Beat in the egg yolks. Cover the bowl with clingfilm and a tea-towel and let the batter rise in a warm place for about an hour, or longer, until it is spongy and bubbly.

Beat the egg whites to soft peaks and fold them into the batter. Cover and let it rise for another hour or more.

Lightly grease a crêpe pan, or a heavy cast-iron griddle or frying pan, and heat it over a medium–low heat. Ladle on one large or a few small ladlefuls of batter. Cook for a minute or so, until holes break through. Turn the *blini* and brown it on the other side for about 30 seconds. Turn it out on to a plate.

If you are not serving the *blinis* right away, wrap them in a tea-towel or aluminium foil and keep them warm in a hot oven. If you will be serving them much later, wrap them in foil and reheat them for 30 minutes in an oven pre-heated to 325°F/170°C/gas mark 3, still wrapped in their foil.

Note

These *blinis* also freeze well. Stack them between pieces of greaseproof paper and wrap them tightly in foil. Seal them in a plastic bag. To thaw, remove them from the plastic bag and place them in a moderate oven, still wrapped in foil, for an hour.

Cornmeal Blinis

20 BLINIS

These *blinis* have a grainy texture, beautiful golden colour and rich flavour. They freeze well and are easy to make.

6oz (170g) stoneground cornmeal
1½ teaspoons salt
12fl. oz (340ml) boiling water
2 eggs
8fl. oz (225ml) milk

2oz (55g) unbleached white flour, sifted
2 tablespoons melted unsalted butter
butter for cooking the blinis

Combine the cornmeal and salt. Bring the water to a boil and whisk it into the cornmeal. Make sure there are no lumps. (This can be done in a food processor or electric mixer.) Let it sit for 10 minutes. Beat in the eggs, milk, flour and butter, and beat until smooth. Let the batter sit for 30 minutes.

Heat a well-seasoned crêpe pan and brush it with butter. Ladle in the batter – about 3 tablespoons for each *blini*. Cook for 1 minute, then turn the *blini* over and cook for about 30 seconds on the other side. Turn the *blini* out on to a plate and continue to use up the batter, brushing the pan with butter after every three or so.

If not serving right away, stack the *blinis* between pieces of grease-proof paper. Wrap them tightly in foil and refrigerate or freeze. To serve, reheat for 30 minutes (1½ hours if frozen) in an oven pre-heated to 325°F/170°C/gas mark 3, still wrapped in their foil. Remove the *blinis* from the foil and arrange them on a serving dish or on individual plates.

Sesame Crackers

3–4 DOZEN

These are delicious, crunchy, nutty-tasting crackers. They go very well with cheese and with foods like humous or tapenade. They are also very easy to make.

6oz (170g) wholemeal flour
2oz (55g) sesame seeds
½ teaspoon salt
2fl. oz (60ml) safflower or
   vegetable oil

1 tablespoon sesame butter
   (optional)
up to 3fl. oz (90ml) water, as
   necessary

Pre-heat the oven to 350°F/180°C/gas mark 4. Oil two baking sheets.

Mix together the flour, sesame seeds and salt. Add the oil and optional sesame butter and rub in. (This can be done in a food processor fitted with the steel blade, using the pulse action, or in an electric mixer.)

Add 2fl. oz (60ml) of the water. The dough should have a pie-crust consistency (though coarser). If it is too dry, add a little more water. Gather up the dough into a ball and roll it out on a well-floured board, or between pieces of greaseproof paper. The dough should be about ⅛ inch thick.

Cut the dough into squares (or use a biscuit cutter). Place them on the prepared baking sheets and bake them in the upper third of the pre-heated oven until they are brown – about 20–25 minutes – switching the positions of the baking sheets halfway through. Don't let the crackers get too brown or they will taste bitter. Cool them on racks.

Buckwheat–Sesame Crackers

3–4 DOZEN

These are much like the sesame crackers on p. 261. Here earthy buckwheat is combined with the nutty sesame seeds.

5oz (140g) wholemeal flour
2oz (55g) buckwheat flour
1oz (30g) sesame seeds
½ teaspoon salt

2fl. oz (60ml) safflower or
* vegetable oil*
3fl. oz (90ml) water, as necessary

Pre-heat the oven to 350°F/180°C/gas mark 4. Oil two baking sheets.

Mix together the flours, sesame seeds and salt. Add the oil and rub in. (This can be done in a food processor fitted with the steel blade, using the pulse action, or in an electric mixer.)

Add the water. The dough should have a pie-crust consistency (though coarser). If it is too dry, add a little more water. Gather up the dough and roll it out on a well-floured board, or between pieces of greaseproof paper. The dough should be about ⅛ inch thick.

Cut the dough into squares (or use a biscuit cutter). Place them on the prepared baking sheets and bake them in the upper third of the pre-heated oven until they are brown – about 20–25 minutes – switching the positions of the baking sheets halfway through baking. Don't let the crackers get too brown or they will taste bitter. Cool them on racks.

10: Dishes Made with Stale or Leftover Bread

I tested all the recipes in this book in our apartment kitchen, and there were times when it looked more like a bakery. My husband would come home to find the kitchen piled high with bread and rolls, with scarcely a surface on which to lay down a newspaper, let alone set the table. If we had had a freezer it would have been fine, but the freezer compartment in our refrigerator is big enough to accommodate only a loaf or two. So I had a lot of bread on my hands. I gave many loaves away, but I held on to some, because there's much you can do with bread that's going stale.

I had already come across many recipes for leftover bread when I did research for a Mediterranean cookery book I completed in 1988. People all over the Mediterranean basin are ingenious when it comes to turning stale bread into something tasty. In Spain they use it to thicken soups, and they rub slices with garlic, olive oil and tomato for lunch. In Italy they make soups and salads with stale bread, and also use it for delicious *croûtons* topped with savoury items like thick tomato sauce, sautéed peppers or mushrooms. The Portuguese have a number of ingenious, fragrant thick soups – almost like porridge – called *açordas*. In the Middle East stale pitta goes into salads and into delicious casseroles called *fatta*. The French use their dry *brioche* for *pain perdu* (French toast), and in England and America we have irresistible bread-and-butter puddings (when I worked in restaurants in Austin, Texas, we never threw away bread ends; every day there was a bread pudding on the menu).

I suppose I'm just scratching the surface here: there is probably enough material out there to fill a book. But these recipes should give you some ideas. In any case, after working on this chapter I rarely throw away old bread. It has to have gone pretty far before it's beyond transforming. Just remember to store bread that is no longer fresh in the refrigerator and it will keep from moulding for some time.

Salt Cod Acorda

SERVES 6

Acordas are Portuguese thick, porridge-like soups, thickened with stale bread. They are a brilliant way of using up bread, and we ate our fill when I was testing recipes for this book. *Acordas* can be eaten in a bowl, like a soup, or they can be served on a plate. They go well with salads or as a side-dish with grilled fish. They usually have a strong garlicky flavour.

This salt cod *acorda* is rich and filling, with the strong flavours of salt cod, garlic and coriander.

a 1½lb (680g) piece of salt cod,
    de-salted (see below)
2½ pints (1.5 litres) water
2 tablespoons olive oil
1 medium-sized or large onion,
    chopped
10 large cloves garlic, 5 of them
    chopped
a 14oz (400g) tin tomatoes, seeded
    and chopped, with their liquid
1 bay leaf
1 teaspoon dried thyme

½–¾lb (225–340g) waxy
    potatoes, scrubbed and sliced
a pinch of cayenne pepper
freshly ground pepper (to taste)
14oz (395g) stale country bread,
    cubed
6oz (170g) spinach, washed
    thoroughly and stemmed
a bunch fresh coriander
salt, if necessary
3 eggs, beaten

To de-salt the cod

Two days before making the soup, place the cod in a bowl of water in the sink under a tap and soak it for two days, letting cold water drizzle over it constantly so that the water is being replenished continually. If this isn't possible, soak it in the water in the refrigerator, changing the water about six times over the course of the two days. It is very important to de-salt the cod thoroughly or your *acorda* will be inedible.

Once the fish has been de-salted, drain and place it in a large pan. Cover it with 2½ pints (1.5 litres) water or more and bring it very slowly to simmering point. Do not boil. Cover the pan tightly and turn off the heat. Leave the cod in the water for 8–10 minutes, then drain, retaining the water. Rinse the fish with cold water. When it is cool enough to handle remove the skin and bones, and flake the fish into a bowl. Set it aside.

Making the acorda

Heat the olive oil in a large, heavy-bottomed pan and sauté the onion with the 5 chopped cloves of garlic over a medium–low heat, stirring often, until the onion is tender and beginning to colour. Add the tomatoes with their juice, the bay leaf and the thyme, and bring to a simmer. Simmer for 15 minutes, stirring often. Add 2¼ pints (1.2 litres) of the cooking water from the fish, then add the potatoes and simmer for 10–15 minutes, until the potatoes are tender. Stir in the flaked cod and adjust the seasonings, adding cayenne, freshly ground pepper to taste and salt if necessary. Stir in the bread and cook together, stirring often, until the soup is thick – about 10 minutes. Stir in the spinach.

Pound together the remaining garlic and the coriander in a mortar and pestle until you have a fairly smooth paste. Beat in the eggs.

Just before serving, ladle a little of the hot soup into the mortar, combine it with the egg mixture, then stir this mixture back into the soup. Stir together off the heat, and serve. The soup should have the consistency of thick porridge.

Coriander and Garlic Acorda

SERVES 4

This is a highly seasoned *acorda*, and a very simple one. You can put it together in no time.

10 large cloves garlic, peeled
a bunch fresh coriander
salt
1 tablespoon olive oil
1lb (450g) stale country bread,
    diced

1½–2 pints (850ml–1.14 litres)
    boiling water
4 eggs
freshly ground pepper

Place the garlic and coriander in a mortar and pestle, add some salt and pound to a paste. Work in the olive oil. Transfer the mixture to a large bowl or soup tureen.

Bring the water to simmering point and poach the eggs. Remove them from the water and drain them on kitchen paper.

Salt the water and stir it into the herb mixture in the tureen. Add the bread. Stir together well for 5–10 minutes and adjust the seasonings. If the soup is too thick, add a little more simmering water. Divide the *acorda* between four soup bowls and place a poached egg on each serving. Sprinkle with pepper and serve.

Gazpacho Andaluz

SERVES 4

Gazpacho is a dish I never tire of – and that's a good thing, too, because it's ubiquitous in Spain and I don't mind eating it every day when I'm there. It's the perfect hot-weather soup, like a liquid salad, and a fine way of using up stale bread.

For the soup base

2 thick slices stale French or country
  bread, crusts removed
1lb (450g) ripe tomatoes, skinned
2–4 garlic cloves (to taste), peeled
2 tablespoons olive oil
1–2 tablespoons wine vinegar
  (to taste)
salt (to taste)

freshly ground pepper
½ pint (285ml) ice-cold water
1 small spring onion, chopped, or
  2 tablespoons chopped
  Spanish onion
½–1 teaspoon paprika ⎫
½ teaspoon crushed cumin |
  seed   ⎬ optional
2 tablespoons chopped |
  fresh basil ⎭

For the garnish

1 small cucumber, peeled and finely
  diced
1 red or green sweet pepper, seeds
  and membranes removed, finely
  diced

1 hard-boiled egg, diced (optional)
4 tablespoons finely chopped onion
2oz (55g) croûtons

Soak the bread in the water for 5–10 minutes, until soft. Squeeze out the water.

Blend together all the ingredients for the soup base until smooth. (You can do this with a pestle and mortar or in a blender.) Adjust the seasonings to taste and chill the soup for several hours: it must be very cold. Serve, garnishing each bowl with a heaped spoonful of each of the garnishes.

Thick Tuscan Bean and Vegetable Soup

SERVES 6

This is a thick, hearty bean soup, with lots of mineral-rich, dark leafy greens. The soup is thickened by puréeing some of the beans.

8oz (225g) dried haricot or borlotti beans, picked over and washed
2 pints (1.2 litres) water
1 bay leaf
salt and freshly ground pepper (to taste)
1–2 tablespoons olive oil
2 medium-sized yellow onions, chopped
4 large garlic cloves, finely chopped or crushed, plus 1 large garlic clove, cut in half
2 sticks celery, diced
3 medium-sized carrots, peeled and diced
4 medium-sized potatoes, diced

1lb (450g) tomatoes, chopped
3lb (1½kg) Swiss chard, stems removed, leaves cleaned and chopped
1lb (450g) kale, stems removed, leaves cleaned and chopped
½ Savoy cabbage, finely shredded
1 tablespoon tomato purée
1 hot dried red chilli
1 teaspoon dried thyme
2–2½ pints (1.2–1.5 litres) water
12 slices of any of the country breads on pp. 38–41 and sourdough country breads, pp. 65–98

Soak the beans overnight or for several hours, drain and combine them with 2 pints (1.2 litres) water in a soup tureen or large saucepan. Bring to a boil, add the bay leaf, reduce the heat, cover and simmer for 1–2 hours, until the beans are tender. Add salt to taste, drain the beans and retain the cooking liquid. Purée half the beans in some of their cooking liquid, using a blender or food processor fitted with the steel blade, and set them aside.

Heat the olive oil in a large, heavy-bottomed saucepan or soup tureen over a low heat and add the onion and half the chopped or crushed garlic. Sauté, stirring, for about 5 minutes, then add the celery and carrots. Sauté, stirring, for another 10 minutes, then add all the remaining vegetables, the tomato purée, chilli, the whole cooked beans, the thyme, 2 pints (1.2 litres) water and the cooking liquid from the beans. Add some salt, bring to simmering point, cover and simmer for an hour.

If the vegetables aren't covered, add another cup of water. Stir in the puréed beans and the remaining chopped or crushed garlic and mix well. Add salt and freshly ground pepper to taste, and more thyme or garlic if you wish.

Toast the bread and rub each piece with the half cloves of garlic. Place two pieces in each soup bowl, ladle in the hot soup and serve.

Pappa al Pomodori

SERVES 4 TO 6

This is another brilliant Italian recipe, fragrant with basil and tomatoes. Although it's called a soup, it's thick enough to serve on a plate.

2 tablespoons olive oil
1 small onion, chopped
4 garlic cloves, coarsely chopped
1½lb (680g) ripe tomatoes,
    quartered
3 tablespoons tomato purée
a pinch of cayenne pepper or hot
    crushed chillis

2 tablespoons fresh basil, coarsely
    chopped or torn into pieces
1lb (450g) bread, wholemeal or
    white (preferably a coarse
    country variety), a few days old
    (if possible), cut into cubes
1½ pints (850ml) water
salt and freshly ground pepper (to
    taste)

Heat the oil in a large, heavy-bottomed pan or soup tureen over a low heat and sauté the onion and garlic gently for 10–15 minutes, being careful not to brown. Add the tomatoes, tomato purée, cayenne pepper or crushed chillis and simmer for another 20 minutes, stirring occasionally. Add the basil, bread, water and salt and simmer for 10–15 minutes, stirring and mashing the bread with a wooden spoon from time to time, and being careful that the bread doesn't stick to the bottom of the pan. Add lots of freshly ground pepper, adjust the salt, cover and remove the pan from the heat. Serve the soup warm, at room temperature or chilled, on plates or in bowls.

Italian Bread Salad

SERVES 6

This is one of the most delicious ways of using up stale bread. It is just one of several Mediterranean bread salads (see also *fattoush*, opposite).

1lb (450g) stale country or French bread
1 small red onion
1lb (450g) tomatoes, chopped
2 tablespoons chopped fresh basil
2 tablespoons chopped fresh parsley

4–5 tablespoons red wine vinegar
1 large garlic clove, finely chopped or crushed
salt and freshly ground pepper (to taste)
6 tablespoons olive oil

Place the bread in a bowl and cover it with cold water. Skin the onion, cut it in half and place it on top of the bread. Soak for 20 minutes. Drain and squeeze all the water out of the bread. Don't worry if the bread crumbles (wholemeal bread usually does).

Slice the onion very thin and toss it with the bread, tomatoes, basil and parsley.

Mix together the vinegar, garlic, salt and pepper, and whisk in the oil. Toss this with the bread, cover and refrigerate for at least 2 hours before serving.

Note

If you are using bread that isn't really stale and hard, omit the soaking step: just moisten it with water and squeeze.

Fattoush

SERVES 6

This is a Syrian salad made with vegetables and crisp pieces of pitta bread. I replace some of the olive oil used in the traditional dish with low-fat natural yoghurt.

2 pitta breads (stale is fine)
juice of 2 lemons
2 garlic cloves, finely chopped or
  crushed
salt and freshly ground pepper (to
  taste)
4 tablespoons olive oil
4 tablespoons low-fat natural
  yoghurt
1 large or 2 small cucumbers,
  chopped, or a small head
  Romaine lettuce, leaves washed
  and cut into 1-inch pieces

a bunch spring onions, chopped, or
  1 medium-sized red onion,
  chopped
1lb (450g) firm, ripe tomatoes,
  chopped
1 sweet green pepper, chopped
  (optional)
a bunch parsley, finely chopped
2 tablespoons chopped fresh mint
3 tablespoons chopped fresh
  coriander

Open up the pittas and toast them until they are crisp and brown. Break them into small pieces and place them in a salad bowl.

Mix together the lemon juice, garlic, salt and pepper, olive oil and yoghurt and toss with the broken-up bread. Then add the vegetables and herbs and toss together again. Adjust the seasonings and serve.

Chick-pea Fattet

SERVES 6

Fatta (singular: fattet) are Middle Eastern dishes made with crisp pitta bread broken up into small pieces, soaked in a tasty stock, topped with any number of delicious foods and thickened yoghurt. They're a great way to use up stale pitta bread.

This chick-pea fattet is almost like a humous casserole.

1lb (450g) chick peas, picked over
1½ pints (850ml) water
salt
1 pint (570ml) low-fat natural
    yoghurt
2 wholemeal pitta breads
1 large whole garlic clove, plus 3
    garlic cloves, finely chopped or
    crushed

juice of 1½ lemons
½ teaspoon ground cumin
2 teaspoons sesame tahini
    (optional)
freshly ground pepper (to taste)
1–2 tablespoons dried or fresh mint
    leaves (optional)

Soak the beans for several hours or overnight, then drain them and put them in a large pan, covered with the water. Bring to the boil, reduce the heat, cover and simmer for 1½–2 hours, until the beans are very soft. At the end of the cooking, add salt to taste.

Meanwhile, drain the yoghurt for about an hour in a strainer lined with muslin or a thin tea-towel.

Open out the pitta breads and toast them in a hot oven until they are crisp and brown. Oil a 4-pint (2.5-litre) baking dish, break the pitta into pieces and line the dish with them.

Drain the beans and retain the cooking liquid. Coarsely purée half of them, or pound them in a mortar and pestle, along with the juice of 1 lemon, the clove of garlic, the cumin and ¼ pint (140ml) of the cooking liquid. Add salt to taste.

Place the drained yoghurt in a bowl and beat in the chopped or crushed garlic, optional tahini and pepper.

Squeeze the juice of half a lemon into the cooking liquid from the beans and sprinkle about 5–6fl. oz (140–180ml) over the broken-up pitta bread (enough to moisten the bread). Top with the chick-pea purée and the whole chick peas. Spread the remaining chick peas over the purée and top with the yoghurt. Crush the dried mint or sprinkle the fresh mint over the top and serve.

Fattet with Chicken

SERVES 6–8

I love this dish hot or cold. The yoghurt on the top becomes like thick white cheese.

For the chicken stock

1 medium-sized chicken, cut into pieces
3 pints (2 litres) water (enough to cover the chicken)
a bay leaf
1 onion, quartered

4 garlic cloves, crushed
juice of 3 lemons
seeds from 2 cardamom pods, ground to a powder
salt and freshly ground pepper

For the rice and fattet

1½ pints (850ml) low-fat natural yoghurt
1 tablespoon vegetable or safflower oil
1 large onion, chopped
6oz (170g) basmati rice, washed

1 teaspoon ground cinnamon
1 teaspoon ground allspice
3 pitta breads
4 garlic cloves, pounded in a mortar and pestle or crushed

Cover the chicken with the water, add the bay leaf, onion, garlic and salt to taste, and bring to a boil. Skim off any foam and add the lemon juice, cardamom, salt and pepper. Simmer gently for an hour, until the chicken is very tender and almost falls off the bones. Remove the chicken from the stock, strain the stock and refrigerate it for several hours or overnight. Skim off the layer of fat that forms at the top. Set aside 12fl. oz (350ml) of the stock for soaking the pitta and the rest for cooking the rice. Skin and bone the chicken, shred the meat and set it aside.

Place the yoghurt in a sieve lined with muslin or a thin tea-towel and let it drain for about an hour.

Meanwhile, heat the oil in a heavy-bottomed saucepan and sauté the onion until tender and beginning to colour. Add the rice, cinnamon and allspice, some salt and pepper, and cover by an inch with the chicken stock set aside for the rice (add some water if there isn't enough). Bring to a simmer, cover the pan and cook over a low heat for 15–20 minutes, or until the rice is tender and the liquid absorbed.

Open up the pitta bread and toast it in the oven until it is brown and crisp. Oil a baking dish or casserole and crumble the bread into it. Spread the rice over the bread and top with the chicken. Heat the remaining chicken stock to a simmer and pour on enough to moisten the pitta bread.

Beat the pounded or crushed garlic into the thickened yoghurt. Spread it over the chicken, and serve.

Note

You can reheat this dish in a medium oven (350°F/180°C/gas mark 4) if you want to eat it hot.

Bruschette

Bruschette is the original garlic bread – grilled slices of crusty bread rubbed with garlic, usually drenched in good virgin olive oil and rubbed with tomato.

*several 1-inch-thick slices of coarse
    bread, such as the country breads
    on pp. 38–41 and sourdough
    country breads, pp. 65–98*

*2 garlic cloves, cut in half
    lengthwise
2–3 tablespoons olive oil
1–2 tomatoes, cut in half*

Grill the bread on both sides until it is just beginning to brown around the edges. It should remain soft inside. Remove it from the heat and while it is still hot rub it with a cut clove of garlic. Brush it with olive oil, then rub it with the cut side of a tomato, squeezing a little of the tomato juice on to the bread.

Bruschette with Tomato Topping

SERVES 4

This rich tasting, savoury dish is very easy to make and makes a nice late supper or luncheon dish.

1½lb (680g) very ripe tomatoes,
  skinned and coarsely chopped
3 cloves garlic, finely chopped or
  crushed

1 tablespoon olive oil
2 tablespoons chopped fresh basil
salt and freshly ground pepper
8–12 bruschettes (opposite)

First make the tomato topping. Heat the oil over a low heat and sauté the garlic for 1 minute. Add the tomatoes, turn up the heat and cook for 15 minutes over medium–high heat, stirring and crushing the tomatoes with the back of a wooden spoon. Add salt and pepper to taste, and the basil. Cook for another minute, then remove from the heat and adjust the seasonings.

Make the *bruschettes*, top with the tomatoes and serve.

Crostini

Crostini – garlic *croûtons* – differ from *bruschette* in that they are thinner, thus a little more delicate, and are toasted in the oven or in a toaster, and can be cooled and kept for several hours. This makes them very convenient for entertaining. They can be served with any number of toppings, or added to soups and salads.

The ingredients are the same as for *bruschette*, but cut the bread only ½ inch thick, and the tomato is optional.

If toasting in the oven, pre-heat it to 350°F/180°C/gas mark 4. Toast the bread until it begins to colour – 10–20 minutes. Like *bruschette*, it shouldn't be crisp all the way through. Remove it from the heat, rub it with garlic and brush it with olive oil. If keeping for a few hours, cover the *crostini* lightly with foil or transfer them to a paper bag. Do not rub with the tomato until just before you add the topping and serve. If adding to salads, cut the slices into small squares.

Pain Perdu

SERVES 6

This is French toast – the ingenious French way of using up stale brioche. Of course you can use other breads as well, but eggy, light breads are best. *Challah* (p. 188) would be a very good choice, but really whatever slightly stale bread you have to hand will be delicious.

12 thick slices slightly stale bread
4 large eggs
½ pint (285ml) milk
1 tablespoon mild-flavoured honey
  or caster sugar (optional)
a pinch of salt
a pinch of nutmeg
a pinch of ground cinnamon
  (optional)
butter for frying, as necessary
icing sugar, honey, jam or maple
  syrup, for topping

If the bread isn't dry, slice it and allow it to dry out for an hour or so.

Turn the oven on low if you aren't serving the French toast as you make it. Beat together the eggs, milk and optional honey or sugar. Add the salt, nutmeg and cinnamon.

Heat the butter in a large, heavy frying pan over a medium–low heat. Dip the bread into the batter and turn it over so that it soaks from both sides. It should be saturated but not so soggy that it falls apart. Place it in the frying pan and sauté slowly until golden-brown – about 5–7 minutes. Turn and fry it on the other side until golden-brown. Place it in the oven on a baking sheet or wrapped in a tea-towel if you aren't serving it at once. Dust with icing sugar, or serve with honey, jam or maple syrup.

Cheese and Bread Pudding

SERVES 6

This is a savoury, comforting dish, and easy to throw together.

*4 oz (115g) mushrooms, cleaned
and sliced*
1 tablespoon unsalted butter
*1 clove garlic, finely chopped or
crushed*
2 tablespoons dry white wine
*salt and freshly ground pepper (to
taste)*

1 tablespoon chopped fresh parsley
*8oz (225g) strong Cheddar cheese,
grated*
4–6 slices wholemeal bread
4 eggs
¾ pint (125ml) milk
½ teaspoon dried thyme
½ teaspoon dry mustard

Pre-heat the oven to 350°F/180°C/gas mark 4. Butter a 3-pint (2-litre) soufflé or *gratin* dish.

Heat the butter in a frying pan and sauté the mushrooms and the garlic together until the mushrooms begin to soften and release their liquid. Add the wine and cook until it is absorbed. Add the parsley, salt and freshly ground pepper to taste. Set aside.

Toss the cooked mushrooms with the cheese and layer this mixture with the bread slices in the prepared casserole. Beat together the eggs, milk, thyme and mustard. Add a pinch of salt and some freshly ground pepper, and pour over the cheese and bread.

Place in the pre-heated oven and bake for about 40–45 minutes, until puffed and browned. Serve at once.

Bread Pudding with Peaches

SERVES 8

This exquisite bread pudding is an adaptation of a recipe by Richard Olney. I suppose it could go by many names: bread-and-butter pudding, 'Spotty Dave', 'Spotty Dick', etc. Olney's pudding is less solid than this, and I must say mine is a result of doubling the original recipe but not having a big enough *gratin* dish to accommodate a doubled amount of liquid. No matter – this turned out to be just scrumptious. If you want a more liquid, bread-and-butter-type pudding, double the amount of milk, add an extra egg and use a larger *gratin* dish (mine was about 12 inches long). I think what makes this pudding fantastic is the *eau-de-vie*-macerated dried fruit.

6oz (170g) currants and raisins
eau-de-vie *or* Kirsch *to cover the*
  dried fruit
3oz (85g) unsalted butter (more if
  necessary)
5oz (140g) leftover bread, hard
  crusts removed, torn into pieces
  or diced
6 tablespoons mild-flavoured honey
5 eggs
1 pint (570ml) milk

4–5 large ripe peaches, peeled and
  sliced
2fl. oz (60ml) single cream
1 tablespoon brown sugar
cream or sabayon sauce (see p. 279)
  for serving

Several hours before you wish to make the pudding, place the dried fruit in a bowl and pour on *eau-de-vie* or Kirsch to cover (I've had very good luck with *eau-de-vie-de-poire*).

Pre-heat the oven to 350°F/180°C/gas mark 4. Butter a 12–15-inch *gratin* dish.

Heat the butter over a low heat in a frying pan or large saucepan and add the bread. Sauté over a low heat, stirring often and adding more butter if needed, until the bread is slightly crisp on the outside. Turn the bread into the prepared *gratin* dish and spread it in an even layer. Drain the raisins and currants and sprinkle them over the bread. Add the peaches and arrange them so that the top is even.

Beat together the eggs and honey. Whisk in the milk and cream. Pour the liquid over the bread and fruit. (If it doesn't cover the bread and fruit, add a little more milk.)

Bake for about 45 minutes, or until the custard is set and the top beginning to brown. Towards the end of baking, sprinkle the additional brown sugar over the top.

Sabayon Sauce with Gewürztraminer

SERVES 8

This fabulous sauce, from Richard Olney, is incredibly delicious on fruit and on bread pudding. It's easy to make and will keep for several hours.

4 egg yolks
2 heaped tablespoons caster sugar

8 tablespoons rather sweet
Gewürztraminer

Construct a *bain-marie* by placing a trivet (it can be a small heat-proof *gratin* dish) in a large saucepan and standing a smaller, heavy saucepan on it so that water will come between one-third and halfway up the sides of the smaller saucepan. Heat water in the large saucepan while you beat together the egg yolks and sugar in the smaller saucepan, until the yolks are light yellow and thick. Add the wine and whisk together. Now place the small saucepan in the hot water on the trivet. Do not allow the hot water to come quite to the boil (let it come to just below the boil) while you whisk the sauce continuously in the smaller saucepan. It is ready when it is thick and doubled in volume, which will happen quickly if the water around it is hot. If the water does reach the boil, raise the saucepan with the sauce out of it and keep whisking while you turn down the heat.

Remove the sauce from the heat and continue to whisk for a couple of minutes longer. Set the sauce aside until you are ready to use it.

Another Bread Pudding

SERVES 6–8

This is a bread pudding without much butter. It's spicy, sweet and filling.

4 thick slices bread (about
  10oz/285g)
2oz (55g) unsalted butter
3oz (85g) raisins
2–3 apples, sliced (optional)
4 eggs
6 tablespoons mild-flavoured honey
  or brown sugar

1 pint (570ml) milk
1 teaspoon vanilla essence
  (optional)
½ teaspoon freshly grated nutmeg
3 tablespoons chopped pecans
  (optional)
cream for topping (optional)

Pre-heat the oven to 350°F/180°C/gas mark 4. Butter a 3-pint (2-litre) baking or *gratin* dish.

Butter the bread. Cut or tear it into pieces and place them in the prepared baking dish. Sprinkle on the raisins and optional apples.

Beat together the eggs and honey or sugar. Add the milk, vanilla essence and nutmeg. Pour the liquid over the bread. (Add more milk if the bread isn't covered.) Sprinkle the optional pecans and any leftover butter, cut into pieces, over the top.

Bake in the pre-heated oven until the custard is set – about 45–60 minutes. Remove from the heat. Serve the pudding warm, topped with cream if you wish.

Bibliography

Anderson, Jean, *The Food of Portugal*, Robert Hale, London, 1986.

Beard, James, *Beard on Bread*, Alfred A Knopf, New York, 1974.

Brown, Edward Espe, *The Tassajara Bread Book*, Shambala Press, Berkeley, California, 1970.

California Culinary Academy, *Breads*, Ortho Books, San Francisco, 1985.

Clayton, Bernard, Jr, *The Breads of France*, Bobbs Merrill, Indianapolis and New York, 1978.

David, Elizabeth, *English Bread and Yeast Cookery*, Penguin Books, Harmondsworth, 1977.

Ecole de Gastronomie Française Ritz-Escoffier, bread and pastry recipes, Paris.

Fitzgibbon, Theodora, *A Taste of England in Food and in Pictures*, Pan Books, London, 1986.

Field, Carol, *The Italian Baker*, Harper & Row Publishers, New York, 1985.

Grigson, Jane, *English Food*, Macmillan, London, 1979.

Luard, Elisabeth, *The Old World Kitchen: the Rich Tradition of European Peasant Cookery*, Bantam Books, New York and London, 1987.

Luard, Elisabeth, *The Princess and the Pheasant and Other Recipes*, Bantam Press, London, 1987.

McNeill, F. Marian, *The Scots Kitchen*, Blackie & Son Ltd, Edinburgh, 1929, Panther Books, London, 1974.

Middione, Carlo, *The Food of Southern Italy*, William Morrow, New York, 1987.

Olney, Richard, *Ten Vineyard Lunches*, Ebury Press, London, 1988.

Robertson, Laurel, Flinders, Carol, and Godfrey, Bronwen, *The Laurel's Kitchen Bread Book*, Random House, New York, 1984.

Shulman, Martha Rose, *The Vegetarian Feast*, Thorsons Publishers, London, 1983.

Shulman, Martha Rose, *Fast Vegetarian Feasts*, Thorsons Publishers, London, 1984.

Shulman, Martha Rose, *Herbs and Honey Cookery*, Thorsons Publishers, London, 1984.

Shulman, Martha Rose, *Spicy Vegetarian Feasts*, Thorsons Publishers, London, 1985.

Shulman, Martha Rose, *Chez Martha Rose*, Macmillan London, London, 1988.

Shulman, Martha Rose, *Mediterranean Light*, Bantam Doubleday Dell Publishing Group, New York, 1989.

Viera, Edite, *The Taste of Portugal*, Robert Hale, London, 1988.

Wells, Patricia, *The Food Lover's Guide to France*, Workman Publishing, New York, 1987.

Index